SAMS
Teach Yourself

Macromedia®
Dreamweaver® MX 2004

in 24 Hours

Betsy Bruce

SAMS   *800 East 96th Street, Indianapolis, Indiana 46240*

Sams Teach Yourself Macromedia® Dreamweaver® MX 2004 in 24 Hours

International Standard Book Number: 0-672-32593-4

Library of Congress Catalog Card Number: 2003092928

Printed in the United States of America

First Printing: November 2003

06   05   04   03   4   3   2   1

Trademarks

Warning and Disclaimer

Bulk Sales

Sams Publishing offers excellent discounts on this book when ordered in quantity for bulk purchases or special sales. For more information, please contact

U.S. Corporate and Government Sales
1-800-382-3419
corpsales@pearsontechgroup.com

For sales outside of the U.S., please contact

International Sales
+1-317-428-3341
international@pearsontechgroup.com

Acquisitions Editor
Betsy Brown

Development Editor
Damon Jordan

Managing Editor
Charlotte Clapp

Project Editor
Andrew Beaster

Copy Editor
Kitty Jarrett

Indexer
Kelly Castell

Proofreader
Mike Henry

Technical Editor
Steve Heckler

Team Coordinator
Vanessa Evans

Designer
Gary Adair

Page Layout
Julie Parks

Contents at a Glance

Introduction 1

Part I: Getting Started with Dreamweaver MX

HOUR 1   Understanding the Dreamweaver Interface 7
2   Creating a Basic Web Page with Text 41
3   Planning and Defining a Project 61
4   Setting Lots o' Links: Hyperlinks, URLs, Anchors, and Mailto Links 79
5   HTML Is Fun! Viewing and Modifying HTML 97

Part II: Adding Images and Multimedia

HOUR 6   Displaying Images on a Page 117
7   Optimizing and Creating Images 131
8   Creating Image Maps and Navigation Bars 151
9   Adding Flash and Other Multimedia Files to a Web Page 163
10   Managing Assets by Using the Assets Panel 185

Part III: Web Page Layout with Tables and Frames

HOUR 11   Displaying Data by Using Tables 201
12   Designing Page Layout by Using Tables 219
13   Understanding and Building Frames and Framesets 235

Part IV: Dynamic HTML: Layers, Cascading Style Sheets, Behaviors, and Timelines

HOUR 14   Using Dynamic HTML and Layers 257
15   Formatting Web Pages by Using Cascading Style Sheets 271
16   Inserting Scripted Functionality by Using Behaviors 289
17   Adding Advanced Behaviors: The Drag Layer Behavior 309

Part V: Collecting User Data by Using Forms

HOUR 18 Creating a Form and Using a Form to Collect Data 323

19 Sending and Reacting to Form Data 345

Part VI: Organizing and Uploading a Project

HOUR 20 Uploading a Project 365

21 Managing and Editing a Project 383

22 Customizing Dreamweaver 397

23 Reusing Items in a Web Site by Using the Library 415

24 Creating and Applying a Template 429

Part VII: Appendixes

A Resources 445

B Glossary 451

Index 463

Table of Contents

Introduction   **1**

    What Is Dreamweaver MX 2004? 1

    Who Should Use Dreamweaver MX 2004? 1

    Who Should Use This Book? 2

    How to Use This Book 2

Part I: Getting Started with Dreamweaver MX

HOUR 1: Understanding the Dreamweaver Interface   **7**

    Acquainting Yourself with Dreamweaver 7

    Installing the Software 8

        Activating Dreamweaver 9

        Hardware and Software Requirements 9

        Getting the Demo Version 10

    Exploring the Dreamweaver Work Area 10

        The Start Page 11

        The Menu Bar 13

        The Insert Bar 16

        The Document Window 28

        The Document Toolbar 29

        The Status Bar 30

        Panels and Inspectors 32

        Context Menus 36

    Getting Help 37

    Summary 38

    Q&A 39

Workshop 39
   Quiz 39
   Quiz Answers 40
   Exercises 40

HOUR 2: Creating a Basic Web Page with Text   **41**
Creating a New Page 41
   Entering and Centering Text 42
   Applying Text Formatting 43
   Understanding Paragraph and Break Tags 43
   Changing Text Size 44
   Selecting a Font 44
   Selecting a Text Color: Using the Color Picker 45
   Using Dreamweaver's CSS Styles 47
Creating Lists and Indenting Text 48
Pasting Text from a File 50
Adding a Separator to a Page: The Horizontal Rule 51
Setting Page Properties 52
   Adding a Page Title 52
   Setting Page Appearance 53
Saving Your Work and Previewing in a Browser 56
Summary 58
Q&A 59
Workshop 59
   Quiz 59
   Quiz Answers 60
   Exercises 60

HOUR 3: Planning and Defining a Project   **61**
Defining a New Web Site 61
Using the Site Definition Wizard 64
Using the Files Panel 68
Using the Expanded Files Panel 69

Summary 196
Q&A 197
Workshop 197
    Quiz 197
    Quiz Answers 198
    Exercises 198

Part III: Web Page Layout with Tables and Frames

HOUR 11: Displaying Data by Using Tables   **201**
Creating a Table for Data 201
    Adding a Table to a Web Page 202
    Selecting Table Elements 203
    Setting Cell Padding and Cell Spacing 206
    Adding Header Cells to a Table 207
    Making a Table Accessible to People with Disabilities 207
Modifying a Table and Adding Content 208
    Adding and Sorting Data 208
    Adding and Removing Rows and Columns 210
    Changing Column Width and Row Height 211
    Resizing a Table and Changing Border Colors 211
    Using a Dreamweaver Preset Table Format 212
Exporting Data from a Table 213
Importing Table Data 214
Summary 216
Q&A 217
Workshop 217
    Quiz 217
    Quiz Answers 218
    Exercises 218

HOUR 12: Designing Page Layout by Using Tables   **219**

    Using Layout Mode 220

        Adding a Layout Table and Layout Cells 220

        Stretching Content to Fit the Page 222

    Editing a Table in Standard Mode 225

        Merging and Splitting Table Cells 225

        Aligning Table Cell Contents 226

    Adding Color to a Table 227

    Nesting a Table Within a Table 228

    Using a Tracing Image to Transfer a Design to a Web Page 229

    Turning a Table into a Group of Layers 231

    Summary 232

    Q&A 233

    Workshop 233

        Quiz 233

        Quiz Answers 234

        Exercises 234

HOUR 13: Understanding and Building Frames and Framesets   **235**

    Creating a Frameset 236

        Viewing Frame Borders 238

        Splitting a Page into Frames 238

        Naming Frames 239

    Using the Frames Panel 241

    Nesting Frames 242

    Using Existing Web Pages with Frames 243

    Setting Frame and Frameset Attributes 244

        Setting the Scrolling and Resize Attributes 244

        Setting Borders 246

        Setting the Frame Size 247

        Creating an Alternative to Frames 247

    Using Frames Objects 248

Introduction

"Ooooooo, Dreamweaver. I believe you can get me through the night." Remember that song by Gary Wright? Okay, some of you weren't born yet. The song brought up memories of seventh-grade dances for me. I'm glad that Dreamweaver, the software, came along and replaced that vision in my head. Dreamweaver, the software, has helped me through a number of nights developing Web sites and Web applications!

What Is Dreamweaver MX 2004?

Dreamweaver MX 2004 is newest version of Macromedia Dreamweaver, an award-winning HTML editor and Web application development tool. Some people do not exploit the more powerful features of Dreamweaver because they don't know about them. You will not be one of those people with this book in your hand!

Dreamweaver is excellent at quickly creating attractive Web pages that include styled text, graphics, forms, frames, tables, and more. But Dreamweaver really shines when you need to make your Web page *do* something. Dreamweaver excels at Dynamic HTML (DHTML), the Web functionality that enables the exact position-ing of content on a Web page and the scripting to make it work. Don't know how to script? No problem! Dreamweaver includes *behaviors*, scripted functionality that you simply click to add to a certain object.

Who Should Use Dreamweaver MX 2004?

Whether you are creating your very first Web page or have decided to try Web edit-ing software after coding by hand for years, you are going to love Macromedia Dreamweaver MX 2004. Dreamweaver gives you the freedom to visually design the look of a Web page and the power to make it act the way you want. Dreamweaver gives you the flexibility to create your own personal Web page or an entire corporate intranet site.

Who Should Use This Book?

This book is for anyone now using Dreamweaver, as well as anyone who is planning to. If you are new to Web development, this book will get you up to speed creating Web pages and Web sites. If you are already a Web developer, you'll find tips, tricks, and instructions to get all you can out of Dreamweaver MX 2004.

This book covers creating regular Web pages in Dreamweaver MX 2004, including forms, tables, interactivity, and JavaScript. After you have mastered the techniques covered here, you might want to explore other advanced capabilities of Dreamweaver MX 2004 to create Web pages that connect to databases. (Connecting your Web pages to databases enables you to create Web pages that change dynamically, depending on user choices.) Connecting Web pages to databases is beyond the scope of this book, but you can find information about it in *Dreamweaver MX 2004 Unleashed* from Sams Publishing.

How to Use This Book

Each hour of this book represents a lesson that should take you approximately an hour to learn. The book is designed to get you productively working in Dreamweaver MX 2004 as quickly as possible. There are numerous figures to illustrate the lessons in the book. Code is presented as follows:

- ▶ Code lines, commands, statements, and any other code-related terms appear in a `monospace` typeface. Placeholders (which stand for what you should actually type) appear in *`italic monospace`*. Text that you should type appears in ***`bold italic.`***

- ▶ When a line of code is too long to fit on one line of this book, it is broken at a convenient place and continued to the next line. The continuation is preceded by a special code continuation character (➡).

Each lesson begins with a list of topics and an overview. The lesson ends with questions and answers, a quiz, and some exercises that you can try on your own.

Within the lessons you'll find the following elements, which provide additional information:

| Notes give extra information on the current topic. | **By the** Way |

| Tips offer advice or describe an additional way of accomplishing something. | **Did you** Know? |

| Cautions signal you to be careful of potential problems and give you information on how to avoid or fix them. | **Watch** Out! |

As you read this book, remember: Have fun!

PART I

Getting Started with Dreamweaver MX

HOUR 1	Understanding the Dreamweaver Interface	7
HOUR 2	Creating a Basic Web Page with Text	41
HOUR 3	Planning and Defining a Project	61
HOUR 4	Setting Lots o' Links: Hyperlinks, URLs, Anchors, and Mailto Links	79
HOUR 5	HTML Is Fun! Viewing and Modifying HTML	97

HOUR 1

Understanding the Dreamweaver Interface

What You'll Learn in This Hour:

▶ What hardware and software you will need to run Dreamweaver
▶ How to install the Dreamweaver demo
▶ How to use the Dreamweaver user interface
▶ How to manage panels, inspectors, and windows

I'm sure you are itching to begin creating dazzling and fun Web sites, the type that you'll show off to your friends, family members, and co-workers. Or maybe you've been assigned the task of creating a Web site in Dreamweaver for your job. First, however, you need to understand the Dreamweaver interface and the numerous functions that are going to help you be successful as a Web developer. Understanding the Dreamweaver user interface enables you to understand the instructions in the rest of this book.

If you have used other Macromedia tools, you'll recognize the standard Macromedia user interface elements, such as panel groups and inspectors. If you have used previous versions of Dreamweaver, you should quickly skim this hour to see what exciting changes and updates Macromedia has made to the new version of Dreamweaver. This hour provides an important orientation to the concepts you'll use in later hours to create Web pages.

Acquainting Yourself with Dreamweaver

Dreamweaver is a complete Web development environment—an HTML (Hypertext Markup Language) editor, an authoring tool, a dynamic Web page development tool, and a Web site management tool, all rolled into one. Web pages are created using HTML, but you can do many things without ever laying your eyes on any HTML. If you want to produce professional-quality Web pages, including scripting, Dreamweaver makes it easy to do so.

HTML is the language of Web pages. It consists mainly of paired tags contained in angle brackets (<>). The tags surround objects on a Web page, such as text, or stand on their own. For instance, the HTML code to make text bold looks like this: `<b>bold text</b>`; these bold tags are an example of paired tags. The ending tag of paired tag always begins with a forward slash. Other tags, such as the tag used to insert an image into a Web page, are single tags: `<img src="smile.gif">`.

Dreamweaver is a WYSIWYG (what you see is what you get) Web page editor that is extremely powerful while also being easy to use. You can create new Web sites by using Dreamweaver, and you can import and edit existing Web sites. Dreamweaver will not change or rearrange your code. One of Dreamweaver's most popular features has always been that it leaves existing sites intact; the folks at Macromedia, the company that creates Dreamweaver, call this feature **Roundtrip HTML**.

Dreamweaver is also an authoring tool. What do I mean by *authoring tool*? **Authoring tools** enable you to create a complete application that includes interactivity. Dreamweaver can be used as simply an HTML editor, and it can also be used to create multimedia applications. You can author an experience for your viewers.

Dreamweaver MX 2004 can create dynamic Web pages. **Dynamic Web pages** are created using server-side scripting and require that you understand server technologies and other advanced topics. Although these topics are outside the scope of this book, they should not necessarily be outside the scope of *your* interests. Consult Appendix A, "Resources," for books and Web sites dedicated to creating dynamic Web pages with Dreamweaver. This book teaches you how to create regular Web pages that do not depend on server-side scripting or any special server features to create. You'll need to understand the material in this book before you move on to dynamic Web pages.

Installing the Software

A standard Windows or Macintosh installation program installs Dreamweaver. The installation program creates all the necessary directories and files needed to run Dreamweaver on your hard drive. Dreamweaver also installs the Macromedia

Extension Manager, a program that helps you install Dreamweaver extensions that you can download free from the Internet. You'll learn more about Dreamweaver extensions in Hour 22, "Customizing Dreamweaver."

Activating Dreamweaver

Before you can use Dreamweaver MX 2004, you need to activate the software. This is a new procedure Macromedia has put in place to fight theft and piracy of its products. The first time you launch Dreamweaver MX 2004, you will be prompted to enter the serial number that came with the product and then activate the software.

Activation is an anonymous and secure process that takes a few short steps to complete. The process creates an anonymous hardware ID based on an encrypted combination of your computer's hard drive geometry, CPU family, and operating system, plus the information about your Dreamweaver product. Your hard drive is not scanned, nor is any information collected that can identify you or your computer hardware.

You can activate your software 24 hours a day, 7 days a week either over the Internet or by calling a toll-free telephone number. The Macromedia End User License Agreement allows you to install a secondary version of the software (on your laptop, for instance) for nonconcurrent use. If you need to move the software to a different computer, on the original computer, select Help, Transfer Software in Dreamweaver MX 2004 to deactivate the software on the original computer so that you can activate it on another computer.

Hardware and Software Requirements

Table 1.1 lists the hardware and software required to run Dreamweaver.

TABLE 1.1 Hardware and Software Requirements for Dreamweaver

Windows	Macintosh
600MHz or better Intel Pentium III processor or equivalent	500MHz Power Mac G3 or better
Windows 98, Windows 2000, Windows XP, or Windows Server 2003	OS X 10.2.6 or greater
128MB available RAM (256MB recommended)	128MB available RAM (256MB recommended)
275MB available disk space	275MB available disk space

TABLE 1.1 Continued

Windows	Macintosh
Display capable of 1024×768 and 16-bit color (thousands of colors) or better	Display capable of 1024×768 and 16-bit color (thousands of colors) or better
Netscape Navigator or Explorer 4.0 or greater	Netscape Navigator or Internet Explorer 4.0 or greater (or Safari!)

Getting the Demo Version

Macromedia offers a demo version of the software that you can evaluate before you decide to purchase Dreamweaver. You can download the time-limited demo at www.macromedia.com/software/dreamweaver/trial.

Exploring the Dreamweaver Work Area

When you first open Dreamweaver in Windows, you are given the opportunity to choose either the Designer workspace or the HomeSite/Coder-Style workspace, as shown in Figure 1.1. I suggest that you pick the Designer workspace; all the figures and examples in this book refer to that workspace configuration. The HomeSite/Coder-Style workspace is designed for Web developers who write HTML by hand. The Macintosh version of Dreamweaver gives you the Designer workspace.

FIGURE 1.1
You can change the workspace by selecting either the Designer or the HomeSite/ Coder-Style workspace in the Workspace Setup dialog box.

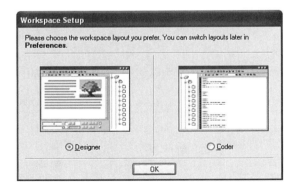

If you select the HomeSite/Code-Style workspace and then want to change to the Designer workspace, you can do so in the Dreamweaver Preferences dialog box. To open the Preferences dialog box, select Edit, Preferences in Windows (Dreamweaver, Preferences on the Mac). Select the General category and click the Change Workspace button. You'll again see the Workspace Setup dialog box, and you can use it to change your workspace configuration. You'll explore many other Dreamweaver preferences throughout this book.

The Start Page

Dreamweaver initially displays a box with a green bar across the top, called the Start page. The Start page lists common Dreamweaver tasks, such as Open a Recent Item, Create New, and Create from Samples. At the bottom of the Start page are links to the Dreamweaver Quick Tour and the Dreamweaver Tutorial. Clicking the image of the Dreamweaver box takes you to the Macromedia Web site for up-to-date information on Dreamweaver, including tips and special offers. Whenever you don't have Web pages open in Dreamweaver, you will see the Start page displayed.

The Start page appears in an important part of Dreamweaver called the Document window. The **Document window** displays a Web page approximately as it will appear in a Web browser. The Document window is bordered on the right by **panels**, as shown in Figure 1.2. These panels contain the commands you use to modify and organize Web pages and Web page elements. The Document window, the panels, and other elements, which you'll explore in a few minutes, are grouped together into an integrated interface if you are working in the Windows operating system.

When you open Dreamweaver MX 2004 for Macintosh, you also see the Document window displaying the Start page, as shown in Figure 1.3. The Macintosh version of Dreamweaver MX 2004 has panels that float on top of the Document window. The floating panels, launched from the Window menu, can be moved to any location on the desktop. The Mac and Windows versions of Dreamweaver look slightly different from each other but have the same features and functionality.

Insert bar　　Document window　　Document toolbar　　　Panel group

FIGURE 1.2
The Dreamweaver workspace contains the Document window along with integrated panels.

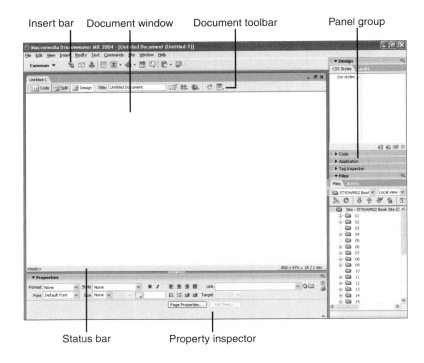

Status bar　　　　　Property inspector

Insert bar

FIGURE 1.3
The Macintosh workspace includes the Document window with panels that float on top.

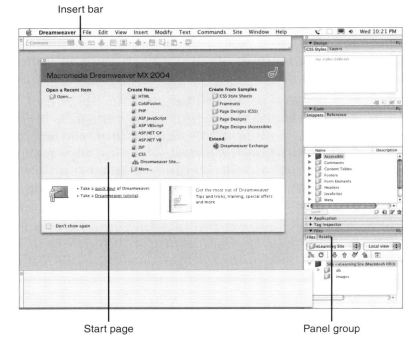

Start page　　　　　　　　　　Panel group

The Menu Bar

Some people prefer using menu commands (I like keyboard shortcuts) and some people prefer clicking icons. For the menu crowd, this section describes the organization of Dreamweaver's menus. The File and Edit menus (see Figure 1.4) are standard in most programs. The File menu contains commands for opening, closing, saving, importing, and exporting files. The Edit menu contains the Cut, Copy, and Paste commands, along with the Find and Replace command and the Preferences command. Many elements of the Dreamweaver user interface and its operation can be configured with the Preferences command.

File	
New...	Ctrl+N
Open...	Ctrl+O
Open Recent	▶
Open in Frame...	Ctrl+Shift+O
Close	Ctrl+W
Close All	
Save	Ctrl+S
Save As...	Ctrl+Shift+S
Save to Remote Server...	
Save as Template...	
Save All	
Revert	
Print Code...	Ctrl+P
Import	▶
Export	▶
Convert	▶
Preview in Browser	▶
Check Page	▶
Design Notes...	
Exit	Ctrl+Q

Edit	
Undo Backspace	Ctrl+Z
Redo Backspace	Ctrl+Y
Cut	Ctrl+X
Copy	Ctrl+C
Paste	Ctrl+V
Clear	
Copy HTML	Ctrl+Shift+C
Paste HTML	Ctrl+Shift+V
Paste Text	
Select All	Ctrl+A
Select Parent Tag	Ctrl+[
Select Child	Ctrl+]
Find and Replace...	Ctrl+F
Find Next	F3
Go to Line	Ctrl+G
Show Code Hints	Ctrl+Space
Indent Code	Ctrl+Shift+>
Outdent Code	Ctrl+Shift+<
Balance Braces	Ctrl+'
Repeating Entries	▶
Edit with External Editor	
Tag Libraries...	
Keyboard Shortcuts...	
Preferences...	Ctrl+U

FIGURE 1.4
The File and Edit menus contain commands that are common to many applications, plus a few Dreamweaver-specific ones.

The View menu (see Figure 1.5) turns on and off your view of the head content; invisible elements; layer, table, and frame borders; the status bar; and image maps. You can tell whether you are currently viewing one of these elements by whether a check mark is shown beside it. The View menu also has commands to turn on the ruler and grid, play plug-ins, and show a tracing image. It's okay if you don't understand what these commands enable you to do—you'll learn more about them in later hours.

FIGURE 1.5
The View menu houses commands to turn interface elements on and off.

The Insert menu (see Figure 1.6) is roughly equivalent to the Insert bar because you can insert all the items available on the Insert bar by using this menu. If you prefer to click icons, use the Insert bar, but if you prefer to see the names of the objects you insert in your Web pages, use the Insert menu. The Modify menu (see Figure 1.6) enables you to modify properties of the currently selected object.

FIGURE 1.6
The Insert and Modify menus give you control over inserting and changing the attributes of objects.

The Text menu (see Figure 1.7) gives you access to multiple ways of fine-tuning the appearance of the text in a Web page. Most important to those of you who are questionable spellers, the Text menu contains the Check Spelling command.

TABLE 1.2   Continued

Icon	Icon Name	Description
Common Category		
	Draw Polygon Hotspot	Allows you to draw a polygon over a specific region of an image and link it to a specific URL. (In the Images drop-down menu.)
	Flash	Places a Macromedia Flash movie at the insertion point. (In the Media drop-down menu.)
	Flash Button	Places one of the available prefabricated Macromedia Flash buttons at the insertion point. (In the Media drop-down menu.)
	Flash Text	Places an editable Flash Text object at the insertion point and creates a Flash file. (In the Media drop-down menu.)
	Shockwave	Places a **Shockwave movie** (that is, a Macromedia Director movie prepared for the Web) at the insertion point. (In the Media drop-down menu.)
	Applet	Places a Java applet at the insertion point. (In the Media drop-down menu.)
	Param	Inserts a tag that enables you to enter parameters and their values to pass to an applet or an ActiveX control. (In the Media drop-down menu.)
	ActiveX	Places an ActiveX control at the insertion point. (In the Media drop-down menu.)
	Plugin	Places any file requiring a browser plug-in at the insertion point. (In the Media drop-down menu.)
	Date	Inserts the current date at the insertion point.
	Comment	Inserts a comment at the insertion point.

TABLE 1.2 Continued

Icon	Icon Name	Description
Common Category		
	Make Template	Creates a Dreamweaver template from the current Web page. (In the Templates drop-down menu.)
	Make Nested Template	Creates a nested Dreamweaver template from the current template. (In the Templates drop-down menu.)
	Editable Region	Adds an editable region to a template. (In the Templates drop-down menu.)
	Optional Region	Adds an optional region to a template; this region can be set to either show or hide. (In the Templates drop-down menu.)
	Repeating Region	Adds a repeating region to a template. (In the Templates drop-down menu.)
	Editable Optional Region	Adds an editable optional region to a template. (In the Templates drop-down menu.)
	Repeating Table	Adds a repeating table to a template and defines which cells can be edited. (In the Templates drop-down menu.)
	Tag Chooser	Enables you to choose a tag to insert from a hierarchical menu of all available tags.
Layout Category		
	Table	Creates a table at the insertion point. (Also in the Common category.)
	Insert Div Tag	Adds a `<div>` tag, the tag that Dreamweaver uses to create layers.
	Draw Layer	Draws a layer container in a Web page.
	Standard Mode	Turns on Dreamweaver's Standard mode, at the same time turning off either Expanded Tables mode or Layout mode.

TABLE 1.2 Continued

Icon	Icon Name	Description
Layout Category		
Expanded	Expanded Tables Mode	Turns on Dreamweaver's Expanded Tables mode, temporarily adding cell padding and borders to all tables.
Layout	Layout mode	Turns on Dreamweaver's Layout mode, enabling you to draw tables and table cells.
	Layout Table	Draws a table while you're in Layout view.
	Draw Layout Cell	Draws a table cell while you're in Layout view.
	Insert Row Above	Adds a row above the currently selected row of a table.
	Insert Row Below	Adds a row beneath the currently selected row of a table.
	Insert Column to the Left	Adds a column to the left of the currently selected column in a table.
	Insert Column to the Right	Adds a column to the right of a currently selected column in a table.
	Left Frame	Creates a frame to the left of the current frame. (In the Frames drop-down menu.)
	Right Frame	Creates a frame to the right of the current frame. (In the Frames drop-down menu.)
	Top Frame	Creates a frame above the current frame. (In the Frames drop-down menu.)
	Bottom Frame	Creates a frame below the current frame. (In the Frames drop-down menu.)
	Bottom and Nested Left Frame	Creates a frame to the left of the current frame and then adds a frame below. (In the Frames drop-down menu.)

TABLE 1.2   Continued

Icon	Icon Name	Description
Layout Category		
	Bottom and Nested Right Frame	Creates a frame to the right of the current frame and then adds a frame below. (In the Frames drop-down menu.)
	Left and Nested Bottom Frame	Creates a frame below the current frame and then adds a frame to the left. (In the Frames drop-down menu.)
	Right and Nested Bottom Frame	Creates a frame below the current frame and then adds a frame to the right. (In the Frames drop-down menu.)
	Top and Bottom Frame	Creates a frame below the current frame and then adds a frame above. (In the Frames drop-down menu.)
	Left and Nested Top Frame	Creates a frame above the current frame and then adds a frame to the left. (In the Frames drop-down menu.)
	Right and Nested Top Frame	Creates a frame above the current frame and then adds a frame to the right. (In the Frames drop-down menu.)
	Top and Nested Left Frame	Creates a frame to the left of the current frame and then adds a frame above. (In the Frames drop-down menu.)
	Top and Nested Right Frame	Creates a frame to the right of the current frame and then adds a frame above. (In the Frames drop-down menu.)
	Tabular Data	Creates at the insertion point a table that is populated with data from a chosen file. (In the Frames drop-down menu.)
Forms Category		
	Form	Places a form at the insertion point.

TABLE 1.2 Continued

Icon	Icon Name	Description
Forms Category		
	Text Field	Inserts a text field.
	Hidden Field	Inserts a hidden field.
	Textarea	Inserts a textarea, which is a multi-line text field.
	Check Box	Inserts a check box.
	Radio Button	Inserts a radio button.
	Radio Group	Inserts a group of related radio buttons.
	List/Menu	Inserts a list or a drop-down menu.
	Jump Menu	Creates a jump menu that allows users to select a Web site from a menu and go to that site.
	Image Field	Inserts an image field, which enables an image to act as a button.
	File Field	Inserts a file field, which enables the user to upload a file.
	Button	Inserts a button.
	Label	Assigns a label to a form element, enabling browsers for people with visual impairments to access extra information about the form elements nested within the label.
	Fieldset	Groups related form fields together to make the form accessible to browsers for people with visual impairments. Fieldset wraps around a group of form elements and appears to sighted people as a box drawn around the group, with the fieldset title at the top.

TABLE 1.2 Continued

Icon	Icon Name	Description
Text Category		
	Font Tag Editor	Opens the Font Tag Editor to set up the attributes of a font tag.
	Bold	Makes the selected text bold by using the b tag. This tag has been dropped from recent versions of HTML. The approved tag for bold text is the strong tag.
	Italic	Makes the selected text italic. This tag has been dropped from recent versions of HTML. The approved tag for italic text is the emphasis tag.
	Strong	Makes the selected text bold by using the approved strong tag.
	Emphasis	Makes the selected text italic by using the approved emphasis tag.
	Paragraph	Makes the selected text into a paragraph.
	Block Quote	Makes the selected text into a block quote, indented from the right and the left by using the blockquote tag.
	Preformatted Text	Makes the selected text preformatted (using the pre tag, displaying the text in a monospaced font and with the ability to enter spaces).
	Heading 1	Makes the selected text a heading size 1 (largest) by using the h1 tag.
	Heading 2	Makes the selected text a heading size 2 by using the h2 tag.
	Heading 3	Makes the selected text a heading size 3 by using the h3 tag.
	Unordered List	Makes the selected text into an unordered (bulleted) list.
	Ordered List	Makes the selected text into an ordered (numbered) list.

TABLE 1.2   Continued

Icon	Icon Name	Description
Text Category		
li	List Item	Makes the selected text into a list item (by using the li tag), a single item in an ordered or unordered list.
dl	Definition List	Creates a definition list. A **definition list** consists of definition terms and definition descriptions.
dt	Definition Term	Creates a definition term within a definition list.
dd	Definition Description	Creates a definition description within a definition list.
abbr.	Abbreviation	Wraps the abbr tag around text, adding a full-text definition to an abbreviation. This aids search engines in indexing a Web page properly.
W3C	Acronym	Wraps the acronym tag around text, adding a full-text definition to an acronym. This aids search engines in indexing a Web page properly.
BR	Line Break	Places a line break, the br tag, at the insertion point. (In the Characters drop-down menu.)
"	Non-Breaking Space	Inserts a special character ( ) that creates a space. The Non-Breaking Space character also prevents a line break from occurring between two words. (In the Characters drop-down menu.)
"	Left Quote	Inserts the special character for a left quote. (In the Characters drop-down menu.)
"	Right Quote	Inserts the special character for a right quote. (In the Characters drop-down menu.)
—	Em-Dash	Inserts the special character for an em dash (—). (In the Characters drop-down menu.)

TABLE 1.2   Continued

Icon	Icon Name	Description
Text Category		
£	Pound	Inserts the special character for the pound currency symbol. (In the Characters drop-down menu.)
€	Euro	Inserts the special character for the euro currency symbol. (In the Characters drop-down menu.)
¥	Yen	Inserts the special character for the yen currency symbol. (In the Characters drop-down menu.)
©	Copyright	Inserts the special character for the copyright symbol. (In the Characters drop-down menu.)
®	Registered Trademark	Inserts the special character for the registered trademark symbol. (In the Characters drop-down menu.)
TM	Trademark	Inserts the special character for the trademark symbol. (In the Characters drop-down menu.)
	Other Characters	Opens a menu that displays many additional special characters. (In the Characters drop-down menu.)
HTML Category		
	Horizontal Rule	Inserts a horizontal rule, a simple divider line across the page.
	Meta	Inserts a `meta` tag into the head section of a Web page. This object can insert a `name` `meta` tag, aiding search engines, or an `http-equiv` `meta` tag that can redirect the user to a different URL or give additional information about the Web page, such as assigning parental control information to a page. (In the Head drop-down menu.)
	Keywords	Inserts a `keywords` meta tag into the head section, adding keywords to the Web page to help search engines properly index it. (In the Head drop-down menu.)

TABLE 1.2 Continued

Icon	Icon Name	Description
HTML Category		
	Description	Inserts a description meta tag into the head section, adding a description to the Web page helping search engines properly index it. (In the Head drop-down menu.)
	Refresh	Inserts a refresh meta tag into the head section. This tag sets the number of seconds before the page will automatically jump to another Web page or reload itself. (In the Head drop-down menu.)
	Base	Inserts a base tag into the head section. This enables you to set a base URL or a base target window affecting all of the paths on the Web page. (In the Head drop-down menu.)
	Link	Inserts the address of an external file, usually a script or style sheet file. (In the Head drop-down menu.)
tabl	Table Tag	Inserts a table tag (in Code view only). (In the Tables drop-down menu.)
tr	Table Row	Inserts a tr tag (in Code view only). (In the Tables drop-down menu.)
th	Table Header	Inserts a th tag (in Code view only). (In the Tables drop-down menu.)
td	Table Data	Inserts a td tag (in Code view only). (In the Tables drop-down menu.)
cap	Table Caption	Inserts a caption tag (in Code view only). (In the Tables drop-down menu.)
fset	Frameset	Inserts a frameset tag (in Code view only). (In the Frames drop-down menu.)
frm	Frame	Inserts a frame tag (in Code view only). (In the Frames drop-down menu.)

TABLE 1.2   Continued

Icon	Icon Name	Description
HTML Category		
ifrm	Floating Frame	Inserts an `iframe` tag (in Code view only). (In the Frames drop-down menu.)
	No Frames	Inserts a `noframes` tag to surround HTML code for browsers that cannot display frames (in Code view only). (In the Frames drop-down menu.)
	Script	Inserts scripted code at the insertion point. (In the Script drop-down menu.)
	No Script	Inserts the `noscript` tag surrounding HTML code that will be displayed by browsers that do not support scripts. (In the Script drop-down menu.)
	Server-Side Include	Places a file that simulates a server-side include at the insertion point. (In the Script drop-down menu.)

The Favorites category enables you to add objects that you use frequently to a single Insert bar category. You'll explore this functionality in Hour 22, when you learn how to modify Dreamweaver to your own way of working. By the end of this book you will have a better idea of the types of objects you'll want to place in the Favorites category to help you work more quickly in Dreamweaver. These are your personal favorites, the objects that you use most often, collected in one handy Insert bar category.

The Document Window

By default the Document window is maximized and its title and filename appear at the very top of the screen. You'll explore saving a file, giving it a filename, and giving it a title in Hour 2, "Creating a Basic Web Page with Text." The Document window is the part of the Dreamweaver interface that you will be using most often in your work. The Document toolbar appears at the top of the Document window.

The Document Toolbar

The Document toolbar, shown in Figure 1.12, gives you quick access to important commands. The three buttons on the left of the Document toolbar enable you to toggle between Code view, Design view, and a split view with both Code view and Design view visible. I probably use Design view 90% of the time and divide the other 10% of my Dreamweaver time between Code view and the split view. The split view showing both Design and Code views is useful when you're learning HTML because it enables you to see the tags that Dreamweaver adds while you create a Web page.

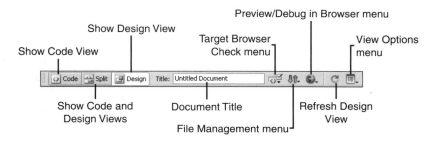

Show Code View
Show Design View
Preview/Debug in Browser menu
Target Browser Check menu
View Options menu
Show Code and Design Views
Document Title
File Management menu
Refresh Design View

FIGURE 1.12
The Document toolbar contains commands you commonly apply to Web pages when editing in Dreamweaver.

The text box in the Document toolbar is where you give a Web page a title (the default title—Untitled Document—isn't very interesting!). This Web page title appears in the user's browser title bar when the user views the page. It is also saved in the browser's Favorites or Bookmarks list as the name of the URL, so it needs to be meaningful.

There are four drop-down menus on the toolbar: the Target Browser Check menu, the File Management menu, the Preview/Debug in Browser menu, and the View Options menu. The Target Browser Check menu enables you to check that your Web page works correctly in various browsers. The File Management menu lists commands such as those for getting files to and from a Web server. You'll explore these commands in Hours 21 and 22, when you upload and manage a Web site. The Preview/Debug in Browser menu gives you quick access to the list of browsers you'll use to preview Web pages. The Refresh Design View button refreshes Design view when you are editing the code (in Code view or the split screen view) so that you can instantly see the changes you make to the code.

Where's My Document Toolbar?

If the Document toolbar isn't visible in your Document window, select View, Toolbar, Document.

The View Options menu changes, depending on whether you have Design or Code view open. While you're in Design view, this menu displays commands that are also in Dreamweaver's View menu, such as those for viewing head content or the rulers. While you're in Code view, the View Options menu contains commands that affect the way the code is displayed, such as Word Wrap and Line Numbers.

The Status Bar

The Dreamweaver Document window has a status bar along the bottom of the page. It contains the tag selector, the Window Size drop-down menu, and download statistics, as shown in Figure 1.13. These convenient tools are just some of the nice touches that Dreamweaver offers to help you have a productive and fun experience designing for the Web.

Tag selector   Window Size menu

FIGURE 1.13
The status bar contains tools that help you get information about a Web page.

Currently selected tag (bold)   Download statistics

The tag selector in the lower-left corner of the Document window provides easy access to the HTML tags that are involved in any object on the screen. If, for example, the cursor is located in a table cell, the tag selector enables selection of any of the HTML tags that control that object. The tag that is currently selected is shown in bold in the tag selector. The tags to the left of the selected tag are the tags that are wrapped around the selected tag.

Did you Know?

The Tag Selector Is Your Friend

The tag selector will be important later, when you start using behaviors in Hour 16, "Inserting Scripted Functionality by Using Behaviors," and Hour 17, "Adding Advanced Behaviors." You apply behaviors to specific tags, and sometimes the tags are difficult to select, especially the <body> tag, which contains the entire Web page content. The tag selector makes it very easy to select the entire body of a Web page by clicking the <body> tag.

The Window Size drop-down menu helps you re-create a target screen resolution by resizing the Document window. You will always want to make sure that your design looks good at a low (800×600) or high screen resolution. You can use the Window Size drop-down menu (see Figure 1.14) to quickly resize the Document window to view the approximate amount of screen real estate you will have at a certain resolution. The Window Size drop-down menu works only when you do not have the Document window maximized.

Maximize button

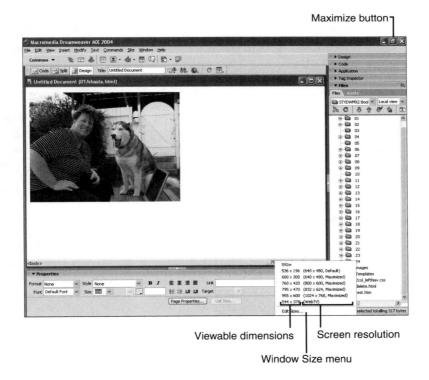

Viewable dimensions   Screen resolution

Window Size menu

FIGURE 1.14
The Window Size menu resizes the screen, approximating how the page will look at different screen resolutions.

Notice the sizes available in the Window Size menu:

▶ The dimensions listed on the right (in parentheses) represent the screen resolutions.

▶ The numbers listed on the left are the estimated browser window dimensions. They are smaller than the screen resolutions because the browser interface (buttons and menus, for instance) takes up space. For example, when the viewer's monitor is set to 640×480, the viewable area is only 536×196 pixels.

Did you Know?

Define Special Window Sizes

Create your own custom settings for the Window Size menu by selecting the last choice in the Window Size pop-up menu, the Edit Sizes command. This command takes you to the Status Bar category in the Dreamweaver Preferences dialog box, where you can add your custom window size. For instance, do you want to create a Web page that is readable on your wireless phone? My phone has the capability to view 120×160 pixels, so I could create a custom size to create a Web page for my phone.

Because bandwidth is often an issue when you're developing for the Web, it's nice to know the estimated file size and download time of a Web page. The estimated download time shown in the status bar is based on the modem setting in the Status Bar category in the Dreamweaver Preferences dialog box. The default modem setting is 28.8Kbps; you might want to change this setting to 56Kbps or whatever the bandwidth speed is for the targeted viewer of your Web page. (Most people in the United States browse the Web at a speed of at least 56Kbps.) Dreamweaver takes into account images and other assets contained in the Web page when calculating the file size and download time.

Panels and Inspectors

You set properties of objects, display panels, and add functionality to Web page through Dreamweaver's panels and inspectors. Most commands in Dreamweaver are available in several places, usually as menu commands and as panel commands. Dreamweaver's panels are grouped into tabbed panel groups beside the Document window (Windows) or floating on top (Mac).

You can open every panel from the Window menu and by default Dreamweaver has all the important panels and the Property inspector open. If a panel or inspector is open, its command has a check mark beside it in the Window menu. To close a panel or an inspector, deselect the command in the Window menu. The panel doesn't actually go away, but the panel group's expander arrow turns and the panel group collapses so that you don't see it anymore. Command names in the Window menu may be slightly different from the names of the panels or inspectors they launch. For instance, you open the Property inspector using the Properties command and the Insert bar using the Insert command.

Panels and Panel Groups

You can expand or collapse a panel group or an inspector by clicking the expander arrow to the left of the panel title, as shown in Figure 1.15. Immediately to the left of the expander arrow is the gripper. You can undock a panel group or inspector by selecting its gripper and dragging the panel group away from where it is docked. To dock a panel group or inspector, select its gripper and drag-and-drop above or below the other panel groups or the Document window. When it is docked, you'll see an outline around the panel group. Because the Macintosh version of Dreamweaver has floating panels, you can move them wherever you want anytime!

Gripper

Expander arrow

FIGURE 1.15
Expand and collapse panel groups using the expander arrow.

In the Windows integrated user interface, resize the width of all the panel groups by dragging the bar that separates the panel groups and the Document window. To resize the height of an individual panel group, move your cursor to the edge of the panel until it turns into a double-arrow cursor and drag the edges of the panel to the desired height. Windows users can use the Collapse button, shown in Figure 1.16, within the bars that separate the Document window from the panel groups and the Property inspector to toggle expanding and collapsing those two areas. Mac users can change the size of floating panel groups by dragging the borders of the group to the desired width and height.

Collapse button

FIGURE 1.16
The Collapse buttons collapse and expand the panel group area and the Property inspector area so that you have more room for the Document window.

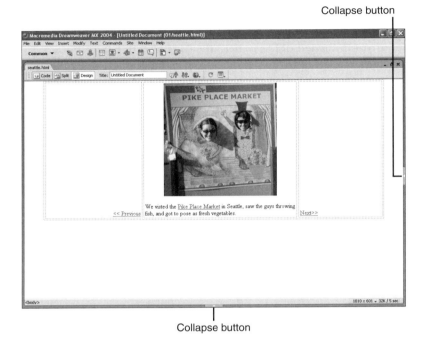

Collapse button

Advanced Panel Maintenance

You can completely close a panel group, removing it from display on the screen, by selecting the Close Panel Group command in the panel drop-down menu located in the upper right of each panel group. There's also a command listed in this menu that enables you to group a panel with a different panel group: Select the Group With command to select a different panel group.

The Property Inspector

The Property inspector displays all the properties of the currently selected object. The Property inspector is like a chameleon that changes depending on the environment; it looks different and displays appropriate properties for whichever object is selected. For example, when text is selected onscreen, the Property inspector presents text properties, as shown in Figure 1.17. In Figure 1.18, an image is selected, and the Property inspector presents image properties.

Selected text

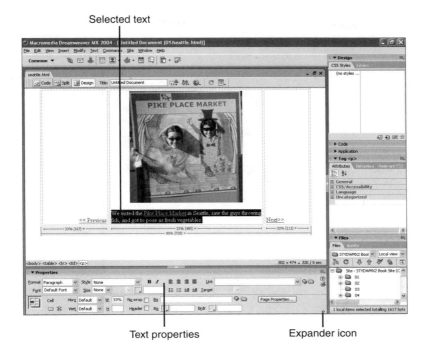

FIGURE 1.17
The Property inspector displays text properties when text is selected.

Text properties   Expander icon

You can expand the Property inspector by using the Expander icon so that you have access to every available property. You do this by selecting the expander arrow in the lower-right corner of the Property inspector. Notice how the arrow is pointing down in Figure 1.18 and pointing up, with the Property inspector expanded, in Figure 1.17.

FIGURE 1.18
The Property
inspector displays
image properties
when an image is
selected.

FIGURE 1.18
The Property
inspector displays
image properties
when an image is
selected.

Context Menus

There are multiple ways to access and modify object properties in Dreamweaver. I'm sure you'll find your favorite ways very quickly. Context menus are one of the choices available. These menus pop up when you right-click (Control+click on the Mac) an object in the Document window. The contents of the menu are dependent on which object you clicked. For instance, Figure 1.19 shows the context menu that pops up when you right-click a table.

Context menu   Table commands

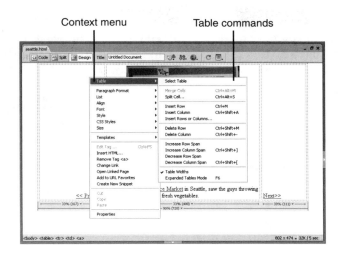

FIGURE 1.19
The context menu for tables gives you quick access to many table commands.

Getting Help

You select Help, Using Dreamweaver (or use the standard help shortcut key, F1) to launch the Dreamweaver help files. The left side of the help page contains the Contents, Index, Search, and Favorites tabs. The right side of the page is where the help content files appear. The Next and Previous arrow buttons enable you to page through all the help topics.

Did you Know?

Using Help to Learn About Dreamweaver

While you are getting familiar with Dreamweaver, you might want to use the arrow buttons in the upper- and lower-right corners of the help content area to navigate through the topics. The topics are grouped, so you might get more information on your current topic on the next page. If you keep clicking either of these arrows, eventually you will go on to another topic.

In Windows, the Contents tab displays the table of contents. The table of contents is organized in subject categories. Selecting one of the categories expands the list, with subtopics under that category. The Index button shows an alphabetical index of all topics in the help system. Select the Search tab to enter a topic you want to search for. Create your own list of favorite help topics by selecting the Favorites tab and clicking the Add button at the bottom to add the current topic.

Dreamweaver help on the Mac looks slightly different from Windows help; it displays in the Macintosh Help Viewer. Click on the Index or Table of Contents links at the top of the left panel to toggle between the two display modes.

One of the easiest ways to get help on your current task is to launch context-sensitive help. When you have an object selected (and you can see its properties in the Property inspector), click the Help icon in the Property inspector, shown in Figure 1.20, to go directly to information about that object.

Help icon

FIGURE 1.20
Clicking the Property inspector Help icon takes you directly to information about the properties of the object currently selected. In this instance, you will go directly to help on images.

Summary

In this hour, you have learned about the Dreamweaver Document window and other elements of the Dreamweaver user interface, such as the Insert bar, menus, the status bar, and panels. You have explored expanding and docking panel groups. You have seen the commands available in Dreamweaver's menus and Insert bar. You have been introduced to the Property inspector and have learned how to get help on Dreamweaver topics.

Q&A

Q. *How do I get as much room in the Document window as I possibly can?*

A. First, make sure that the Document window is maximized. You can collapse the Property inspector and the panel groups by clicking the expander and the Collapse buttons. Or you can do all this much more quickly by pressing F4 (the shortcut for the Hide Panels command in the Window menu). The F4 command works in most of Macromedia's products to hide much of the user interface so you only see your project. The F4 command also toggles the panels back on.

Q. *There's something wrong with my Dreamweaver installation because it looks very different from the examples in your book. All the panels appear on the left side of the screen, and I don't know how to move them. Help!*

A. When Dreamweaver was initially launched, someone selected HomeSite/Coder-Style for the workspace instead of Designer, which is used in this book (and is the workspace that most people choose). You can switch it back by selecting Edit, Preferences and then selecting the Workspace button in the General category.

Workshop

The Workshop contains quiz questions and activities to help reinforce what you've learned in this hour. In case you get stuck, the answers to the quiz appear after the questions.

Quiz

1. Which menu do you use to open a Dreamweaver panel?

2. What three standard items are found in the status bar of the Document window?

3. Is Dreamweaver an HTML editor, an authoring tool, or a Web site management tool?

Quiz Answers

1. The Window menu enables you to turn on and off all the panels and inspectors. There is a check mark beside a command if it is currently turned on.

2. The status bar contains the tag selector, Window Size menu, and download statistics.

3. Sorry, this is a trick question! Dreamweaver is all these things.

Exercises

1. Open the Dreamweaver Preferences dialog box from the Edit menu. Select the General category and examine each of the available settings. Experiment with changing any of these settings. Click the Help button and read about each of the settings. Don't change settings randomly, especially if you don't understand what the setting accomplishes.

2. Experiment with expanding and collapsing panel groups. Resize the panel groups. Explore some of the panel drop-down menus found in the upper-right corner of the panel. Use the F4 key (Hide Panels/Show Panels command) to toggle the options.

3. Launch the Quick Tour from the Start page that appears when you open Dreamweaver MX 2004. You need to be connected to the Internet to take this tour. Click HTML under the Create New category in the Start page. This creates a blank HTML document in the Document window. Now you're ready for Hour 2, where you'll make your first Web page!

Creating a Basic Web Page with Text

What You'll Learn in This Hour:

▶ How to create a new Web page

▶ How to use the Property inspector to change object properties

▶ How to change fonts and font sizes

▶ How to create unordered and ordered lists

▶ How to preview a Web page in different browsers

The most common elements in a Web page are text and images, so this hour we'll start with text. You'll get started creating Web pages with Dreamweaver by becoming familiar with adding text and setting text properties.

Creating a New Page

To create a new Web page, select File, New. The New Document dialog box appears, enabling you to select the type of document you want to create. This dialog box is organized into a Category column and a column that lists the pages in the selected category. Select the Basic Page category, and then select HTML as the Basic Page type, as shown in Figure 2.1. Click the Create button. A new document is created, and you can add text, images, and other objects to it.

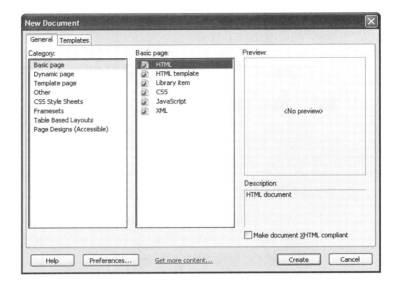

Entering and Centering Text

You can simply type into the Document window to enter text into a Web page.
Type some text as a title at the top of the page, press the Enter key, and type a
couple sentences. To align your title in the center of the page, follow these steps:

1. Open the Property inspector.

2. Select the title text.

3. Click the Align Center icon (see Figure 2.2) in the Property inspector.

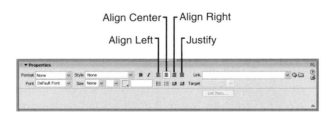

Alternatively, with the text selected, select Text, Alignment, Center. The Text
menu contains all the text formatting commands that you will use in this hour.

Applying Text Formatting

You apply standard HTML formatting to text by using the Format drop-down menu in the Property inspector. There are four basic formatting options here:

► **None**—This option removes any formatting styles currently applied to the selection.

► **Paragraph**—This option applies paragraph tags (<p></p>) to the selection. This adds two carriage returns after the selection.

► **Heading 1 through Heading 6**—These options apply heading tags to the selection. Heading 1 is the largest heading, and Heading 6 is the smallest. Applying a heading tag makes everything on the line that heading size.

► **Preformatted**—This option displays text in a fixed-width, or monospaced, font—on most systems, 10-point Courier. The text resembles typewriter text.

Select the top line in your Web page and apply Heading 1 formatting, as shown in Figure 2.3. Try applying all the different formats to see what they look like.

Text formats

FIGURE 2.3
The Format drop-down menu in the Property inspector applies heading, paragraph, and preformatted tags to text.

Understanding Paragraph and Break Tags

It's important to understand the difference between paragraph (<p>) and break (<br>) tags. Paragraph tags surround a block of text, placing two carriage returns after the block. Think of the paragraph tags as creating a container for the block of text. You create a new paragraph by pressing the Enter or Return key.

The break tag inserts a single carriage return into text. You can insert a break into a Web page by using the keyboard shortcut Shift+Enter or selecting the Line Break object from the Characters drop-down menu in the Text category of the Insert bar. The break tag does not create a container as the paragraph tags do. Formatting such as the Heading 1 text applied to a block of text applies to all the text within the container.

It's important to understand the difference between paragraph and break tags. Pressing Shift+Enter twice, inserting two line breaks, instead of pressing Enter to create a paragraph looks identical to paragraph text. However, because you haven't created a paragraph container, any formatting applied to the paragraph gets applied to the entire container. This will become more important as you begin formatting portions of Web pages in different ways.

Changing Text Size

You change text size by selecting one of the size settings in the Property inspector Size drop-down menu shown in Figure 2.4. The default text size is medium. If you select one of the numbers at the top of the list (or enter your own number), the Units drop-down menu becomes active so that you can select the unit type. Point and pixel are the most common unit types. You can also select one of the relative sizes (xx-small, medium, large, and so on). These text size settings enable the text to appear relative to the size settings that the user configures in his or her browser, and this is particularly useful for users who have vision impairment.

Did you Know?

Use Pixels Instead of Points

I prefer to standardize by using pixels as my measurement unit of choice. Pixels seem to be the most predictable in various browsers and on various platforms. If you develop on Windows or on a Mac and it's important that your fonts look similar on the other operating system, use pixels as your unit of measure for fonts.

Text sizes

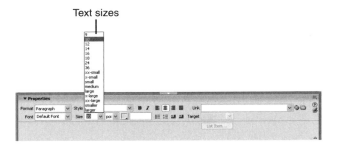

FIGURE 2.4
The Size drop-down menu in the Property inspector enables you to set the size of the selected text.

Selecting a Font

To apply a font, select some text and then select the Font drop-down menu in the Property inspector, as shown in Figure 2.5.

Font List

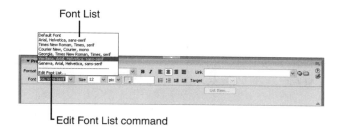

Edit Font List command

FIGURE 2.5
The Font drop-down menu has several font groups from which to choose.

The fonts in the Font drop-down menu are defined in groups. Specifying a group instead of an individual font increases the odds that your viewers will have at least one of the fonts in the group. The browser will attempt to display text with the first font listed, but if that font isn't available, the browser will continue through the list. Dreamweaver has predefined groups to choose from, and you can also create your own groups.

Remember, just because you can see the font and it looks great on your machine doesn't mean that everyone has that font. If a font isn't available, the browser will use the default font—usually Times New Roman—instead. The fonts that are in the predefined font combinations in Dreamweaver are commonly available fonts in Windows and on the Macintosh.

Selecting a Text Color: Using the Color Picker

In a number of areas in Dreamweaver, you can change the color of an object or text. In HTML, colors are specified by using a hexadecimal numbering system, but if you don't know the hexadecimal translation of the color you'd like to use, you can use Dreamweaver's color picker. Change the text color to practice using the Dreamweaver color picker by first clicking the color box to the right of the Size drop-down menu in the Property inspector, as shown in Figure 2.6.

You can experiment with picking a color by using the color picker in a number of ways:

▶ Pick one of the available colors by clicking it with the eyedropper. You are in Eyedropper mode when the Eyedropper button is depressed in the color picker. Five panels are available: Color cubes, Continuous tone, Windows OS, Mac OS, and Grayscale.

▶ Use the eyedropper to pick up any color onscreen by simply clicking the eyedropper on it. You can pick up any color on the screen, not just colors in Dreamweaver. Try selecting a color from one of the icons in the Insert bar.

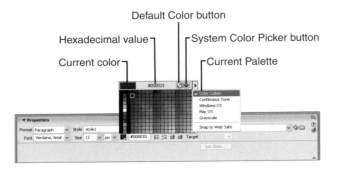

FIGURE 2.6
Select a color box to choose a color from the currently selected palette or create a custom color to use.

▶ Select the System Color Picker button to create a custom color. This opens the system color picker, where you can either pick one of the basic colors or click anywhere in the color spectrum to mix your own color. Click the Add to Custom Colors button and then click the OK button to use the color.

You can also type the color information directly into the color text box in the Property inspector:

▶ Colors are represented in HTML by three hexadecimal numbers preceded by the pound (#) sign. For instance, the RGB (red, green, blue) value for light blue is represented as #0099FF, where the value for R is 00, the value for G is 99, and the value of B is FF. If you know the hexadecimal value for a color, you can simply type it in.

▶ Most browsers display standard color names in addition to hexadecimal values. For instance, you could type in **red** instead of **#FF0000**.

To clear the current color without picking another color, click the Default Color button in the color picker.

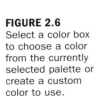

Web-Safe Colors

The Dreamweaver **Web-safe palette** (also known as a *browser-safe palette*) is made up of 212 colors that work on both Windows and Macintosh operating systems displaying 256 colors. Choosing custom colors that are not part of the panel may have an undesirable appearance in older browsers. Most newer computers automatically display more than 256 colors (either thousands or millions of colors), so some Web professionals argue that the Web-safe palette is no longer necessary. But if your Web pages will potentially be viewed on older computers, you should be conservative and design your Web pages by using the Web-safe palette.

Did you
Know?

Are You Locked Into Web Safe?

If you enter a color and Dreamweaver doesn't take the value, the color you entered isn't part of the Web-safe palette. If the Snap to Web Safe setting is selected in the color picker, Dreamweaver won't let you pick a non-Web-safe color. You'll need to turn off the Snap to Web Safe setting before Dreamweaver will allow you to use the color.

Using Dreamweaver's CSS Styles

Dreamweaver uses Cascading Style Sheets (CSS) to set point size and other text properties. CSS is covered in depth in Hour 15, "Formatting Web Pages by Using Cascading Style Sheets." Using the CSS text specifications is the approved way of applying fonts, font sizes, and colors. Note that older browsers—pre-1997 browsers older than Internet Explorer 4 or Netscape Navigator 4—don't support CSS.

By the
Way

Goodbye, `<font>` Tag

The older method of formatting text is to use the `<font>` tag. This tag has been deprecated by the W3C, the Web standards organization. **Deprecated** means that the W3C is removing it from the approved tag list and eventually it may not be supported by browsers. Dreamweaver MX 2004 does not insert any `<font>` tags into your code.

When you apply text formatting in Dreamweaver, a CSS style is created in the code. This style defines the appearance of the text. You can see the style definition that Dreamweaver creates by looking at the CSS Styles panel, shown in Figure 2.7. Dreamweaver gives the style a default name, and you can edit that name by selecting the style in the CSS Styles panel and then selecting the Rename command from the menu in the upper-right corner of the panel.

Instead of redefining the same formatting over and over, you can simply apply an existing CSS style to any text that you want to have the same font and font size. Select the CSS style from the Style drop-down menu in the Property inspector, as shown in Figure 2.8, to apply it to the selected text. You'll learn how to edit the style definition in Hour 15.

FIGURE 2.7
The CSS Styles panel displays the CSS formatting that you've created in the Property inspector.

Style name

Style definition

FIGURE 2.8
The Style drop-down menu in the Property inspector enables you to apply CSS styles to text.

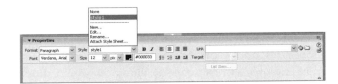

No Guarantees in Web Site Design

There is really no way to guarantee that a Web page will look the same on a viewer's computer as it does on your computer. Browser preferences enable the user to over-ride font settings, size settings, background colors, and hyperlink colors. Don't depend on the page fonts and colors to be exact. If it makes you feel better, though, keep in mind that most users don't change the browser defaults.

Creating Lists and Indenting Text

By using Dreamweaver, you can implement bulleted lists, called *unordered lists* in HTML, and numbered lists, called *ordered lists* in HTML. The Unordered List and Ordered List buttons appear in the Property inspector when you have text selected.

First, create an unordered list by following these steps:

1. Type three items, pressing the Enter (or Return) key after each item so that each is on its own line.

2. Drag the cursor over all three items to select them.

3. Click the Unordered List button in the Property inspector, as shown in Figure 2.9.

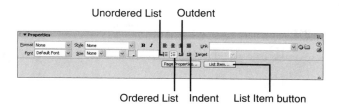

Unordered List   Outdent

Ordered List   Indent   List Item button

FIGURE 2.9
The Property
inspector has but-
tons to create
ordered and
unordered lists.
You can select the
Indent and Outdent
buttons to nest
lists or to indent
and outdent text.

Now each line is preceded by a bullet. Next, add another list that is nested in the
first list:

1. Place the insertion point after the last item.

2. Press the Enter key to make a new line. The new line should be preceded by
   a bullet.

3. Type three items, as you did in the previous list.

4. Drag the cursor over these new items and select the Indent button in the
   Property inspector.

Now the second list is nested within the third item of the first list. You can tell
because it is indented and preceded by a different style of bullet. Use the Outdent
button to place the nested list back in line with the main list.

Customize Your Bullets and Numbers

You can change the bullet or number style by clicking the List Item button in the
Property inspector (refer to Figure 2.9) when your cursor is located within the list.
Oddly, the List Item button does not appear if you have the entire list selected. Pick
the bullet style (either bullet or square) for an unordered list or pick a number style
for an ordered list. You can also start the number count at a number other than one
by entering the initial number in the Start Count box.

Did you Know?

To turn the nested unordered list into an ordered list, as shown in Figure 2.10,
select the three items again and click the Ordered List button in the Property
inspector. To bring the nested list back in line with the main list, select the
Outdent button.

Unordered list

Nested ordered list

FIGURE 2.10
A list can have
another list nested
within it. Select the
Indent button in the
Property inspector
to nest a list.

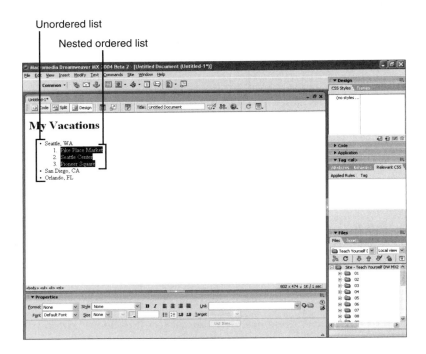

With regular text, you use the Indent and Outdent buttons to modify the margins
of a block of text. In HTML there is no easy way to tab or indent text, so
Dreamweaver uses the `<blockquote>` tag to indent. This tag actually indents both
the left and right sides of the text, so it may look strange if you indent multiple
times.

Pasting Text from a File

Often, you need to transfer text that exists as a word processing document into a
Web page. You can easily copy text from another application, such as Microsoft
Word or even the spreadsheet application Microsoft Excel, and paste it into
Dreamweaver. Dreamweaver can paste text two different ways: with and without
formatting.

To copy and paste text from a word processing program or another program, follow these steps:

dialog box remains open and ready for your next page edits. If you click OK, the changes are applied but the dialog box closes.

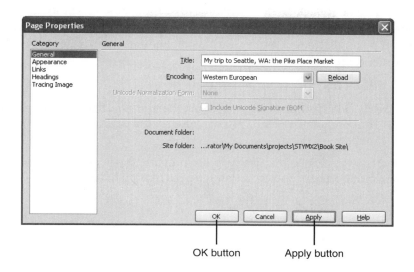

OK button   Apply button

FIGURE 2.12
After you enter a title into the Page Properties dialog box, you can see changes without closing the dialog box by clicking the Apply button instead of the OK button.

Page Titles and Filenames

Did you notice that the word *Untitled* is still in Dreamweaver's title bar in parentheses next to the Web page title? That's because Dreamweaver displays the filename alongside the document title in the title bar. Because the file hasn't been saved, it's still called Untitled in the Dreamweaver title bar.

By the Way

There are various alphabets in the world, and using the Encoding command is how you tell a Web browser which one you are using for your Web page. By default, Dreamweaver lists the Western European encoding type used in the United States and Europe. If you create a page using another alphabet, you need to change the Encoding setting. You can change Dreamweaver's default encoding type in the New Document category in Dreamweaver's Preferences dialog box.

Setting Page Appearance

You use the settings in the Appearance category of the Page Properties dialog box to set the text font, size, and color, along with several other settings, for the entire Web page. The text on a page is black by default. You can change the default text color by using the color picker to select a different color. The settings you make here apply to all the text on the page.

Setting the Default Page Font, Size, and Color

Select the Appearance category in the Page Properties dialog box by clicking the category name on the left side of the dialog box. You can select the default font for the entire page along with the default text size and color. This setting will be overridden by any local text setting, such as the settings you applied to a paragraph earlier this hour.

To set the default font properties, follow these steps:

1. In the Page Properties dialog box, select the font family you want from the Page Font drop-down menu. You can also set the default text to be bold, italic, or both.

2. Select the font size in the Size drop-down menu. If you select a numeric font size, you also need to select a unit type, such as points or pixels.

3. Select a font color by using the Text Color color picker.

The default text settings will be overridden by any other styles that you place on the text. As before, Dreamweaver creates a CSS style that affects all the text on the page.

Setting the Background Color and Background Image

You can set the background color of an entire page in the Appearance category of the Page Properties dialog box. For example, if you'd like to set the Web page background color to white, you can enter the hexadecimal color code (#FFFFFF) into the Background Color text box, type **white** into the box, or use the color picker. Of course, you can pick any color that you want as the background color, but make sure that the combination of the background color and the text color doesn't make your Web page difficult to read. If you apply a dark background color, you need to use a light text color for contrast so that the viewer can read the text.

You can also set a background image for a Web page. This image is tiled both vertically and horizontally on the page. In order for the Web page background to really look nice, you should find or create an image especially designed as a Web page background. You can find these specially designed background images on the Web or in image galleries that you purchase. A background image should never interfere with the readability of a page.

Setting the Page Margins

Margins set the amount of space between the contents of the Web page and the edges of the browser window. You set the margins for a page in the Page Properties dialog box. The default setting for page margins is 15 pixels from the top and 10 pixels from the left in Internet Explorer and 20 pixels from the top and 8 pixels from the left in Netscape. Sometimes you might want to change the margins by entering a value into all the margin boxes, as shown in Figure 2.13. There are four settings for page margins: Left Margin, Top Margin, Right Margin, and Bottom Margin.

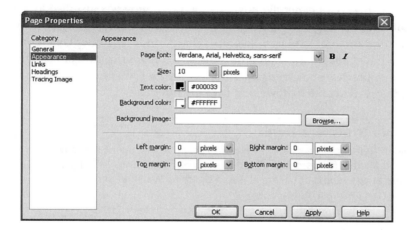

FIGURE 2.13
You set the default text properties, the page background color and image, and the page margins in the Appearance category in the Page Properties dialog box.

Custom Hyperlink Colors

You can set custom colors for hyperlinks in the Links category of the Page Properties dialog box. We'll cover creating hyperlinks in Hour 4, "Setting Lots o' Links: Hyperlinks, URLs, Anchors, and Mailto Links," and you'll have a chance to experiment with changing the link colors in the Page Properties dialog box.

By the Way

Setting Heading Properties

In the Heading category of the Page Properties dialog box, you can set a default font for all six of the sizes of headings. You can also set a unique font size and color for each of the heading sizes. Dreamweaver creates a CSS style that enables this functionality to affect every heading on your Web page.

Saving Your Work and Previewing in a Browser

Even though Dreamweaver is a WYSIWYG tool, you need to see how your page really looks in particular browsers. It's a good idea to save your work before you preview it. Saving your work lets Dreamweaver set the paths to linked files, such as images, correctly. We'll explore the concept of linked files and paths further in Hour 3, "Planning and Defining a Project."

Macromedia says you can define up to 20 browsers for previewing. Good luck finding 20 browsers! I generally have the following browsers installed for testing: Microsoft Internet Explorer, Netscape, and sometimes Opera on my Windows machine and Internet Explorer, Netscape, Safari, and sometimes Opera on my Mac. You have to have these programs installed on your computer before you can use them to preview your Web pages. All the browsers mentioned have free versions and are available to download over the Internet.

> ### Get Your Browsers Here!
>
> Download Netscape Navigator at home.netscape.com/computing/download and download Microsoft Internet Explorer at www.microsoft.com/windows/ie. Safari is available at www.apple.com/safari and Opera is available at www.opera.com/download.

First, set up a browser as follows:

1. Select File, Preview in Browser, Edit Browser List command. Dreamweaver's Preferences dialog box opens to the Preview in Browser category. Dreamweaver may have already located a browser and entered it here during the installation process, so the list may not be empty. My Windows installation of Dreamweaver always finds Internet Explorer and places it in this list for me.

2. Click the plus button to add a browser, as shown in Figure 2.14.

3. Leave the Name text box empty for now; Dreamweaver will automatically pick up the name of the browser.

4. Click the Browse button next to the Application text box and navigate to the browser program. For computers running Windows, the default installation location for most browsers is in the Program Files directory. For the Mac, look in your Applications folder.

Add Browser button

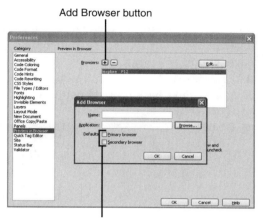

Primary Browser and Secondary
Browser check boxes

FIGURE 2.14
Set the browsers
you will use to pre-
view your Web
pages in the
Preview in Browser
category in the
Preferences dialog
box.

5. Click either the Primary Browser check box or the Secondary Browser check box. This determines which keyboard shortcut you use to launch the browser. The keyboard shortcut for one primary browser is F12, and the shortcut for one secondary browser is Ctrl+F12.

6. Repeat steps 2–5 until all browsers have been added. Click the OK button when you are done.

Below the browser list is a single check box option that controls whether you directly view your Web page in the browser or whether you want Dreamweaver to create a temporary file to display in the browser. When the box is checked, you won't need to save your Web page prior to previewing in a browser because Dreamweaver will create a temporary file for you to display in the browser. If you uncheck this box, you will need to save your Web page prior to previewing it in the browser. I prefer to uncheck this box and know that I'm viewing the actual Web page instead of a temporary file. Even after you've saved your page in Dreamweaver and previewed it in the browser, you can still undo changes that you made prior to saving the page.

Select File, Preview in Browser or select Preview in Browser on the Document toolbar to view the current Web page. Select the browser you want to use from the menu. If the browser is already open, you might have to switch to the application to see your page. If the browser isn't already open, Dreamweaver will open it and load the requested page so you can preview it.

Dreamweaver MX 2004 actually checks each page you open in Dreamweaver for potential browser errors. The Check Browser menu on the Document toolbar displays whether you have any browser check errors in the target browsers selected. By default, Dreamweaver checks your page for errors in Internet Explorer 5 and Netscape 4. Modify the browsers and version in the Target Browsers dialog box, shown in Figure 2.15, by selecting Check Browser, Settings.

FIGURE 2.15
Select which browser definitions Dreamweaver uses to automatically check for errors.

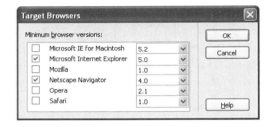

Congratulations! You've created your first Web page in Dreamweaver and learned a lot about formatting the page and text on the page. Many of the tasks described in this hour will become habit to you with every Web page you create, and you will be able to quickly move through the steps you've practiced in this hour.

Summary

In this hour, you have learned how to enter and import text into a Web page. You have set text properties, including headings, fonts, lists, and alignment. You've been introduced to CSS, the language of presentation on the Web. You have used a horizontal rule to separate the page into sections and previewed your work in a browser.

FIGURE 3.1
The Manage Sites dialog box lists all the Web sites you have defined and enables you to manage them.

Basic tab

Advanced tab   Sections

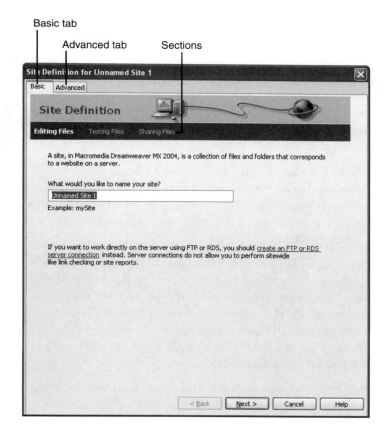

FIGURE 3.2
The Basic tab of the Site Definition dialog box walks you through setting up a site definition.

The Site Definition wizard has three main sections, shown as the section names at the top of the wizard:

> ▶ **Editing Files**—This section helps you set up the local directory where you'll work on the Web site. You tell the wizard whether your site uses server-side technologies. None of the sites or Web pages in this book use these technologies, which connect Web pages, servers, and often databases.

> ▶ **Testing Files**—This section is needed only for sites that use server-side technologies.

> ▶ **Sharing Files**—This section enables you to tell Dreamweaver how you want to transfer files to a server or another central location to share. You'll explore this functionality in Hour 20, "Uploading a Project."

Using the Site Definition Wizard

In the Site Definition wizard, give your site a name. This name is used only inside Dreamweaver, so you can use spaces and characters in it if you want. The site name should be meaningful—it should identify the purpose of the Web site when you drop down the Site menu to change sites. My Dreamweaver has about 30 to 40 sites defined at times, so clear names help me quickly find the site I want to edit. Click the Next button.

The next page of the wizard, Editing Files, Part 2 (shown in Figure 3.3), enables you to specify whether you will be using server-side scripting to create dynamic Web pages. Your Web pages in this book will be regular HTML pages, so you should select the top radio button that says No, I Do Not Want to Use a Server Technology. Click the Next button.

The next page, Editing Files, Part 3, helps you specify where the files in your site are located. The site that you are creating here is your **development site** not the final site that other people will view over the Web. You will need to move the files in your development site up to a server for people to view the files over the Web (the subject of Hour 20). The Web site located on a Web server and available to the public is called the **live site**. I always work on an up-to-date copy of a Web site that is located on my local hard drive.

You can store your development files in three places: on your local machine, on a network drive, or on a server somewhere. Select the top radio button to elect to store the development files on your local machine. If you are working in a networked environment (at your office, for instance), you could use either of the other two choices.

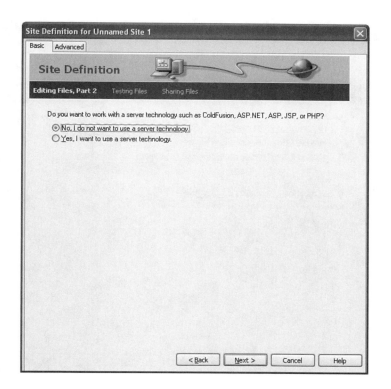

FIGURE 3.3
You tell Dreamweaver whether you will be using server-side scripting in your site.

Don't Develop on the Live Site

Do not ever link to the final live site for development. You do not want to make a mistake on the real site; always make sure you are working on a copy of the site.

Watch Out!

As shown in Figure 3.4, the text box at the bottom of the dialog box asks you to enter the location of the site directory. Click the folder icon to the right of the text box to navigate to the directory. Use an existing directory on your hard drive or create a new directory for your site. Click the Next button.

Name Your Files Properly to Avoid Problems

Spaces, punctuation, and special characters in file and directory names may cause problems. You can use underscores instead of spaces in names. All files should be named using a combination of letters, numbers, and underscores. If you are planning on adding scripting (using Dreamweaver behaviors, covered in Hour 16, "Inserting Scripted Functionality by Using Behaviors"), you shouldn't name any files, including image files, beginning with a number.

By the Way

FIGURE 3.4
You enter the directory that will house your development files.

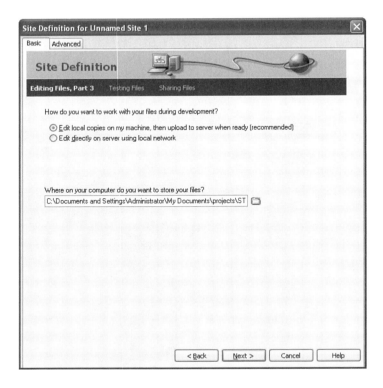

Servers May Be Case-Sensitive

Filenames are case-sensitive on some servers. Servers running the various flavors of the Unix operating system enable you to create files named `mydog.gif`, `Mydog.gif`, and `MYDOG.gif` all in the same directory because the capitalization differs. Microsoft servers are not case-sensitive.

The next section in the Site Definition wizard enables you to configure how you share files. You can set up a central location where members of your team can share files. Or you can set up a location on a public Web server where you share your Web site with the world. You'll learn how to configure this section and transfer files in Hour 20. For now, simply drop down the top menu and select None, as shown in Figure 3.5. Click the Next button.

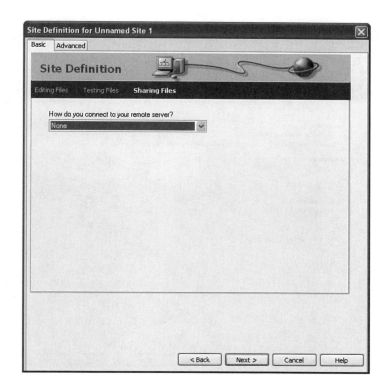

FIGURE 3.5
To set up the connection information later, simply select None.

The last page of the wizard displays a summary of your site, as shown in Figure 3.6. You can come back to this wizard at any time to change your site definition by selecting the Edit Sites command from the Site menu (either the one in the Files panel or the one in the Document window). Click the Done button.

After you click the Done button, Dreamweaver displays a message, telling you that it will now create the initial site cache. When you click OK, a progress bar like the one in Figure 3.7 appears (and disappears very quickly if you have nothing in your site yet). The initial site cache is created each time you create a new site. The **site cache** is used to store information about the links in your site so that they can be quickly updated if they change. Dreamweaver continues to update the cache as you work.

FIGURE 3.6
The Site Definition wizard displays a summary of your site definition.

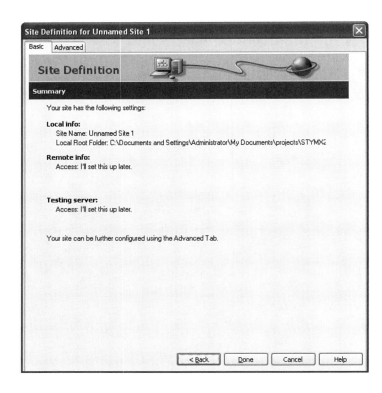

FIGURE 3.7
You may see a progress bar as Dreamweaver creates a cache for your site. This file speeds the updating of links when you move or rename a file.

Using the Files Panel

You select the site you'd like to work on in the Files panel, which is shown in Figure 3.8. This is where you open Web pages to edit in Dreamweaver. The Site drop-down menu gives you quick access to all your defined sites. It also gives you another way to launch the Manage Sites dialog box.

Site drop-down menu

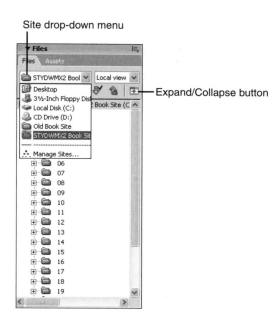

—Expand/Collapse button

FIGURE 3.8
The Files panel
enables you to
change sites and
open Web pages.

Using the Expanded Files Panel

To get a bigger view of a site and get access to more functionality, select the
Expand/Collapse button in the Files panel to open the Expanded Files panel. The
Expanded Files panel, shown in Figure 3.9, is a larger representation of the Files
panel and has two panes: Local Files (on the right, by default) and Remote Site
(on the left), which you will set up in Hour 20. Because you have not yet defined
a remote site, you should not have any files in the Remote Site pane at this point.

FIGURE 3.9
The Expanded Files
panel has two
panes: Local Files
and Remote Site.

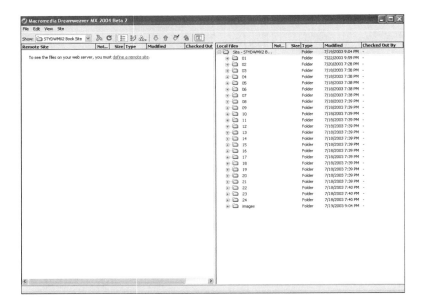

Creating New Files in the Files Panel

You can create new files and new folders right in the Dreamweaver Files panel.
Right-click (Control+click on the Mac) in the Files panel to open the Files panel
menu. This context menu, shown in Figure 3.10, has two commands of interest at
the top: New File and New Folder. You'll use those commands to create files and
folders (also called *directories*) in the Files panel.

The Web sites you create will need directories, and probably every site will have an
images directory for all the images in the site. Create an images directory by using
the New Folder command. An untitled folder is added to your site. Give this folder
the name images. You need to be careful about what is selected when you select the
New Folder command so that you do not nest the folder within another folder. To
add a folder at the site root, select the top line, which begins with the word *Site*.

Now try adding a new file to your site. Right-click (or Control+click) on the root
folder, the top line in the Files panel, which lists the name of the site, and select
the New File command. A new untitled Web page is created in the Web site. Title
the Web page **index.ht**m, which is one of the popular default page names for
many servers. Using the **default page name** enables the user to find your page
more easily by just entering a basic Web page address without the specific page
appended. Another common default page name is index.html. Both the .htm and

the `.html` file extensions are acceptable. The `.htm` file extension became popular because the older versions of Microsoft Windows could only handle three-character file extensions; this is no longer a limitation in newer versions of Windows. After you add the new folder and a new file, the site should look as shown in Figure 3.11.

FIGURE 3.10
The Files panel context menu contains commands to create new folders (directories) and files in a Web site.

FIGURE 3.11
You can add files and folders in Dreamweaver's Files panel.

Did you Know?

Name Files Consistantly

I think it's a good idea to name everything with lowercase letters. Some servers and scripting languages are case-sensitive. When you name everything with lowercase letters, you don't need to remember whether you used uppercase letters.

Editing a Site Definition

So far in this hour, you have used the Basic tab in the Site Definition dialog box to initially define a Web site. Now let's explore the Advanced tab and use it to edit site settings. Open the Manage Sites dialog box again by selecting Manage Sites from the Site drop-down menu. Select the site you just created and then click the Edit button. The Site Definition dialog box opens again. Click the Advanced tab at the top of the dialog box. As shown in Figure 3.12, this is another view of the information that you entered into the wizard.

FIGURE 3.12
The Advanced tab contains all the site properties.

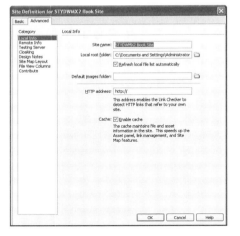

 Did you Know?

A Quick Way to Edit Site Definitions

A fast way to open the Site Definition dialog box is to simply double-click the name of the site in the Files panel's Site drop-down menu.

The left side of the Site Definition dialog box shows categories, and the right side lists the selected category's properties. Select the Local Info category and then select the folder icon next to the Default Images Folder text box. Navigate to the images folder you just created. Now Dreamweaver knows where you'll keep your images for the site. Click the OK button to save your changes. Click the Done button to close the Edit Sites dialog box.

You'll learn about other advanced options later in this book. In Hour 20, you'll set up the Remote Info category in order to upload your files to a remote Web site. In Hour 21, "Managing and Editing a Project," you'll explore the Cloaking and Design Notes categories.

Considering Site Organization

There are many opinions about the proper way to organize a Web site. Some people like to compartmentalize all the files into directories and subdirectories. Some people like to have a very shallow structure, with many files in a single directory. As you get more experienced at Web development, you'll find your ideal organization. It's nice to exchange ideas with other Web developers or hobbyists so that you can learn from the successes and failures of others and they can learn from yours.

I have a directory on my hard drive called `Projects`, represented in Figure 3.13. The `Projects` directory contains a directory for each project I'm working on. Within each project directory there is a directory called `Web`. This is the directory where I keep all the development files for the site and the directory that I set as the root in Dreamweaver.

This directory structure enables me to put other files, such as correspondence, contracts, invoices, and spreadsheets, in the client's folder without making them part of the Web site. It's good practice to keep other files separate from those you plan to transfer to the Web. You might prefer to have one directory that contains all your Web sites. Do whatever works best for you.

FIGURE 3.13
An example of a
directory structure
in which the Web
site is housed in
the Web directory.

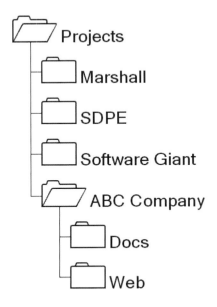

Put some thought into how you'll organize the files in your Web site before you start a project. You will probably want to create a separate images folder to hold your images, as shown in Figure 3.14. If you have other types of assets, such as sound or video, you might want to create separate folders for those, too. I always create a scripts directory to hold external JavaScript files and external Cascading Style Sheets files; you'll explore these in the later hours of this book.

FIGURE 3.14
You can organize
your Web site into
images and other
directories.

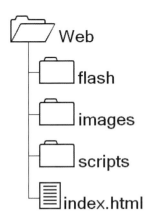

I try to logically break up sections of Web sites into separate directories. If your Web site has obvious divisions (departments, lessons, products, and so on), you can create directories to hold the Web pages in each of the sections. You'll be surprised at how even a small Web site becomes quickly unmanageable when all the files are dumped into one directory.

Most Web sites use many image files. If you have different sections in your Web site, do you want to have separate images directories in each section? It might be a good way to organize your site. Then again, if images are used across multiple sections, it might make the images hard to find. Make sure that your organizational logic isn't going to break down as you add files to your site.

Luckily, if you do have to rearrange assets, Dreamweaver will update any links for you. When you move a file, Dreamweaver asks you if you want to search and update links to that file. That's what the site cache is created for. However, it is still best to make wise design decisions at the beginning of a big project.

Summary

In this hour, you have learned how to define a Web site and determine its root. You have learned how to quickly add files and folders to a site. You have learned how to use the Files panel and expand it into the Expanded Files panel. And you have explored ideas about how to organize a site.

Q&A

Q. *How do I import a Web site into Dreamweaver?*

A. There is no procedure for importing a site. You simply define a site exactly as you did this hour, pointing to the root directory of the site you'd like to import. Dreamweaver will present all the files in the Files panel, enabling you to open and edit them. If the site you need to import is on a Web server, you'll first need to read Hour 20 and set up remote site settings pointing to the server.

Q. *If I need to move files within my site, is it okay to do it within Dreamweaver?*

A. If you need to do some housekeeping or rearranging, it's best to do it within Dreamweaver. Dreamweaver automatically updates links to files and warns you if deleting a file will affect other files within your site. Make sure you take care of these tasks within Dreamweaver and not elsewhere.

Workshop

The Workshop contains quiz questions and activities to help reinforce what you've learned in this hour. In case you get stuck, the answers to the quiz appear after the questions.

Quiz

1. Why do you need to define a Web site?

2. What does the Dreamweaver cache do?

3. You must go through a conversion process to import an existing Web site into Dreamweaver. True or false?

Quiz Answers

1. You define a Web site so that Dreamweaver knows where the root of the site is and what your site management preferences are.

2. Enabling the cache speeds up some Dreamweaver features, such as updating hyperlinks.

3. False. No conversion process is necessary to import an existing Web site into Dreamweaver.

Exercises

1. Try defining a new Web site.

2. Add some files and folders to the new site.

3. Explore the other categories in the Site Definition dialog box (Notes or Cloaking, for instance). We'll cover the other categories in upcoming hours.

HOUR 4

Setting Lots o' Links: Hyperlinks, URLs, Anchors, and Mailto Links

What You'll Learn in This Hour:

- ▶ When to use relative and absolute paths
- ▶ How to create a hyperlink to another page within a Web site and a hyperlink to a page outside a Web site
- ▶ How to create hyperlinks within a page
- ▶ How to add a link that opens a preaddressed email message

Clicking a **hyperlink** allows the viewer to jump to another Web page, jump to another section of the current Web page, or launch an email message. A Web site is made up of a group of Web pages, and hyperlinks enable viewers to navigate from page to page. Hyperlinks, in the simplest form, are the familiar underlined and colored text that you click. You can also make an image a hyperlink.

Hyperlinks help make the Web a powerful source of information. If you've surfed the Web at all, I'm sure you've clicked many, many hyperlinks. But hyperlinks can also make the Web confusing. Sometimes it is difficult to remember the exact path you took to find information, and that can make it difficult to get back to the information when you want to see it again.

A Web address is called a **uniform resource locator (URL)**. You can link many types of files over the Web, but only a few file types will actually be displayed in a browser. A browser can display the supported image formats, HTML, player applications (such as Flash), and a few other specialized types of files. If a link leads to a file that the browser can't display (a `.zip` file, for example), the browser will usually ask you if you'd like to save the file to your hard drive.

Exploring Relative and Absolute Paths

Whenever you create a hyperlink to another Web page or place an external file (such as an image file) in a Web page, you need to enter a path to the file. Dreamweaver helps make sure that these paths are correct, but it's important that you understand the difference between the two main types of paths: absolute paths and document-relative paths. An **absolute path** is the full URL (more about URLs in a few minutes) to a file. A **document-relative path** points to the location of a file in relationship to the page being viewed.

An analogy for an absolute path is a house address. If I gave the address of my house to someone who lives in another town, I would tell them, "I live at 123 Spruce, Seattle WA 98122, USA." This is all the information that anyone would need to get to my exact location or to send me a letter (this isn't my real address, so if you really want to send me a letter, send it in care of the publisher!). If I gave directions to my house to someone who lives on my street, I might tell them, "I live two doors south of you." The directions in this case are relative to my neighbor's location. This is analogous to a document-relative path.

The link to the Macromedia Dreamweaver Support Center shown in Figure 4.1 is an absolute path. It contains the entire path to a file on the Internet. Because you have no control over this site, linking to it means that you need to check to see that the link remains valid. If the site moves in the future, you will need to update the link.

A URL consists of up to five sections, as shown in Figure 4.2:

▶ **Protocol**—The first part of the URL is the protocol. It is `http` for Web pages to indicate Hypertext Transfer Protocol (HTTP). Sometimes you might want to link to a file on an FTP (File Transfer Protocol—another method of communicating over the Internet to move files to and from a server) server, using `ftp` as the protocol instead of `http`.

▶ **Domain**—The second part of the address is the domain. This is the Web server where the Web page is located; for example, in Figure 4.2, the domain is `www.betsybruce.com`. A colon and two forward slashes (`://`) separate the protocol and the domain.

A hyperlink with an absolute path

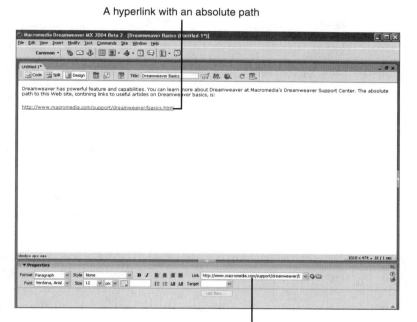

FIGURE 4.1
Entering an absolute path links to a specific Web page.

A hyperlink with an absolute path

▶ **Port**—An optional third part of a URL is the port. The default port for a Web server is port 80. When you enter http as the protocol, port 80 is implied and doesn't usually need to be included. You might need to enter port information when entering addresses to specialized Web applications that listen on a different port than port 80.

▶ **Path and filename**—The fourth part of the address is the path and filename. The path includes all directories and the filename. Most Web pages end in .htm or .html. Other common file endings are .cgi, for Common Gateway Interface, .asp, for Active Server Pages, .jsp, for JavaServer Pages, .aspx, for ASP.NET files, .php, for PHP pages, and .cfm, for Cold Fusion Markup Language.

▶ **Query string**—The filenames might be followed by an optional fifth part of a URL—a query string. A query string is added to a URL to send data to a script to be processed. We'll explore query strings in Hour 19, "Sending and Reacting to Form Data."

FIGURE 4.2
A URL consists of
multiple sections.
Every URL must
contain a protocol,
a domain name,
and the complete
path to a file.

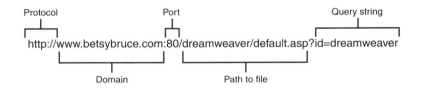

You might see a URL that does not have a filename referenced at the end, such as
http://www.macromedia.com/support/dreamweaver/. This type of address works
because the Web server looks for a default page in the directory. Most Web servers
have a default page name that doesn't need to be explicitly entered at the end of
the URL. Usually the default page name is default.htm, default.html,
index.htm, or index.html. On some servers, any of these names will work. This
functionality can be configured in Web server software.

Default pages in the root of a site are often referred to as *home pages*. To create a
home page for a Web site, ask your Webmaster or Web hosting service for the
default page name for your Web server. If you don't have a default page on your
Web site and a visitor doesn't enter a filename at the end of the URL, he or she
might see all the contents of your directories instead of a Web page. Or the user
might get an error message!

You usually do not need to enter the protocol into the browser's address box to go
to a Web page. Most browsers assume that you want to use HTTP. However, if you
are surfing to an FTP file, you need to enter ftp as the protocol at the beginning
of the URL. Even though browsers assume HTTP, you still need to preface absolute
links entered into Dreamweaver with http://.

Within your own Web site, you use document-relative paths so that you can
move your site anywhere and your links will still work. While developing in
Dreamweaver, you will create a Web site on your local hard drive and then eventually move the site to a Web server. Document-relative paths will work the same
in both locations.

It's important to use document-relative paths instead of absolute paths in your
Web site. If you have an absolute path to a file on your local drive, the link will
look like the following:

file:///C¦/My Documents/first_page.html

This file, first_page.html, is on the C: drive in a directory called My Documents.
If you preview this page in your browser, it works fine for you. So, what's the

problem? The reason it works fine is that you have that page available on your hard drive, but other people don't have access to your hard drive and will not be able to access the page.

Document-relative paths don't require a complete URL. The path to the linked file is expressed relative to the current document. You use this type of path when inserting images into a Web page. You also use a document-relative path when creating a hyperlink to a Web page within your Web site.

By the Way

Links Work with Other Files, Too

You don't have to limit your links to Web pages. You can link to movies, word processing files (.doc files, for instance), PDF files, or audio files. The URLs work the same no matter what the content is.

The following are some examples of document-relative paths:

▶ When linking to a file that is in the same directory as your current file, you enter only the filename as the path. For instance, if the file mktg.htm in Figure 4.3 has a link to sales.htm, the path would simply be the filename because both files are in the same directory.

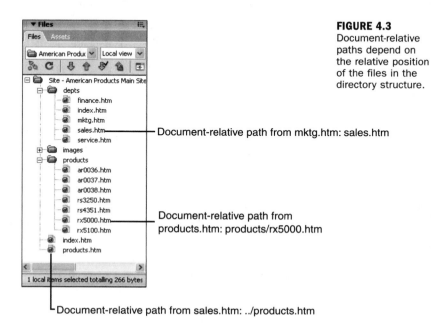

FIGURE 4.3
Document-relative paths depend on the relative position of the files in the directory structure.

Document-relative path from mktg.htm: sales.htm

Document-relative path from products.htm: products/rx5000.htm

Document-relative path from sales.htm: ../products.htm

▶ To link to a file that is in a directory nested within the directory where the current file is located, you enter the directory name and the filename as a path. For instance, if the file `products.htm` in Figure 4.3 has a link to the file `rx5000.htm` in the `products` directory, the path is `products/rx5000.htm`.

▶ When linking to a file in a directory above the current directory (called the *parent directory*), you enter `../` plus the filename as a path. The `../` means go up to the next parent directory. For instance, if the file `sales.htm` in Figure 4.3 has a link to the file `products.htm` in the site root, the path is `../products.htm`.

Before it saves your Web page, Dreamweaver inserts all links as absolute links. It does this because it cannot calculate a relative link until the file is saved. After the file has been saved, Dreamweaver can tell where your document is relative to all linked files and will change the links to document-relative addresses. Accidentally using absolute paths is an easy mistake to make. Dreamweaver looks out for you, however, and attempts to correct these problems for you.

There is a third type of path, called **site root-relative**. In a site root-relative link, the path is relative to the root of the entire Web site. The *root* of the Web site is defined as a certain directory of a Web site, usually where the site's home page is located. Site root-relative linking is used in professional environments where many different sections of the Web site need to access a common group of files, such as a corporate logo or common button images.

Site root-relative paths are not the best choice for beginners to Web development work. The main difficulty is that you can preview pages that have site root-relative links only if they are loaded on a Web server. Therefore, if you use these links, you won't be able to preview your work in a browser without loading it onto the server. Stay away from site root-relative paths until you are more experienced.

Watch Out!

Be Careful with Your Slashes

A site root-relative path is preceded with a forward slash (/). An example of a site root-relative path is

`/depts/products.html`

Be careful not to enter a path this way by accident when typing in an address.

Adding a Hyperlink Within a Web Site

In this section you'll create several new Web pages and save them to your Web site. You'll need several so that you can practice linking to them, so create a couple now. You can use these pages to practice linking by using document-relative paths.

By the Way

Click Here...

It's generally bad form to explicitly reference a hyperlink by saying "Click here to see our statistics." It's better to incorporate a hyperlink into a natural sentence, such as, "The 2004 statistics show that sales increased by 32%." Ideally, hyperlinks are meant to seamlessly blend into the text of your documents.

Create a new page that links to an existing page:

1. Select File, New to open the New Document dialog box.

2. Select the Page Designs category in the New Document dialog box, as shown in Figure 4.4. These designs come with Dreamweaver and are a great starting place for your Web page development. Select Image: Picture and Description Vertical from the Page Designs list. Make sure to create a document (instead of a template) by selecting the Document radio button. Click the Create button.

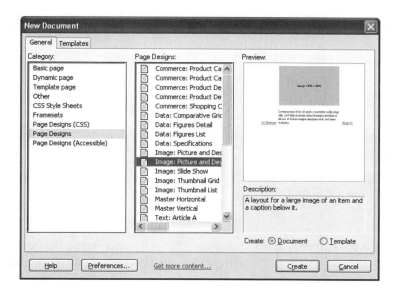

FIGURE 4.4
Using a Page Designs category gives you a head start when creating a Web page.

3. You now have a Web page with an image placeholder and some placeholder text. Save this document in the root of your site.

4. Repeat steps 1–3 to create several Web pages.

5. Select and replace the placeholder text, the text beginning with "Lorum ipsum," on one of the Web pages with some text of your own. You'll learn how to replace the placeholder image in Hour 6, "Displaying Images on a Page."

6. Select the <<Previous link on the Web page.

7. Select the Browse icon (which looks like a folder) next to the Link drop-down menu. Navigate to the directory where the index.htm file is located. Select the filename and click the Select button. Dreamweaver enters a relative URL into the Link drop-down menu, as shown in Figure 4.5.

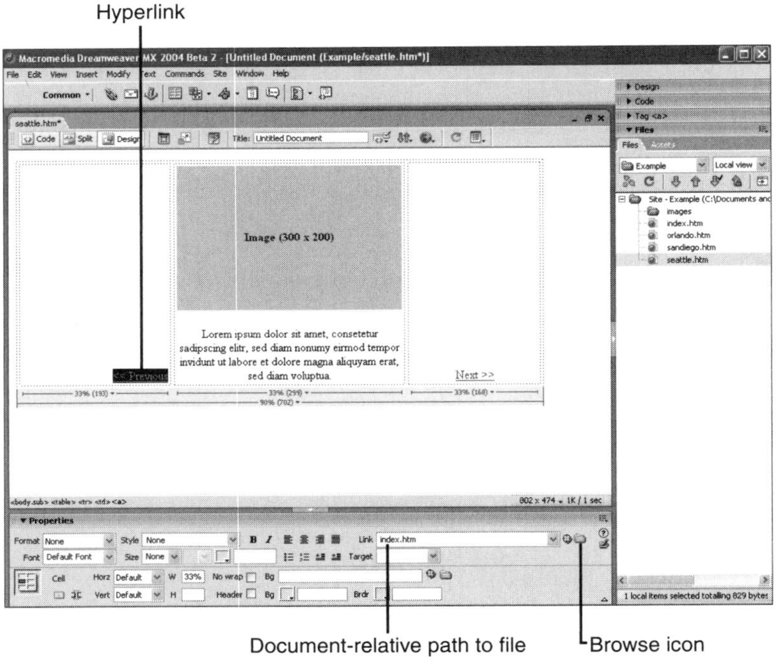

FIGURE 4.5
In the Dreamweaver Document window, you select text that you want to become a hyperlink.

Hyperlink

Document-relative path to file

Browse icon

The selected text appears as an underlined blue hyperlink in the Dreamweaver Document window. Preview the Web page in the browser and click your link. You should jump to another page!

Named anchor

FIGURE 4.10
You enter the name of a named anchor, preceded by a pound sign, to create a link to it.

Link to a named anchor

Using the Point-to-File Icon

There's a little tool that you might have noticed on the Property inspector: the Point-to-File icon. This icon enables you to create links visually. You can drag the **Point-to-File icon**, shown in Figure 4.11, to a named anchor or a file located in the Files panel.

When the Point-to-File icon is dragged over a named anchor, the name of the anchor appears in the Link box of the Property inspector. To select the named anchor, simply release the mouse button while the Point-to-File icon is over the named anchor. Using this icon is a nice way to link to objects or files without having to know or type in the filenames. You can also use the Point-to-File icon to link to files listed in your Files panel by dragging the icon over to the panel and highlighting a particular file.

Drag cursor to the named anchor

FIGURE 4.11
Drag the Point-to-File icon to a named anchor. While the icon is over the anchor, its name appears in the Link box.

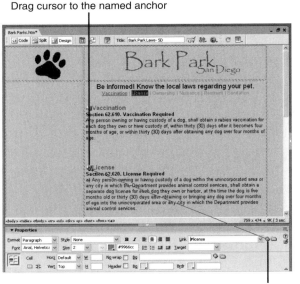

Point-to-File icon

Adding a Mailto Link

It's nice to put a link in a Web page to allow a viewer to send email. This type of link is called a **mailto link**. The Dreamweaver Email Link object helps you implement a mailto link. The user must have an email application set up to work with the browser in order for these links to work.

To create a mailto link, select some text to be the link. Click the Email Link object (in the Common panel of the Insert bar), and the Email Link dialog box appears (see Figure 4.12). Enter the email address and click OK. The text looks like a hyperlink, but instead of linking to another page, it opens a preaddressed email message.

FIGURE 4.12
You create a link that creates an email message by using the Email Link object. The linked text is in the top box, and the email address is in the bottom box of the Email Link dialog box.

Email Link

Text:	Ask us a question!	OK
E-Mail:	help@barkpark.org	Cancel
		Help

Watch
Out!

Spammers Love Mailto Links

Spammers troll the Internet for mailto links. If you use mailto links in your Web pages, expect to get a lot of **spam**, or junk email, sent to the email address used in the mailto links.

An **email link** is a hyperlink like any other except that it opens the user's default email application, such as Outlook or Eudora, with an email address already entered. Most users have a default email client, so these links are an easy and quick way for the user to send email. The email application has to be properly configured, with a server specified to send email, for the email to actually be sent.

Summary

In this hour, you have learned the difference between absolute and relative addresses. You have created links to external Web sites and relative links to pages within a Web site. You have learned how to insert a named anchor and then link to it, and you have created a mailto link to allow a viewer to launch an email message directly from a Web page.

Q&A

Q. *The named anchor that I want to link to is low enough on the page that I can't see it onscreen. How can I use the Point-to-File icon to reach it?*

A. If you drag the Point-to-File icon to either the top or the bottom of the Document window, the window will scroll. Hold the icon near the edge of the window until it has scrolled to the point where the named anchor is visible on the screen.

Q. *I found a page on another site that I want to link to, but the URL is really long. Do I have to retype it in Dreamweaver?*

A. The easiest way to enter a lengthy URL is to copy the URL from the browser's address textbox (by pressing Ctrl+C in Windows or Control+C on the Mac). You can then paste the URL into Dreamweaver's Link drop-down menu.

Q. *Is there any way to add a subject line into an email link?*

A. Yes! In the Dreamweaver Email Link dialog box, add a question mark immediately after the email address (no space) and then `subject=` and the subject that you want to appear. You can also simply edit the link in the Property inspector's Link drop-down menu. The link will look like this:

```
mailto:betsy@betsybruce.com?subject=Sams Teach Yourself
Macromedia Dreamweaver MX 2004 in 24 Hours
```

Workshop

The Workshop contains quiz questions and activities to help reinforce what you've learned in this hour. In case you get stuck, the answers to the quiz appear after the questions.

Quiz

1. How can you view a named anchor if it isn't currently visible onscreen?

2. What is the difference between a document-relative path and a site root-relative path?

3. When does a Web page viewer see the active link color?

Quiz Answers

1. Select View, Visual Aids, Invisibles to see items that are invisible elements.

2. A site root-relative path begins with a forward slash and a document-relative path does not.

3. A Web page viewer see the active link color while he or she is actively clicking a hyperlink.

Exercises

1. Surf the Web for 10 to 15 minutes with your new awareness of the different types of links. When you place the cursor over a link, you can usually see the address of the link in the status bar of the browser. Look for links to named anchors, too.

2. Create a favorite links page, including links to all your favorite Web sites. You can either use the URL of the link as the text that displays or you can create a hyperlink out of a descriptive word or phrase. Hint: The major browsers have methods of exporting all your bookmarks or favorites. These methods can give you a huge head start on this exercise.

.

HTML Is Fun! Viewing and Modifying HTML

What You'll Learn in This Hour:

▶ How to structure the code in a Web page
▶ How to use the Quick Tag Editor
▶ How to view and edit HTML code
▶ How to clean up Word HTML

Even though Dreamweaver handles HTML behind the scenes, you might occasionally want to look at it. Dreamweaver also makes the transition easier for those stoic HTML hand-coders who are making a move to a visual HTML development tool such as Dreamweaver. You won't be sorry! I'm a very competent HTML hand-coder, but I can get my work done much quicker by using Dreamweaver.

Dreamweaver offers several ways to access HTML code. During this hour, you will explore the HTML editing capabilities of Dreamweaver. You'll use Dreamweaver's capability to clean up the code produced when saving a Word document as HTML. If you don't already know HTML, you'll find that viewing HTML that Dreamweaver creates is a great way to learn.

Exploring Code View

The Dreamweaver Document window enables you to view a Web page in either Design view or Code view. You can see Design and Code views at the same time by selecting the Show Code and Design Views button in the toolbar. When you do this, it's easy to pop back and forth between the views with just a click of a button.

Did you Know?

Toggle the Panels Off

If you are using a floating panel version of Dreamweaver (as Mac users do), the panels continue to float over the code in Code view. You can toggle all the panels on and off by pressing the F4 key.

Create a new HTML page in Dreamweaver. Then click the Code View button in the toolbar to view the page's HTML code, as shown in Figure 5.1. The first line in the code is the **document type declaration**, which uses the doctype tag. It tells a validator which version of HTML the page uses. Dreamweaver adds this line automatically, so you shouldn't have to worry about it. After the document type declaration, the entire Web page is enclosed in HTML tags.

FIGURE 5.1
Code view displays the code of a Web page.

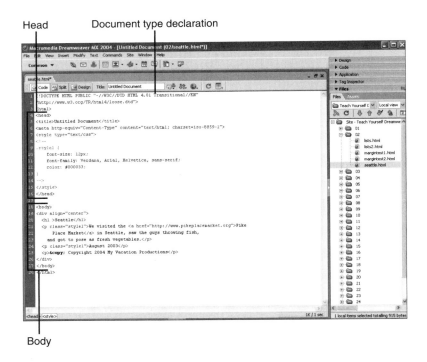

Head   Document type declaration

Body

Dreamweaver creates Web pages by adding HTML tags (and other types of tags, such as ASP.NET or XML, when you get more advanced). When you select an object from Dreamweaver's Insert bar, Dreamweaver inserts the appropriate tag or tags into your Web pages. Tags have properties called **attributes** that Dreamweaver uses to fine-tune the way the object displays on the page. For instance, an image tag (<img>) has the src (source) attribute, which sets the files that the image tag displays. Most image tags also have height and width attributes that tell the browser the size of the image. These are just a few of the many attributes of an image tag. Here is an example of an image tag with standard attributes:

```
<img src="market.jpg" height="156" width="124">
```

Exploring the Head and Body of a Web Page

There are two main sections to a Web page: the head and the body. You'll see these sections in the code. The head is surrounded by head tags, and the body is surrounded by body tags. All the content visible in a Web page is in the body. The head of the document contains code that supports the Web page. In the head of the document, Dreamweaver automatically adds the <title> tag because the document title is part of the head. Right beneath the title, Dreamweaver inserts a meta tag, like this:

```
<meta http-equiv="Content-Type" content="text/html; charset=iso-8859-1">
```

This meta tag specifies the character set that the browser should use to display the page. The preceding example specifies the Latin character set for Western European languages. You can set the default character set for a Web page in the New Document category of Dreamweaver's Preferences dialog box. You can also set the font that Dreamweaver uses while you are working in Dreamweaver; you do this in the Fonts category of the Preferences dialog box, as shown in Figure 5.2.

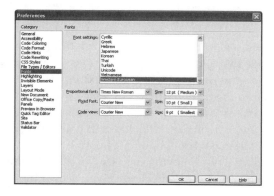

FIGURE 5.2
You set the character set to display Web pages in the Fonts category of the Dreamweaver Preferences dialog box.

Dreamweaver places other content into the head of the page as you author. The head is where most JavaScript and other scripting code, CSS definitions, and other code resides. You usually do not have to worry too much about editing the head of a document. While in Design mode, if you'd like to see a visual representation of the head content, select View, Head Content. You then see icons at the top of the Document window representing the elements in the head. When you select one of the icons, its properties appear in the Property inspector, as shown in Figure 5.3.

Head content

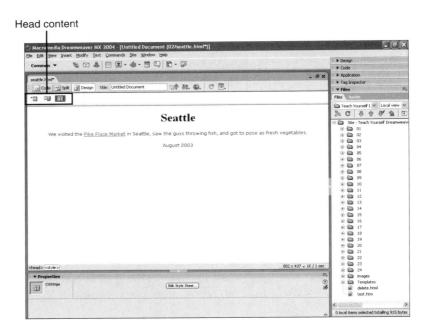

You display both Design view and Code view by selecting the middle button, the lengthily named Code and Design Views button. Place your cursor over the divider to modify the window sizes. Type some text into the Design view pane. The text is inserted into the body of the document. If you select an object in the Document window, the code for that object will be selected in Code view. This is a quick way to get to the code of a selected object. If your Web page is large, there might be a lot of HTML to go through, and it might not be easy to find the code that you are looking for. Try displaying only Design view. Highlight a single word that you typed. When you select Code view, Dreamweaver highlights that word.

Inspecting Code

If you'd prefer to see the code in a window on top of the Document window, use the Code inspector instead of Code view. You launch the Code inspector by selecting Window, Code Inspector.

Discovering Code View Options

When you are in Code view, the View Options menu, shown in Figure 5.4, enables you to change the way the code is displayed. These commands are also available in View, Code View Options.

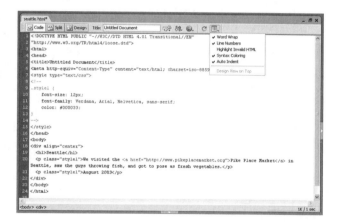

FIGURE 5.4
The View Options menu enables you to configure how code is displayed.

The following options are available in the View Options menu:

- ▶ **Word Wrap**—Wraps the lines of code so that you can view it all without scrolling horizontally. This setting does not change the code; it simply displays it differently.

- ▶ **Line Numbers**—Displays line numbers in the left margin.

- ▶ **Highlight Invalid HTML**—Turns on highlighting of invalid code that Dreamweaver doesn't understand.

- ▶ **Syntax Coloring**—Colors the code so that elements are easier to discern. You set the colors in the Code Coloring category of the Dreamweaver Preferences dialog box.

- ▶ **Auto Indent**—Makes the code automatically indent based on the settings in the Code Format category of the Preferences dialog box.

Did you Know?

JavaScript Error? Check the Line Number

If you receive a JavaScript error when previewing a Web page in a browser, the error often displays the number of the code line that is causing the problem. You can view the code in Code view with the line numbers displayed to troubleshoot the error.

If you make changes to the code in Code view, Dreamweaver doesn't display the changes in the Document window until you click the Refresh button in the tool-bar. If you select View Options, Highlight Invalid Code, Dreamweaver highlights all invalid tags in bright yellow in both the Code inspector and the Document window, as shown in Figure 5.5. When you select a highlighted tag, the Property inspector calls the tag invalid. It might give a reason why the tag is invalid and offer some direction on how to deal with it.

FIGURE 5.5
Invalid tags appear highlighted, and the Property inspector may offer insight into what to do about the problem.

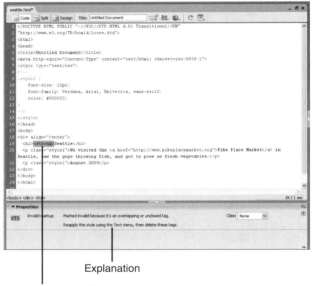

Explanation

Invalid tag (it has no closing tag)

Viewing and Editing HTML Tags by Using the Quick Tag Editor

Using Dreamweaver's Quick Tag Editor is the quickest and easiest way to look at a single HTML tag and edit it. There are different ways you can access the Quick Tag Editor:

▶ Click the Quick Tag Editor icon on the Property inspector, as shown in Figure 5.6.

FIGURE 5.6
Click the Quick Tag Editor icon to view and edit the tag of the object that is currently selected.

Quick Tag Editor icon

▶ Right-click (Control+click on the Mac) any object and select the Edit Tag Code command from the context menu, as shown in Figure 5.7.

FIGURE 5.7
Using the Edit Tag Code command in the context menu launches the Quick Tag Editor.

▶ Select Modify, Quick Tag Editor.

▶ Right-click (Control+click on the Mac) a tag in the tag selector and select the Edit Tag command, as shown in Figure 5.8.

When you select the Quick Tag Editor icon in the Property inspector, the tag pops up beside the Quick Tag Editor icon. When you open the Quick Tag Editor from the context menu or Modify menu, the tag pops up directly above the object in the Document window.

FIGURE 5.8
Using the Edit Tag command in the tag selector launches the Quick Tag Editor.

The Quick Tag Editor has three modes:

- ▶ **Insert HTML**—This mode enables you to insert HTML in the Web page.

- ▶ **Edit Tag**—This mode enables you to edit the existing contents of a tag.

- ▶ **Wrap Tag**—This mode wraps another HTML tag around the selected tag.

When the Quick Tag Editor opens, you can toggle between the three modes by pressing Ctrl+T (Control+T on the Macintosh). The following sections explore each of the three modes.

Using the Insert HTML Mode

The Quick Tag Editor's Insert HTML mode, shown in Figure 5.9, shows a pair of empty tag angle brackets with the insertion point between them. You can either enter text into the brackets, select from the tag drop-down menu, or both. Dreamweaver adds the closing tag automatically. The Quick Tag Editor starts in this mode when you do not have an object selected.

Tag menu

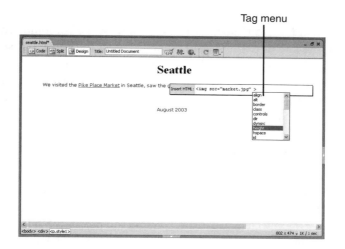

FIGURE 5.9
The Insert HTML
mode in the Quick
Tag Editor presents
empty tag brackets.
You can enter a tag
name and attrib-
utes or select from
the tag drop-down
menu.

Using the Edit Tag Mode

The Quick Tag Editor's Edit Tag mode enables you to edit the HTML of an existing
tag and the tag's contents. To add attributes of the selected tag, place the insertion point at the end of the tag contents in the Quick Tag Editor and add a space.
The tag drop-down menu appears, as shown in Figure 5.10, with attributes appropriate for the tag.

h1 tag attributes

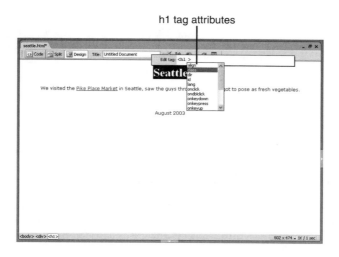

FIGURE 5.10
The tag drop-down
menu presents
attributes appropri-
ate for the current
tag. It appears
automatically after
the delay that is
set in the
Preferences dialog
box.

When the Quick Tag Editor is open, you can use a keyboard shortcut to move up and down through the tag hierarchy. The Ctrl+Shift+< key combination (⌘+Shift+< on the Macintosh) selects the parent tag of the currently selected tag. As you press this key combination, the contents of the Quick Tag Editor change and the tag selector does, too. Use Ctrl+Shift+> (⌘+Shift+> on the Macintosh) to move down through the tag hierarchy. You can also use the Select Parent Tag and Select Child commands from the Edit menu.

Using the Wrap Tag Mode

The Quick Tag Editor's Wrap Tag mode, shown in Figure 5.11, enables you to wrap HTML around the current selection. For instance, when you have text selected, you can wrap a hyperlink (<a href></a>) or text formatting (<h1></h1>) around the text. Dreamweaver adds the opening tag before the selection and the closing tag after the selection. You can right-click (Control+click on the Mac) on the selection and select the Wrap Tag command. To add an attribute to the tag, press the spacebar to get the tag menu to drop down; you can pick the attribute you want from this list of attributes.

FIGURE 5.11
The Wrap Tag mode wraps an HTML tag around the current selection.

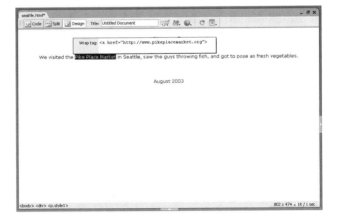

Setting Code Preferences

There are a number of preferences you can set for HTML. The four categories in Dreamweaver preferences that apply to HTML—Code Coloring, Code Format, Code Hints, and Code Rewriting—help control the way Dreamweaver creates and displays the code in your Web pages. If you are used to hand-coding your pages a certain way, don't complain about the way Dreamweaver formats it—change it!

> ### Understand a Preference Before You Change It
> Don't change a setting in the Preferences dialog box if you aren't sure what it does. Many of Dreamweaver's default settings reflect the standard way of creating Web pages. Change them if you need to, but know that you could inadvertently cause a problem if you change them blindly.

Setting Code Color Preferences

The tags in Code view display code colored according to the settings in the Dreamweaver Preferences dialog box. You must have syntax coloring turned on in the View Options menu in order to see colored code. Select the Code Coloring category in the Preferences dialog box. You select which type of code you'd like to edit here. Also, this category enables you to set the background color for Code view. Either enter a color in hexadecimal format or use the color picker to select a color.

Select the HTML document type from the list and click the Edit Coloring Scheme button. The left side of the dialog box enables you to select a tag and then individually set a color for it on the right. To change a tag color, select a type of tag (HTML Image Tags are selected in Figure 5.12) and select a new text color or background color. You can also make the text bold, italic, or underlined.

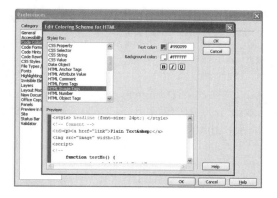

FIGURE 5.12
You set the tag colors displayed in Code view in the Dreamweaver Preferences dialog box.

Setting Code Format Preferences

In the Code Format category of the Dreamweaver Preferences dialog box, shown in Figure 5.13, you set how Dreamweaver will create code. Dreamweaver indents code to make it easier to read. You can change the size of the indent in the

Preferences dialog box. You can also select whether Dreamweaver should indent the code for tables and frames.

FIGURE 5.13
The Code Format category of the Dreamweaver Preferences dialog box enables you to set indentation, wrapping, and tag case.

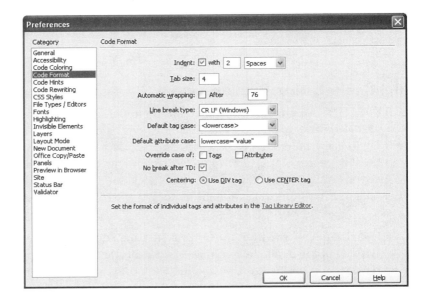

Did you Know?

Apply Dreamweaver Formatting to Any Page

The Code Format category options apply only to new documents created in Dreamweaver. However, you can select Commands, Apply Source Formatting to apply the same formatting to an existing Web page.

If automatic wrapping is selected, Dreamweaver will wrap a line that exceeds the column width entered in the After field in the Code Format category. Some lines may end up a little longer than that number because Dreamweaver does not wrap lines that will affect the appearance of the Web page. You can also set the type of line break that Dreamweaver uses. This can affect the way your code looks in different operating systems.

Because many W3C standards specify lowercase tags, it's a good idea to always use lowercase tags and lowercase attributes. By default, Dreamweaver uses lower-case for tags, the Default Tag Case setting, and attributes, the Default Attribute Case setting. In limited cases, you might want to override the case for tags or attributes. For instance, if you do not want Dreamweaver to change the tag or attribute case in an existing document, check the Override Case of Tags check box

Q&A

Q. *Which should I learn first—Dreamweaver or HTML?*

A. It's helpful to know HTML when you are developing Web pages. I think the best way to learn HTML is to first learn to use a Web editing program such as Dreamweaver. Continue to view the code as you work and use the Reference panel (by selecting Window, Reference) to look up tags or attributes that you are curious about. If you still need grounding in HTML after that, get a good HTML reference book or take a class.

Q. *Can I add tag attributes that don't appear in the tag drop-down menu? I saw a tag attribute listed on a Web site that isn't listed in Dreamweaver for that tag.*

A. Yes. Use the Tag Library Editor by selecting Edit, Tag Libraries. This editor controls the attributes that appear in the tag drop-down menu. Dreamweaver does not list every attribute that is available, so there might be one or two that you want to add.

Workshop

The Workshop contains quiz questions and activities to help reinforce what you've learned in this hour. In case you get stuck, the answers to the quiz appear after the questions.

Quiz

1. How do you toggle through the three Quick Tag Editor modes?

2. What does it mean when a tag appears highlighted in yellow in a Web page?

3. Does Dreamweaver automatically format the HTML that you type into Code view?

Quiz Answers

1. You toggle through the Quick Tag Editor's three modes by pressing Ctrl+T in Windows or Command+T on a Macintosh.

2. When a tag appears highlighted in yellow in a Web page, it means that Dreamweaver thinks it is an invalid tag.

   3. No, Dreamweaver does not automatically format the HTML that you type
   into Code view. However, you can format it by using the Apply Source
   Formatting command on any Web page.

Exercises

   1. Experiment with using the different Quick Tag Editor modes. Pay attention
   to how the Property inspector reflects selecting attributes in the Quick Tag
   Editor. You can select many of the same attributes by using the Property
   inspector's radio buttons, text boxes, and check boxes.

   2. Examine the HTML of a Web page in Code view. First, select an object in the
   Document window and then open Code view. Do you see the HTML for the
   selected object?

   3. Create a new HTML page in Dreamweaver, open Code view, and briefly
   examine the general structure of the Web page: head and body tags nested
   within HTML tags. Select and delete all the code and then re-create this general structure. What are the common tags that go into the head section of
   the page? Enter them. Notice that Dreamweaver enters closing tags for you
   if you've enabled that option in the Preferences dialog box. Press the spacebar after the tag name within any of the tags. What attributes are available
   for that tag? What happens when you select an attribute?

PART II

Adding Images and Multimedia

HOUR 6   Displaying Images on a Page   **117**

HOUR 7   Optimizing and Creating Images   **131**

HOUR 8   Creating Image Maps and Navigation Bars   **151**

HOUR 9   Adding Flash and Other Multimedia Files
             to a Web Page   **163**

HOUR 10 Managing Assets by Using the Assets Panel   **185**

Image to the right of the text

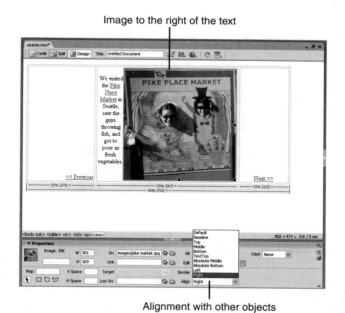

FIGURE 6.4
You can change
how an image
aligns with adjacent
objects in the Align
drop-down menu.

Alignment with other objects

TABLE 6.1 Image Alignment Options in the Property Inspector

Align Option	Description
Default	Baseline-aligns the image, but this depends on the browser.
Baseline	Aligns the bottom of the image with the bottom of the element.
Top	Aligns the image with the highest element. Additional lines of text wrap beneath the image.
Middle	Aligns the baseline of the text with the middle of the image. Additional lines of text wrap beneath the image.
Bottom	Aligns the baseline of the text at the bottom of the image.
TextTop	Aligns the image with the highest text (not the highest element, as with the Top option). Additional lines of text wrap beneath the image.
Absolute Middle	Aligns the middle of the image with the middle of the text beside it.
Absolute Bottom	Aligns the bottom of the highest element with the bottom of the image.
Left	Aligns the image to the left of other elements.
Right	Aligns the image to the right of other elements.

To increase the distance between the image and other page elements, set the V Space and H Space. V stands for vertical and H stands for horizontal. To add space to the right and left of an image, put a value in the H Space text box, as shown in Figure 6.5. Horizontal space is added to both the right and the left of the image. Vertical space is added to both the top and the bottom of the image.

FIGURE 6.5
Put a value in the H Space text box to increase the space to the right and the left of the image. Put a value in the V Space text box to increase the space above and below the image.

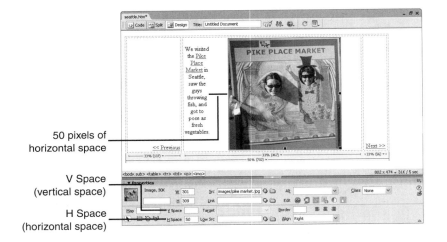

50 pixels of horizontal space

V Space (vertical space)

H Space (horizontal space)

Adding Alternative Text

Believe it or not, some people who may surf to your Web pages are still using text-only browsers, such as Lynx. Others are stuck behind a very slow modem or Internet connection and have the images turned off in their browsers. Others are visually impaired and have text-to-speech (TTS) browsers that read the contents of Web pages. For all these viewers, you should add alternative text to your images.

You enter alternative text, called *alt text*, in the Alt drop-down menu in the Property inspector, as shown in Figure 6.6. Make the text descriptive of the image that it represents. Don't enter something such as "a picture." A better choice would be "Pike Place Market in Seattle." In some browsers, the Alt text also pops up like a ToolTip when the viewer puts the cursor over an image.

FIGURE 6.6
Alt text is useful for viewers who don't have images in their browsers or are visually impaired.

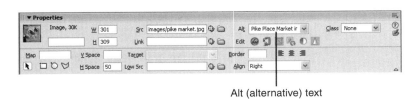

Alt (alternative) text

TTS browsers used by people who are visually impaired read the alt text description of an image to the user. When an image does not have the `Alt` attribute set, a TTS browser says the word *image*; listening to the browser say *image* over and over isn't very enjoyable! Some images on a Web page are purely ornamental and do not add information to the page—a divider line, for instance. Select `<empty>` from the Alt drop-down menu in the Property inspector to add alt text with no content; this makes text-to-speech browsers skip the image.

Missing Alt Text Reporting

You can run a Missing Alt Text report by selecting Site, Reports. This report shows you all the images that are missing alt text.

Creating a Linked Image

The Link property appears in the Property inspector when you have text or an image selected. Linked images are common on the Web. When the user clicks a linked image, the browser loads the linked Web page. With an image selected, you can add a hyperlink in a couple ways:

- ▶ Type a URL into the Link box in the Property inspector.
- ▶ Browse for the linked page by selecting the Browse icon beside the Link box.
- ▶ Use the Point-to-File icon to link to a file. The Point-to-File icon enables you to simply drag the file over to the Files panel to create a link.

To enter a known URL as an image link, select an image on your Web page and make sure the Property inspector is open. Enter a URL in the Link box underneath the Src box, as shown in Figure 6.7.

Link   Border

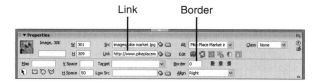

FIGURE 6.7
You set hyperlinks in the Link box in the Property inspector.

Notice that when you enter a URL in the Link box, the Border property automatically changes to 0. This is so that you do not have the hyperlink highlight as a border around the image. If you prefer to have a highlighted border, set the border to a value greater than 0. You can also set a border for an image that isn't linked to anything. The border will then appear as a black box around the image.

After you save the Web page, preview it in a browser. When you click the image that has the hyperlink, your browser should go to the hyperlinked page.

Exploring Image Flavors: GIF, JPEG, and PNG

All browsers support the two standard image formats: GIF (pronounced either "gif" or "jif") and JPEG (pronounced "j-peg"). There is also a newer format, the portable network graphics (PNG—pronounced "ping") format. Here's a little more information about these three formats:

- ▶ **GIF**—This format is best for images that have blocks of continuous color, usually drawings.

- ▶ **JPEG**—This format is best for photographic images and images that do not have blocks of continuous color—for example, images that contain color gradients.

- ▶ **PNG**—This format is a replacement for the GIF format. It supports alpha channels that are useful for transparency. Although PNG is not as popular as the other two formats, its popularity is growing. This is the Macromedia Fireworks native file format.

Did you Know?

Optimize Your Images

Image optimization software programs can help you decide which image format is the most efficient to use for a particular image. These programs also help you reduce the number of colors in an image and improve other factors that reduce file size and download time.

If you have Fireworks, for example, in Dreamweaver you can select Command, Optimize Image in Fireworks when you have an image selected. This opens the image file in Fireworks. Another program that has image optimization is Adobe Photoshop.

The File Types/Editors category in the Preferences dialog box allows you to associate file extensions with different external programs, as shown in Figure 6.8. For example, you can associate the .jpg, .gif, and .png file extensions with Fireworks. When an image is selected in Dreamweaver, you can click the Edit button to open the image file in Fireworks. You make your edits and save the file. To associate an editor with a file extension, select a file extension in the File Types/Editors category, click the plus button, and browse to the image editor program.

Add or remove extensions

Add or remove editors

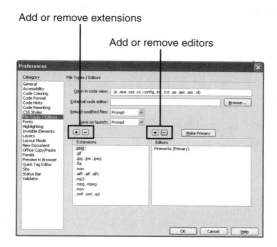

FIGURE 6.8
The File Types/Editors category in the Dreamweaver Preferences dialog box configures other applications to edit linked files.

While you're in an external image editor, you might want to create a low-resolution version of an image to link to from the Low Src box in the Property inspector. This image will appear during the initial loading of the Web page and then will turn into the higher-resolution version of the image. This functionality evolved to help speed up download times. Usually the low-resolution image is grayscale or a smaller version of a color image.

Editing Images Within Dreamweaver

Although you will probably want to become somewhat familiar with a graphics tool to create and optimize images to put in your Web sites, Dreamweaver has a few basic image editing capabilities to explore. In Hour 7, "Optimizing and Creating Images," you'll explore how to use Macromedia Fireworks for image editing. Dreamweaver MX 2004 has several image editing tools built right in:

▶ **Edit**—Opens the selected image in Fireworks for editing (of course, you need to have Macromedia Fireworks or another image-editing program defined in the Preferences dialog box for this command to work).

▶ **Optimize**—Opens the selected image in the Fireworks optimization window. You'll learn more about this in Hour 7. This command requires that you have Fireworks installed.

▶ **Crop**—Lets you trim off unwanted portions of the image and saves the smaller file. This command works within Dreamweaver, enabling you to save the cropped image.

▶ **Resample**—This command becomes active after you've resized an image in Dreamweaver. It optimizes an image by adding or removing pixels in the image. This command works within Dreamweaver.

▶ **Brightness and Contrast**—Changes the brightness and contrast of an image to correct an image that is too bright or too dark. This command works within Dreamweaver.

▶ **Sharpen**—Sharpens a blurry image. This command works within Dreamweaver.

You can access all these image editing commands from the Property inspector when you have an image selected, as shown in Figure 6.9. Make sure you have a backup copy of any images you modify because Dreamweaver changes the actual image file.

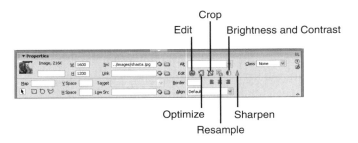

FIGURE 6.9
Dreamweaver has image-editing commands that enable you to jump out to an image-editing program or edit an image directly in Dreamweaver.

Creating a Rollover Image

Dreamweaver makes it easy to implement rollover images by using the Rollover Image object. A **rollover image** is an image that swaps to another image when the viewer's cursor is over it. You need two image files with exactly the same dimensions in order to create a rollover.

To create a rollover image, follow these steps:

1. Place the insertion point where you want the rollover image to appear.

2. Select the Rollover Image object from the Insert bar or select Insert, Interactive Images, Rollover Image. The Insert Rollover Image dialog box appears.

3. Type a name for the image in the Image Name text field.

4. Select both the original image file and the rollover image file by clicking the Browse buttons next to those options and selecting the image files.

5. Check the Preload Rollover Image check box if you'd like the rollover image downloaded into the viewer's browser cache. With a preloaded image, there is less chance that the viewer will have to wait for the rollover image to download when he or she moves the cursor over the image.

6. Add a link to the rollover image by clicking the Browse button next to When Clicked, Go to URL or type in the external URL or named anchor.

7. The Insert Rollover Image dialog box should look as shown in Figure 6.10. Click the OK button.

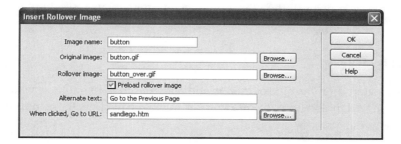

FIGURE 6.10
A rollover image swaps one image for another when the viewer's cursor is over the image. You need to enter both image paths into the Insert Rollover Image dialog box.

Summary

In this hour, you have learned how to insert an image into a Web page and how to set a link, low-resolution source, vertical space and horizontal space, and alt text. You have learned how to change the size of an image border and edit the image by using an external editor. You have learned how to align an image on a page and align it in relationship to other elements beside it. You have also created a rollover image.

Q&A

Q. *I created a Web page with some images in it. When I preview it in the browser, the images don't show up. Why?*

A. Until you save your page, Dreamweaver doesn't know how to express the path to the image files. That's why the images don't show up. Save your page before you preview it, and you should be all right.

Q. *I accidentally stretched an image. Help!*

A. It's easy to restore the original dimensions of an image by selecting the image and clicking the Refresh button that appears next to the width and height text fields in the Property inspector after you've resized an image.

Workshop

The Workshop contains quiz questions and activities to help reinforce what you've learned in this hour. In case you get stuck, the answers to the quiz appear after the questions.

Quiz

1. How do you create a box around an image?

2. What are the three widely supported image formats for Web pages?

3. If you want an image on the left and text beside it on the right, what Align value would you give the image?

Quiz Answers

1. Enter a value in the Border text box to create a box, or border, around an image.

2. The three widely supported image formats for Web pages are GIF, JPEG, and PNG.

3. You give the image the Align value Left.

Exercises

1. Insert an image into a new page. Resize it by using the resizing handles. Click the Refresh button. Resize the image by holding down Shift while dragging the corner resizing handle. Click the Refresh button. Change the width and height dimensions by entering different values into the W and H boxes in the Property inspector.

2. Add alt text to an image. Open your browser, select the browser preferences or Internet options, and turn off viewing of images. The command for this may be called Show Pictures or Automatically Load Images. Return to Dreamweaver and preview the Web page in that browser so that you can see how the alt text looks.

3. Insert an image into a Web page and experiment with Dreamweaver's image editing tools. Try using sharpen, cropping, and brightness/contrast. Then resize the image and try image resampling. Does Dreamweaver actually change the original files? Be careful not to make any permanent changes to your files.

HOUR 7

Optimizing and Creating Images

What You'll Learn in This Hour:

▶ How to optimize images
▶ How to create an image in Fireworks
▶ How to add strokes, fills, effects, and text to an image
▶ How to slice and export images

Macromedia Fireworks is an image creation and optimization tool that is an excellent addition to your Web development toolbox. You will need to create and optimize the images that you use in your Web sites, and Fireworks enables you to quickly create images that have cool effects such as bevels and glows. If you do not have Fireworks, you can download a trial version at www.macromedia.com/software/trial_download.

Dreamweaver and Fireworks are tightly integrated. You can open Fireworks files in Dreamweaver, make changes, and see those changes in the original Fireworks file. You can also import tables, rollover images, and HTML code created in Fireworks directly into Dreamweaver.

Fireworks is a professional image tool that could fill an entire 24-hour learning period on its own! This hour simply touches on some of the important elements and describes a few image manipulation techniques. There is so much more to learn about Fireworks than is possible in this hour.

Acquainting Yourself with Fireworks

This hour demonstrates how to accomplish image optimization and creation in Macromedia Fireworks, but many of the techniques described here are achievable in other image editing programs as well. We're exploring Fireworks in this hour because many people purchase Fireworks along with Dreamweaver and it is another Macromedia product. Although the command names may differ in other image-editing programs, such as Adobe Photoshop, the techniques are similar to those in other programs.

Fireworks has an integrated interface that looks very similar to Dreamweaver's interface. The Fireworks Document window, shown in Figure 7.1, contains a Tools panel on the left, a Property inspector at the bottom, and panel groups on the right. You can open an existing image in Fireworks or create a new one from scratch.

Tools panel   Document window   Panel groups

FIGURE 7.1
The Fireworks has an integrated interface similar to Dreamweaver's interface.

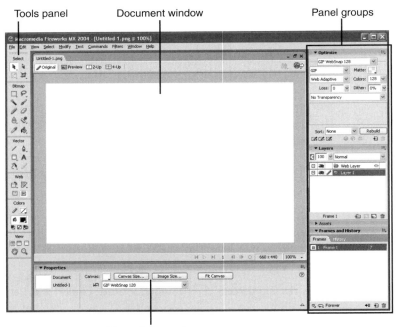

Property inspector

Optimizing Images for Use in a Web Page

One of the powerful features of Fireworks is its capability to optimize an image and show you the smallest and best-looking format for the image. This is probably how I use Fireworks most frequently. To practice using this feature, open an image, preferably a photograph, in Fireworks. Because your image will be different from the one I'm working with, you will get different results than are shown here.

You can get a photo from your digital camera, or from a collection of clip art, or from a digital photo service bureau such as PhotoDisc (`http://creative.getty-images.com/photodisc/`). You need to optimize images to make sure that they aren't larger than they need to be because larger images mean longer downloads. Do your Web page viewers a favor and optimize any images you use so that they aren't any larger than they need to be.

Digital cameras are often set to take pictures at a high resolution. Although a higher resolution gives excellent results for printing, it is usually too high to display on a computer screen. Have you ever looked at a digital photo on your computer and had it appear huge? That's because the photo is saved at 150 or 300 pixels per inch, but your monitor resolution is approximately 72 pixels per inch. You need to sample a photo down to the standard 72 pixels per inch before you use it in a Web page. Open your selected image file in Fireworks and click the Image Size button in the Property inspector (see Figure 7.2).

FIGURE 7.2
The Image Size button is available in the Fireworks Property inspector when nothing on the screen is selected.

The Image Size dialog box appears, enabling you to change the resolution and size of the image. First change the Resolution setting to 72 pixels per inch, as shown in Figure 7.3. Make sure that the Constrain Proportions check box is selected and then examine the pixel dimensions of the image. You can change them here by entering a new width or height, or you can change them later, during the optimization process. With the proportions constrained, you can change one of the dimensions, and Fireworks will change the other dimension proportionally for you. Because you are working with an image for a Web page, you don't need to worry about the Print Size settings.

FIGURE 7.3
The Image Size dia-log box enables you to change the size and resolution of an image.

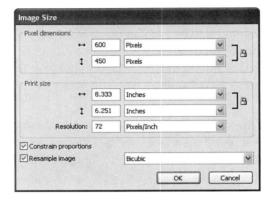

To optimize the image and save it for the Web, follow these steps:

1. In Fireworks, select File, Export Wizard.

2. Accept the defaults, with the Select an Export Format setting selected, and click the Continue button.

3. Select the Web radio button because you will be using this image as part of a Web page. Click the Continue button.

4. In the Analysis Results dialog box, Fireworks suggests that you use either a GIF or JPEG image, the accepted formats for Web pages. After you read the information in this dialog box, click the Exit button. The Export Preview dialog box appears, as shown in Figure 7.4.

5. Two versions of the image are displayed in the Export Preview dialog box: a JPEG version and a GIF version. The image properties are displayed on the left side of the box. Click the JPEG (top image) to display the JPEG properties and click the GIF (bottom image) to display the GIF properties.

6. Examine the image size and download time for each of the formats. Choose the format with the quickest download time. If you are optimizing a photo, the JPEG format will probably make the smallest file. Select an image file format to further optimize the file.

7. Experiment with the image format optimization settings while examining the file size. It's safe to experiment here prior to saving the final image. Examine the preview image to make sure the quality of the image isn't degraded too much.

Properties   JPEG

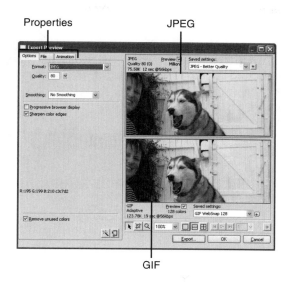

GIF

FIGURE 7.4
The Export Preview dialog box enables you to compare the file size and download time of different file formats.

8. Click the File tab to modify the image size. Decreasing the size of the image will make it load more quickly.

9. When you are satisfied that your image is optimized, click the Export button. Give the file a name and click Save.

Your newly optimized image is now ready to be incorporated into a Web page!

Setting JPEG Quality

Depending on your original image, a JPEG quality setting somewhere between 50 and 80 usually works best. You need to examine the preview image while optimizing, paying attention to both the foreground and background. Check that there aren't any areas of the image that are extremely **pixilated**, where the square pixels are visible to the user or blurry.

Creating an Image

In Fireworks you can create a new image from scratch, such as a button graphic that you can use in your Web site. First you create a new file, and then you add some color and text. Next, you apply an effect to make it look interesting. To try this, follow these steps:

1. Select File, New.

2. The New Document dialog box appears, as shown in Figure 7.5. You set the width, height, and resolution of the new file in this dialog box. Enter 70 pixels for the width and 26 pixels for the height. The resolution should be 72 because that is the standard resolution for images that will be displayed on a computer screen.

FIGURE 7.5
You set the width, height, and resolution in the New Document dialog box. You also set the canvas color here.

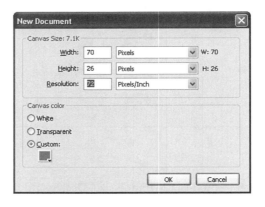

3. Give the button a background color by selecting the Custom radio button under Canvas Color, clicking the color picker, and then picking a color.

4. When you are done with the settings in the New Document dialog box, click OK.

5. Select 200% from the magnification drop-down menu at the bottom of the Document window, as shown in Figure 7.6. This will make it easier to see what you are working on.

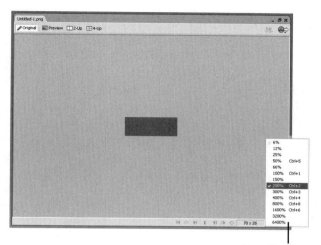

Magnification menu

FIGURE 7.6
You can magnify
the Document win-
dow by using the
magnification drop-
down menu. The
magnification level
is displayed at the
bottom of the
Document window.

Adding Text to an Image

You can add text to a button. The Text tool in Fireworks enables you to place editable text into the Document window. You should turn on guides so that you can judge whether you have the text centered in the button. You can use any font on your system, and you can apply antialiasing and other text effects. *Antialiasing* is a process of blending the edges of text with its background so that the letters look smoother.

Add text to your rectangle as follows:

1. Turn on the rulers by selecting View, Rulers. You need the rulers to be visible because guides are added to an image by clicking and dragging from the ruler. *Guides* are useful for lining up text and other elements within an image.

2. Click within the left ruler and drag a vertical guide to the middle of the image. Repeat by dragging a horizontal guide down from the top ruler to the middle of the image. You can open the Info panel to help precisely place the guides. The guides should look as shown in Figure 7.7.

Remove or Hide the Guides

To remove the guides, simply drag them off the screen. To leave the guides in place but hide them, select View, Guides.

By the Way

FIGURE 7.7
You can add guides to an image so that you know where the middle of the image is.

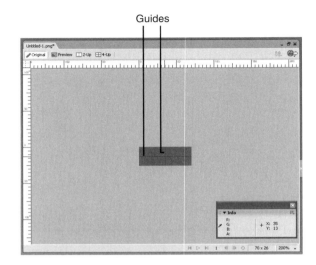

2. Select the Text tool from the Tools panel. (That is, click the button that shows the letter A.) Don't click within the Document window quite yet.

3. In the Property inspector, select a font, make the font size 14, and choose white for the color (unless white won't be visible on your canvas color).

4. Click the canvas and enter some text for a button title (try **Next** for a next button). Leave enough room on the right side for a small arrow.

5. Pick up and position the text object. You can use the arrow keys on your keyboard to fine-tune the positioning while you have the text selected. Select the text by using the arrow tool. The button should look something like the one in Figure 7.8.

Pointer tool

Subselection tool   Text object

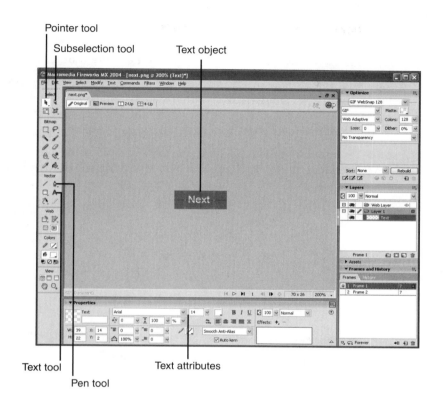

FIGURE 7.8
Create a text object and set the font, font size, and font color.

Text tool   Text attributes

Pen tool

Adding a Shape to an Image

Fireworks has tools for drawing any type of shape you might want. Now you'll create a triangle shape to the right of the text on your button that will look like an arrow. After you create the triangle, you can modify the stroke (that is, the outline) and the fill. To create a triangle, follow these steps:

1. Select the Pen tool from the Tools panel. The cursor becomes an ink pen. The Pen tool adds points to create a shape. You'll create three points for a triangle.

2. Click to create one point in the triangle. Hold down the Shift key while you click to create a second triangle point. This should force the creation of a straight line. Click on the original point to close the shape.

3. This last line may not be perfectly straight, but you can adjust it. There are two arrow tools in Fireworks: the Pointer tool and the Subselection tool. You can use the Subselection tool (the white arrow tool) to select a single point

in your triangle. Use this tool to select any of the points, and then press the arrow keys on your keyboard to fine-tune the position of the points so that the triangle is even. Use the Pointer tool to select the entire triangle.

4. Make sure that the triangle object that you just created is selected (in case you clicked your cursor somewhere else after step 3). You should see the three points when it is selected. If the triangle is not selected, select the Pointer tool from the Tools panel and click the triangle to select it.

5. The stroke settings are in the Property inspector. Select None from the stroke drop-down menu, as shown in Figure 7.9. Notice that the stroke color picker now has a red line through it, signifying that this object does not have any stroke attributes applied.

Stroke drop-down menu

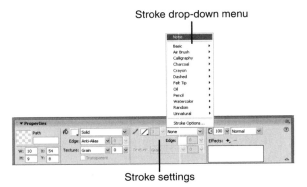

FIGURE 7.9
Set the stroke in the Property inspector.

Stroke settings

6. The fill settings are directly to the left of the stroke settings in the Property inspector. Select Solid from the fill drop-down menu, and select a color (I suggest white) from the color picker. The image should look like the one in Figure 7.10.

Did you Know?

Check the Final Size
You might want to reduce the magnification to 100% so that you can see what your button will look like at its final size.

7. Underneath the fill settings is the Edge property. Make sure that Anti-Alias is selected so that the edges of the triangle will blend nicely into the background.

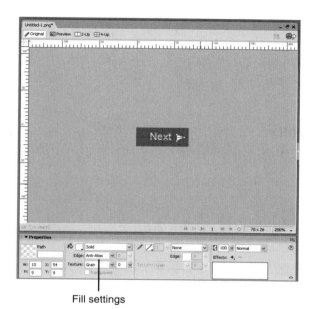

Fill settings

FIGURE 7.10
The triangle now
has no stroke and
a solid fill.

8. Save your file as a Fireworks PNG file. The PNG format is the native format that Fireworks uses to save files. When you do this, you save the source file, but you still need to export a file to use in your Web page. Although Fireworks uses standard PNG files, these files contain a lot of extra information—information about shapes and fonts that Fireworks needs to edit the image. When you optimize, this extra information is removed.

You Can Cloak Your Fireworks Files

You can save your original Fireworks files to your Web site. Dreamweaver has a cloaking feature that you will learn about in Hour 21, "Managing and Editing a Project," that enables you to easily store source files in your Web site.

Did you Know?

---

9. Select File, Export Preview to optimize your button. Adjust the settings, as shown in Figure 7.11, to get the smallest file and then click the Export button to save the image. This is the image that is inserted into your Web page in Dreamweaver.

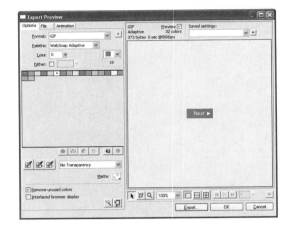

Creating a Rollover Image

It's easy to use Fireworks to create rollover images. In this section, you'll create a
rollover version of the button that you just created. Remember that the trick to
creating a rollover image is that the two images involved need to be exactly the
same size. You'll continue using the same button file you just created. To begin
creating a rollover image, follow these steps:

1. Open the Frames panel. You should already have a Frame 1. Add a new
   frame by clicking the New/Duplicate Frame button (the button with the plus
   sign) in the lower-right corner of the panel.

2. Select Frame 1 in the Frames panel and select everything by using Edit,
   Select All (Ctrl+A in Windows, Command+A on a Mac). Copy the contents
   of Frame 1 (Ctrl+C in Windows, Command+C on a Mac), click Frame 2, and
   paste the contents (Ctrl+V in Windows, Command+V on a Mac). Now you
   have an exact copy of Frame 1 in Frame 2.

3. Select the text on Frame 2 by using the Pointer tool. The text attributes
   appear in the Property inspector. Change the text color to a different, highlight color. Remember which color you use because you'll use it again in a
   few minutes for the arrow.

Adding an Effect to a Rollover Image

Fireworks lets you add a number of interesting effects to images to make them
look unique and beautiful. Even better, they are very easy to remove if they don't

turn out quite the way you'd like. Each time you add an effect to an object, it is listed in the Effects area of the Property inspector, with a check mark beside it. You simply uncheck the check box to turn off the effect for an object.

Fireworks Can Use Photoshop Plug-ins

If you have Photoshop, you can use Photoshop plug-ins in Fireworks. Point to the directory that contains the Photoshop plug-ins in the Folders category of the Fireworks Preferences dialog box (which you open by selecting Edit, Preferences). You need to restart Fireworks to load the Photoshop plug-in commands. After you restart Fireworks, it displays the Photoshop plug-in commands in the Effect Panel drop-down menu.

By the Way

To add an effect to your image, follow these steps:

1. Make sure you have the triangle object on Frame 2 selected. You'll apply the effect to this object.

2. Select the Add Effects button (the + button) to drop down the Effects menu, as shown in Figure 7.12.

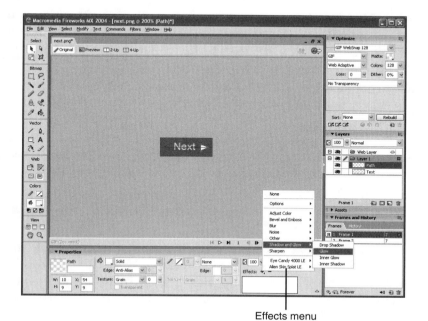

Effects menu

FIGURE 7.12
The Effects area of the Property inspector enables you to select the effect you'd like to add.

3. From the Effects menu, select Shadow and Glow and then select Glow. The effect is applied to the triangle, and the attribute box appears.

4. Select the same color you applied to the text in the preceding section. If you need to edit the effect, simply double-click it in the list.

You can add bevels, glows, and blurs to images, and you can emboss images, too. You'll probably want to experiment with the different effects. Usually you can change the colors involved, too. For instance, you can make an object glow in yellow from its center or glow from the bottom of the image as if it were on fire. Fireworks effects enable you to get professional image results without having to know all the steps necessary to do the effects with the other tools in Fireworks.

To simulate what the rollover effect will look like on the Web page, click between Frame 1 and Frame 2. Does it look good? Now you must complete the final step to export both of the frames as separate images to use in a Dreamweaver rollover image. Fireworks uses something called *slices* to facilitate rollover images and other interactivity. To export your rollover images to Dreamweaver, follow these steps:

1. Select the Slice tool and draw a rectangle that completely covers the canvas. The slice appears as a tinted box over the image. You can toggle slices on and off by using the buttons directly beneath the Slice tool in the Tools panel.

2. Right-click (Control+click on the Mac) the slice you just created. The context menu shown in Figure 7.13 appears. Select the Export Selected Slice command.

3. The Export dialog box appears, as shown in Figure 7.14. Name your file next.gif. Make sure that the Current Frame Only check box is *not* checked. Save the buttons in the images directory you created in your Web site.

4. Go to the images directory. You should see two images: next.gif and next_f2. The next_f2 image is the content from Frame 2.

So that you can make updates or changes to this button later, you should save the Fireworks file. When you reopen the file in Fireworks, you'll have access to change all the text objects, shapes, and other elements of the image. The native Fireworks PNG file can be displayed in a Web page, but I don't recommend that because it isn't an optimized file format, and it is bigger than necessary for a Web page.

Slice tool

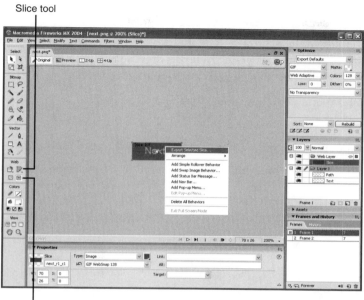

Show Slices button

FIGURE 7.13
This context menu enables you to export all the frames beneath the slice.

Current Frame Only check box

FIGURE 7.14
Use the Export dialog box to export the two frames as separate images.

Slicing an Image into Pieces

Fireworks enables you to slice an image into smaller pieces so that you can add interactivity to the individual pieces. You can draw slice objects over an image in Fireworks and then export the slices as individual graphic files.

To create a sliced image, follow these steps:

1. Open an image in Fireworks.

2. Make sure that the Show Slices button is selected in the Tools panel.

3. Select the Slice tool and draw a rectangle on top of the image, as shown in Figure 7.15.

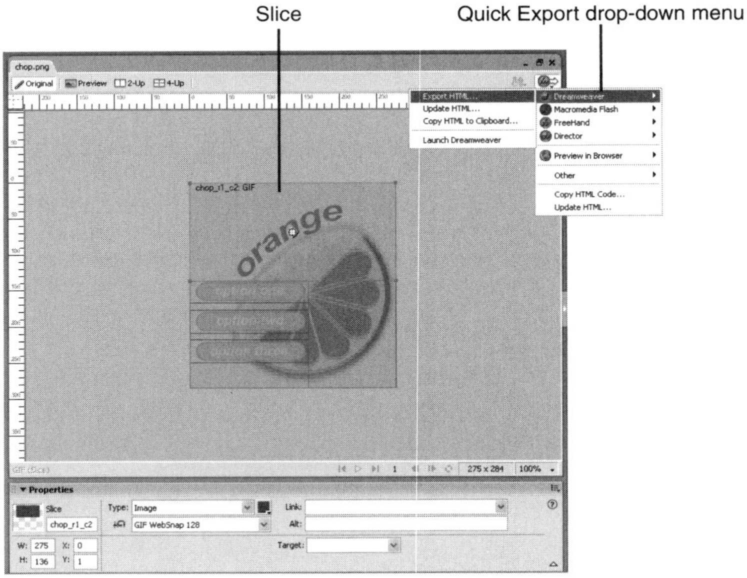

FIGURE 7.15
Draw slices over an image to create individual image files that are held together by an HTML table.

Slice   Quick Export drop-down menu

4. Slice up the entire image by repeating step 3.

5. Select the Quick Export drop-down menu in the upper-right corner of the Fireworks Document window. Select Dreamweaver, Export HTML from the Quick Export drop-down menu. The Export dialog box appears.

6. Fireworks enables you to export all the slices as individual image files along with the HTML table that will display the images as if they were all one image. Make sure that Export HTML File is selected at the bottom of the Export dialog box.

7. Select the Save button and save the HTML file and all the sliced images into a directory.

If you open the HTML file that you just created, you'll see all the slices pushed together as if they were a single image. You can open this file in Dreamweaver and edit it. In a minute, you will learn how to import the HTML into Dreamweaver.

Placing a Fireworks File into Dreamweaver

Dreamweaver and Fireworks are tightly integrated so that you can efficiently use the two tools together. After you've imported HTML that was created in Fireworks into Dreamweaver, you can edit the HTML in Dreamweaver and update the original Fireworks files, too. Dreamweaver knows when you have inserted a Fireworks file into your Web page, and it keeps track of any edits that you make to the file.

To import the HTML and the sliced images that you created in Fireworks, follow these steps:

1. In Dreamweaver, create a new Web page and then select Inset, Image Objects, Fireworks HTML. The Insert Fireworks HTML dialog box appears.

2. Click the Browse button and navigate to the HTML file that you saved in Fireworks. Select the Delete File After Insertion check box if you would like the file to be deleted after it is inserted into the Web page.

3. The HTML table and images are inserted into the Dreamweaver Document window.

Now the HTML that Fireworks created is in the Web page. Dreamweaver knows that the HTML originally came from Fireworks. When you select the table or the images, the Property inspector shows that the table or image originated in Fireworks, as you can see in Figure 7.16. There is also an Edit button you can click to open Fireworks and make any edits you'd like.

FIGURE 7.16
The Property
inspector shows
that the object was
originally created in
Fireworks, and the
Edit button lets you
edit the object in
Fireworks.

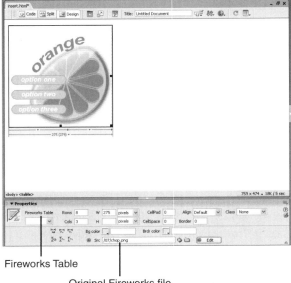

Fireworks Table

Original Fireworks file

Summary

In this hour you have learned how to create a button image in Fireworks by using strokes, fills, and other effects. You have learned how to add text to a button. You have learned how to optimize an image to make it download quickly over the Internet. You have also learned how to slice a single image into multiple images, export those images and the HTML that holds them together, and import the HTML into Dreamweaver.

Q&A

Q. *How can I tell which file format makes the smallest file?*

A. That's what you use optimization capabilities of Fireworks for. You don't need to know off the top of your head which format to use because you can experiment in Fireworks and find out what format creates the smallest file.

Q. *Why would I want to use Fireworks instead of Dreamweaver to add behaviors to images?*

A. Some people, mainly graphic designers, are more comfortable working in the program they know the best. If you know Fireworks, using Fireworks to add behaviors will be easier. Macromedia has given graphic designers the power to add HTML to their graphics with Fireworks. Because you are reading this book, you probably know (or want to know) Dreamweaver. Therefore, it will probably be easier for you to apply behaviors by using Dreamweaver. Dreamweaver has many more Web page coding capabilities than Fireworks.

Workshop

The Workshop contains quiz questions and activities to help reinforce what you've learned in this hour. In case you get stuck, the answers to the quiz appear after the questions.

Quiz

1. How do you create a guide in Fireworks?
2. What is the native file format in Fireworks?
3. Edits made in Dreamweaver will update the original Firework PNG files when you've imported from Fireworks. True or false?

Quiz Answers

1. Turn on the rulers, click within the rulers, and drag a guide into position.
2. The native file format in Fireworks is PNG.
3. True. You don't need to make changes in two places!

Exercises

1. Try applying some of the various effects available in Fireworks to an image. What does Glow do? What's the difference between Drop Shadow and Inner Shadow? Try using the Bevel and Emboss effects. What do they do? Try changing the color by using the color picker.

2. In Fireworks, select Commands, Creative, Add Picture Frame and then experiment. Export your experiment to Dreamweaver and try editing the image in Dreamweaver. What happens when you make changes in Fireworks? Are they automatically reflected in Dreamweaver?

Creating Image Maps and Navigation Bars

What You'll Learn in This Hour:

▶ How to define an image map
▶ How to open a new browser window by using targeting
▶ How to create a navigation bar

In Hour 6, "Displaying Images on a Page," you inserted an image into a Web page and created a rollover image. In this hour, you'll expand on that knowledge, creating an image map and a navigation bar. These are more complicated uses of images.

Adding Links to a Graphic by Using Image Maps

An **image map** is an image that has regions, called *hotspots*, defined as hyperlinks. When a viewer clicks a hotspot, it acts just like any other hyperlink. Instead of adding one hyperlink to an entire image, you can define a number of hotspots on different portions of an image. You can even create hotspots in different shapes.

Image maps are useful for presenting graphical menus that the viewer can click to select regions of a single image. For instance, you could create an image out of a picture of North America. You could draw hotspots around the different countries in North America. When the viewer clicked a country's hotspot, he or she could jump to a Web page with information on that country.

Dreamweaver creates **client-side** image maps, meaning that the Web page holds all the defined coordinates and hyperlinks. The other type of image map, a **server-side** image map, depends on a program that runs on a Web server to interpret coordinates and hyperlinks. Client-side image maps react more quickly than server-side image maps to user input because they don't have to contact the server for information.

Creating an Image Map

When an image is selected, you see four image map tools in the lower corner of the expanded Property inspector. These four tools are used to define image map hotspots. The arrow is the Pointer Hotspot tool, which is used to select or move the hotspots. There are three image map hotspot tools: One tool draws rectangles, one draws circles, and one draws polygons.

To create an image map, follow these steps:

1. Insert an image into a Web page. The image must be selected for the image map tools to appear in the Property inspector.

2. Give the map a name in the Map Name text box, as shown in Figure 8.1. The name needs to be unique from other map names in the page.

Map Name text box

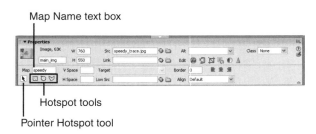

FIGURE 8.1
Give an image map a name and use the hotspot tools to draw hotspots within an image map.

Hotspot tools

Pointer Hotspot tool

3. Select one of the hotspot tools. You'll spend the next minutes exploring each of the hotspot tools in depth.

4. With a newly drawn hotspot selected, type a URL in the Link box, as shown in Figure 8.2, or click the Browse icon to browse to a local Web page. You can also link a hotspot to a named anchor by entering a pound sign followed by the anchor name.

URL   Hotspot alt text

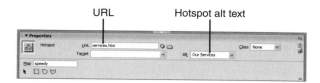

FIGURE 8.2
Enter a URL to link
a hotspot with
another Web page
or a named anchor
within the current
page.

5. Enter alternative text for the hotspot in the Alt text box. As discussed in Hour 6, some browsers display this text as a ToolTip.

6. Optionally, select a window target from the Target drop-down menu in the Property inspector. Target windows will be covered a little later in this hour, in the section "Targeting a Link to Open in a New Browser Window," where you will open a new browser window by using the Target drop-down menu selections. Most of the time, you probably won't select a target.

You set all the image properties for an image map just as you would an ordinary image. You can set the vertical space, horizontal space, alt text, border, and alignment. If you copy and paste the image map into another Web page, all the image map properties come along, too.

Adding a Rectangular Hotspot to an Image Map

To add a rectangular hotspot to your image map, first select the Rectangle Hotspot tool. Click and drag the crosshair cursor to make a rectangle the dimensions of the hotspot you want to create. When you release the mouse, a highlighted box appears over the image, as in Figure 8.3. With the hotspot selected, enter a URL into the Link box in the Property inspector.

To move or adjust the size of the hotspot, you need to first select the Pointer Hotspot tool. You can't use the other hotspot tools to adjust the hotspot, or you will end up creating another hotspot. Click the hotspot with the Pointer Hotspot tool and either move the hotspot to another location or resize the hotspot by using the resizing handles.

In the Web page HTML, the rectangular hotspot is defined by two sets of x and y coordinates. The upper-left corner of the rectangle is recorded as the first two coordinates in the code and the lower-right corner of the rectangle is recorded as the last two coordinates. The coordinates are in pixels, and they are relative to the image, not to the Web page. The HTML code for a rectangular area looks like this:

```
<area shape="rect" coords="127,143,251,291" href="services.htm">
```

Rectangular hotspot

FIGURE 8.3
Create a rectangle
and link it to a
URL. Now it's a
hotspot!

FIGURE 8.3
Create a rectangle
and link it to a
URL. Now it's a
hotspot!

Rectangle Hotspot tool

In this example, the upper-left corner of the rectangle is 127 pixels from the left of the image and 143 pixels from the top of the image. The bottom-right corner of the rectangle is 251 pixels from the left of the image and 291 pixels from the top. It's nice to have a visual representation in Dreamweaver and not have to figure this out yourself, isn't it?

Adding a Circular Hotspot to an Image Map

A circular area might better define some areas in your image map than a rectangular one. You create a circular hotspot just as you create a rectangular one. Select the Circle Hotspot tool and then click and drag to create the hotspot, as shown in Figure 8.4. Notice that the hotspot is always a perfect circle and not an ellipse. Reposition or resize the hotspot by using the Pointer Hotspot tool.

You can understand why you can have only a circle and not an ellipse when you see how the circular hotspot coordinates are defined. A circle is defined by three values: The circle's radius and the x and y values that define the circle's center. The HTML code defining a circular area looks like this:

```
<area shape="circle" coords="138,186,77" href="about.htm">
```

Circular hotspot

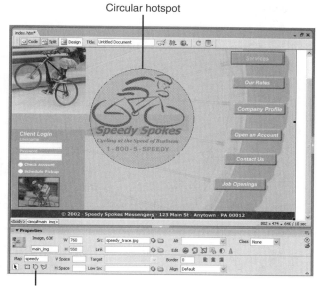

Circle Hotspot tool

FIGURE 8.4
The Circle Hotspot tool creates hotspots that are perfectly circular.

Adding an Irregular Hotspot to an Image Map

Sometimes the area you'd like to turn into a hotspot just isn't circular or rectangular. The Polygon Hotspot tool enables you to create any shape you want to define an irregular hotspot.

You use the Polygon Hotspot tool a little differently than you use the Circle or Rectangle Hotspot tools. First, select the Polygon Hotspot tool from the Property inspector. Instead of clicking and dragging to create a shape, click once for every point in the polygon, as shown in Figure 8.5. You should move around the area you want to define as a hotspot in either a clockwise or counter-clockwise manner; clicking randomly may create an odd polygon. When you are finished creating the points of the polygon, select the Pointer Hotspot tool to complete the polygon. You select the Pointer Hotspot tool in order to deselect the Polygon Hotspot tool so that you don't accidentally add stray points on the screen. Or you can double-click when you are finished drawing the polygon.

Polygon hotspot

FIGURE 8.5
To create an irregu-
lar hotspot with the
Polygon Hotspot
tool, click once for
every point and
double-click to
finish.

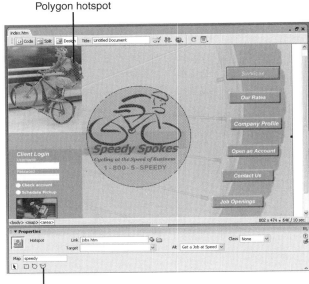

Polygon Hotspot tool

A polygon is defined by as many x and y coordinates, each representing one of the corner points, as you need to define the hotspot shape. The HTML code for a sample polygon hotspot looks like this:

```
<area shape="poly"
coords="85,14,32,33,29,116,130,99,137,130,140,70,156,66,198,84" href="jobs.htm">
```

The polygon defined in this HTML is made up of eight points, so there are eight pairs of x and y coordinates.

Aligning Hotspots

Dreamweaver has built-in alignment tools that you can use to align the hotspots in an image map. First, you need to select the hotspots you want to align. To select all the hotspots in an image map, use the keyboard shortcut Ctrl+A in Windows or Command+A on the Macintosh. Or you can hold down Shift as you click hotspots to add them to the selection. You can tell when hotspots are selected because you can see the resizing handles.

Sometimes it is difficult to finely align hotspots with your mouse. You can use the arrow keys to move a hotspot or multiple hotspots one pixel at a time. The Align

Navigation bar

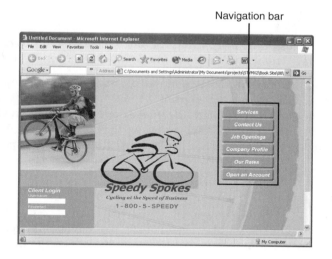

FIGURE 8.9
Test a navigation bar in a browser to make sure the elements have the proper rollover and down states and link to the correct URL.

Make Button States in Fireworks

In Hour 7, "Optimizing and Creating Images," you created a rollover image by placing slightly different-looking images in two frames. To create a down state for a button, simply add a third frame. Fireworks will then export all three graphics to use in a navigation bar.

Did you Know?

Summary

In this hour, you have learned how to create a client-side image map that includes rectangular, circular, and polygonal shapes. You have learned how to use targeting to open a new browser window. You have also created a navigation bar with various button states.

Q&A

Q. *Every time I use the Polygon Hotspot tool, I make a mess of it. I get extra points in the wrong section of the image map. What am I doing wrong?*

A. When you use the Polygon Hotspot tool to create a hotspot, remember to click, click, click around the edges of the hotspot border. After you have defined the border, do not click the image again. Instead, immediately select the Pointer Hotspot tool or double-click on the hotspot to signal Dreamweaver that you are finished creating the polygon hotspot.

Workshop

The Workshop contains quiz questions and activities to help reinforce what you've learned in this hour. In case you get stuck, the answers to the quiz appear after the questions.

Quiz

1. Which image map tool enables you to draw irregular shapes?

2. Where is the code that controls the image map: in the Web page or on the server?

3. What's the reserved target name that will open a new browser window?

Quiz Answers

1. The Polygon Hotspot tool enables you to draw irregular shapes.

2. Dreamweaver creates client-side image maps for which the code is in the Web page.

3. The _blank reserved target name will open a new browser window.

Exercises

1. Create several hotspots. Align the hotspots by using the alignment commands. Make one of the hotspots open a new browser window.

2. Find images for buttons for all the states available in the navigation bar (up, down, over, over when down) or make them yourself in Fireworks. Create a navigation bar.

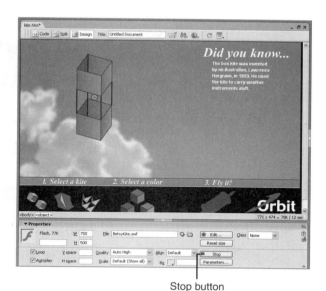

FIGURE 9.2
You can view a Flash or Shockwave movie, and other plug-in–based content, directly in the Document window.

Stop button

Creating Flash Text

Dreamweaver has the capability to create special Text objects—Flash movies with text—directly in Dreamweaver. You do not need to have Flash installed on your computer to have this functionality. You can create Flash text and Flash buttons (you'll try this in a few minutes) right in Dreamweaver.

The Flash Text object enables you to create and insert a Flash movie consisting of text into your Web page. Inserting Flash text has the following advantages:

▶ You can use any font available on your computer. The viewer does not need to have the font installed on his or her computer.

▶ Flash text uses vector graphics, creating a very small file size—much smaller than if you created an image.

To insert a Flash Text object into a Web page, follow these steps:

1. Save your Web page. Select the Flash Text object from the Media menu of the Insert bar or the Insert menu. The Insert Flash Text dialog box appears (see Figure 9.3).

2. Select the font, size, style (bold or italic), and alignment. Select the color, which is the initial color of the text, and the rollover color, which is the color the user will see when he or she places the cursor over the text.

FIGURE 9.3
Set up the Flash
Text object with a
custom font,
rollover color, and a
background color.

Enter text   Text characteristics

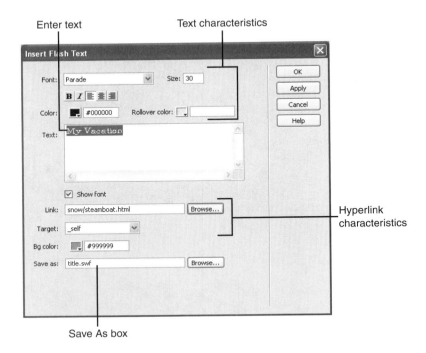

Hyperlink
characteristics

Save As box

3. Type in the Text box the text that you want to appear. Make sure the Show Font check box is selected so that you can see what the font you have selected looks like.

4. Enter a URL in the Link text box or click the Browse button to browse to a Web page or enter a URL.

Watch Out!

Make Sure Flash Doesn't Prevent Search Engine Crawling

Flash may prevent search engines from crawling your Web site. *Crawling* is when the search engine follows the links in a site in order to index all the pages in the site. Enabling a search engine to effectively crawl a site is important for professional Web sites and any Web sites where you'd like searchers to be able to find information in the search engine.

5. Optionally, use the Target text box to target a window for the link. You will learn more about this capability when you learn more about frames in Hour 13, "Understanding and Building Frames and Framesets."

6. Select a background color from the Bg Color drop-down list. It's important to add a background color to the Flash movie if your Web page has a

background color. Flash movies are not transparent, so if the background of your Web page is not white, the Flash movie will stand out as a white box. Simply use the eyedropper from the color picker and click your Web page behind the Insert Flash Text dialog box. Otherwise, your Flash text will be in a white box.

7. Enter a name for the Flash movie in the Save As box. Dreamweaver creates a separate Flash movie, with this name, for your Flash text.

8. Click OK. The text appears in the Dreamweaver Document window.

You can edit a Flash text movie after you have inserted it into a Web page by clicking the Edit button (shown in Figure 9.4) in the Property inspector when the movie is selected in the Document window. You can view the changes you make without closing the Insert Flash Text dialog box by selecting the Apply button.

Edit button

FIGURE 9.4
Click the Edit button to edit a Flash text movie after you insert it into a Web page.

In the Document window, you can resize Flash text by either dragging the resizing handles or entering new values for W (width) and H (height) in the Property inspector. Click the Reset Size button to return to the original dimensions of the movie.

Creating a Flash Button

Dreamweaver comes with a number of templates for creating Flash buttons right in Dreamweaver. (You can download even more templates at the Macromedia Exchange; see Hour 22, "Customizing Dreamweaver.") As with the Flash Text object you just created, you can have Dreamweaver create Flash button movies automatically. Flash buttons use custom fonts and many have animations when the user places his or her mouse over the button. To insert a Flash button into a Web page, follow these steps:

1. Save your Web page. Select the Insert Flash Button object from the Media tab of the Insert bar or select Insert, Media, Insert Flash Button. The Insert Flash Button dialog box appears (see Figure 9.5).

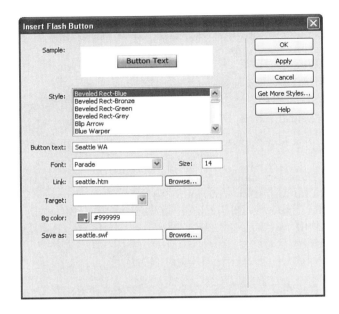

2. Select a button style from the Style list. A preview of the button appears in the Sample window at the top of the dialog box. You can click the preview to see what the down state of the button looks like and to see any animation effects that the button has.

3. Add text for the button in the Button Text field. Only buttons that already have the default "Button Text" text in the Sample window will display this text. You cannot add text to buttons that do not already display text.

4. Set the font and font size for the button text in the Font drop-down menu and Size text box. You can choose any font that's installed on your computer.

5. Enter a URL for a hyperlink and a target, if necessary, in the Link and Target text boxes, respectively. As when you create Flash text, you need to be careful about document-relative addressing. It's best to save the Flash movie in the same directory as the linked Web page.

6. Add a background color from the Bg Color drop-down list. This color appears around the button, not within the button art. Again, be sure to complete this step if you have a background color on your Web page so that there isn't any white surrounding your button.

7. Click OK. The button appears in the Dreamweaver Document window.

You can edit the Flash button as you did the Flash text earlier in this hour. Both button and the text movies are saved as Flash `.swf` files and can be edited in Flash. Some buttons can be used as groups. For instance, a number of e-commerce buttons are available to create purchasing and checkout applications.

Adding a Link to a PDF File

So far in this hour, you've been embedding multimedia content into a Web page. You can also link to content that appears by itself. You link to multimedia files just as you would link to another Web page. If the multimedia file is within your defined Web site, you can use a document-relative URL. If the multimedia file is on another site, you must use an absolute URL.

Adobe Acrobat Reader is a freely distributed player that has become the standard for viewing formatted text files over the Web. PDF (portable digital format) files enable a viewer to see a file exactly as it was meant to be seen—fonts, page layout, and graphics appear predictably. You create PDF files by using an application called Adobe Acrobat Distiller and view them with the Acrobat Reader. An Acrobat Reader plug-in is usually installed when the Reader application is installed.

To display a PDF file, you simply create a hyperlink with the URL to a PDF file. The file will then open within the browser if the Acrobat plug-in is present, as shown in Figure 9.6. If the plug-in isn't installed but the Acrobat Reader is, Acrobat Reader will run as a standalone application and display the PDF file. You can download the Acrobat Reader at `www.adobe.com/products/acrobat/readstep2.html`.

FIGURE 9.6
The PDF viewer,
Acrobat Reader,
loads right in the
browser window,
displaying the PDF
document.

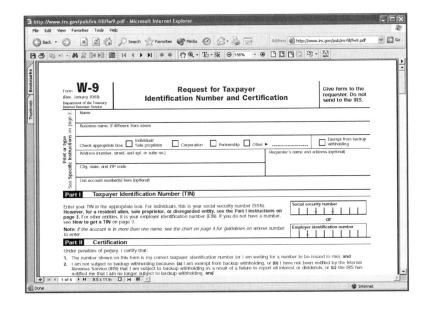

Adding a Sound File to a Web Page

Adding a sound file to a Web page can sometimes add to the experience. And it's a good way for you to get familiar with adding multimedia files. You use the Plugin object from the Media tab of the Insert bar (or Insert, Media, Plugin) to insert a sound into a Web page.

> ### Find Sounds on the Web
>
> Your operating system should have some sound files available for you to use. To find them, search for a directory called *media* or *sounds* or *multimedia*. If you'd prefer to download sounds from the Internet, try www.southparkstudios.com/down/sounds.html to download sounds from the TV show *South Park*. Or, if you prefer the comedy of a more innocent time, try theme songs from classic TV shows at www.tvland.com/theme_songs.

To insert a Plugin object, follow these steps:

1. Position the insertion point in the Dreamweaver Document window where you would like the sound control to appear when the page is viewed in the browser.

2. Select the Plugin object from the Media tab of the Insert bar (or select Insert, Media, Plugin). The Select File dialog box appears. Navigate to a directory that contains a sound file and select a file, as shown in Figure 9.7. Select All Files from the Files of Type drop-down menu. Then click the Select button.

FIGURE 9.7
Select a sound file, in this case an MP3 file, in the Select File dialog.

3. Save your changes, and then preview your Web page in a browser to see what it looks and sounds like.

Notice that the Property inspector for the Plugin object has some properties that are similar to ones you have seen while working with images (see Figure 9.8). Selecting a file fills in the Src box. There is an Align drop-down menu, similar to the one for images, which affects how other objects align with the Plugin object. Other familiar properties are W (width), H (height), V (vertical) Space, and H (horizontal) Space. You can also add a border to the Plugin object. Plg URL and the Parameters button are two additional properties that we will discuss later in this hour.

It's a good idea to give your user control over whether a sound plays. Many plug-ins enable you to include playback controls. A Web page that contains a sound that cannot be turned off can be an extreme annoyance. You'll need to explore the documentation, usually available on the Web site of the company that created the plug-in, to find the parameter names and how to add playback controls.

FIGURE 9.8
Some plug-in prop-
erties are similar to
image properties,
and some are not.
Two additional prop-
erties appear when
you insert a plug-in
in your page: the
Parameters button
and the Plg URL
text box.

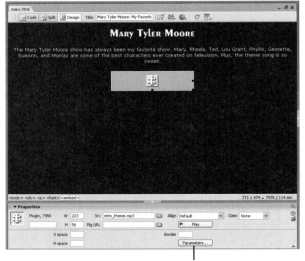

Parameters button

When you're delivering multimedia, much depends on which browser and plug-
ins the user has. Some plug-ins and some sound file formats are more popular
than others. The popularity of file formats is constantly evolving. As of this writ-
ing, the RealMedia and MP3 sound formats are popular and quite common on
the Web. MIDI files are common, too. Table 9.1 lists some of the most popular
sound file formats.

By the
Way

What's Your Default Audio Program?

The last audio application that you installed on your computer probably set itself as
the default application to play audio files. You might have different applications than
are depicted in this hour.

TABLE 9.1   Common Web Sound Formats

Sound Format	Streaming?	Description
RealMedia	Yes	Real-time streaming audio and video format.
Shockwave Audio	Yes	Real-time streaming audio format.
MP3 (MPEG 3)	Yes	Compact file size with excellent sound quali-ty. This open-standard sound format has become very popular.
Liquid Audio	Yes	Small file sizes with excellent sound quality.

TABLE 9.1 Continued

Sound Format	Streaming?	Description
Beatnik	No	Sound format that combines MIDI and digital audio.
AIFF	No	A popular Macintosh sound format. Not ideal for longer sounds because of its large file size.
WAV	No	A popular Windows sound format. Not ideal for longer sounds because of its large file size.
u-Law (.au)	No	Originally, a popular Web sound format from Sun, but not very common today.
QuickTime	Yes	Apple's movie format, which can also play sounds. File sizes can be large.
MIDI	No	An open-standard sound format that uses defined MIDI sounds on the user's computer. Files are very compact.

Resizing a Control

The default size of the Plugin object is 32×32 pixels. That's pretty small, but you can resize a Plugin object by dragging one of the resizing handles. You can also enter a width and a height in the Property inspector with the Plugin object selected. Predicting an appropriate size for a plug-in can get tricky. If you have embedded a sound file into your Web page, some viewers might use Netscape's default LiveAudio Java applet to play the sound. Others might have the QuickTime plug-in registered to play sounds in a Web page. Others might use Windows Media Player.

Increasing the width and height of a plug-in can cause more controls to be visible. In Figure 9.9, for example, giving the plug-in a width of 144 pixels and a height of 25 pixels looks okay with the QuickTime player in Netscape.

The height of 25 pixels in this case is necessary to display the RealMedia Player buttons in Internet Explorer, as shown in Figure 9.10. Depending on what plug-in or ActiveX control your browser has registered to play MP3 files, yours might or might not look the same. This browser shows RealMedia Player embedded in the page and controlling the sound.

QuickTime player

FIGURE 9.9
The QuickTime play-
er with a width of
256 pixels and a
height of 56 pixels
displays all the
audio controls.

RealMedia Player

FIGURE 9.10
Internet Explorer
uses the
RealMedia Player to
play a sound.

So far you have used an *inline*, or *embedded* player, meaning that the player appears within the flow of your Web page. However, if you create a hyperlink to a sound file, when the user selects the link, the user's browser launches the player controller in a separate window. Figure 9.11 shows the QuickTime controller in a separate Netscape window. Figure 9.12 shows Internet Explorer with the Windows Media Player controls in the lower left of the Web page.

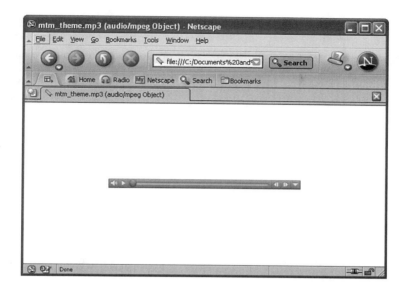

FIGURE 9.11
In Netscape, the QuickTime player opens with the controller taking up the entire window.

FIGURE 9.12
The Windows Media Player launches in a separate part of the Internet Explorer window to play an MP3 file.

Adding Looping to Sound

Dreamweaver offers the flexibility to deal with advanced attributes of objects—even attributes that haven't been created yet—through the Parameters dialog box. Clicking the Parameters button in the Property inspector opens the Parameters dialog box. Parameters consist of two parts: a parameter name and a value.

Different plug-ins have different parameters available. Table 9.2 lists some common sound parameters. Many plug-ins have optional or required parameters that you can set in the Parameters dialog box. The parameters available for sounds, such as loop and autostart, may or may not be available for other formats.

TABLE 9.2   Common Sound Parameters

Parameter	Values
loop	true, false, n (number of times playing)
autostart	true, false
hidden	true, false
volume	0–100
playcount	n (number of times playing—Internet Explorer only)

After you click the Parameters button, click the + button to add a parameter. Then do the following:

▶ To make the sound loop, type **loop** as the parameter name. Tab or click in the Value column and type **true**. The default is false, so if you want the sound to play only once, you do not need to enter the loop parameter.

▶ Add the playcount parameter in addition to loop. The default for playcount is for the sound to play once. Enter a number for the number of times the sound will play.

You can enter multiple parameters in the Parameters dialog box. Figure 9.13 shows the Parameters dialog box with parameters entered. You add the parameter name in the left column and then click or tab to the right column to add the parameter value. After you have finished adding parameters, click the OK button. To edit a parameter, again click the Parameter button in the Property inspector and then click in the parameter you want to change. To delete a parameter, click the – button. Use the arrow keys to rearrange the order of the parameters. Disregard the lightning bolt icons; they are involved in loading dynamic data into parameter fields when you are using server-side scripting.

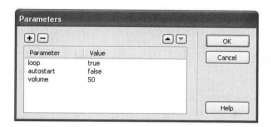

FIGURE 9.13
The Parameters
dialog box can con-
tain many parame-
ters that affect the
functionality of a
plug-in.

Adding a Java Applet to a Web Page

Java is a programming language that is used to create self-contained programs
called *applets*. Java applets run within the browser window just like the other multimedia objects you've been working with in this hour. You can put a Java applet
into your page, add parameters, and add some interesting multimedia to your
Web page.

Java Versus JavaScript

Java and JavaScript are not the same thing. Nor are they really related. **JavaScript**
is a scripting language that is used in Web page development to set the properties
of a Web page. **Java** is a compiled programming language that is used to develop
applications.

Watch Out!

To insert a Java applet into your Web page, you must have all the appropriate
files for the applet. The number and type of files may vary. You need to read the
documentation for the applet that you are using. The example here uses David
Griffith's classic snow applet, available from www.pagesbyjustme.com/downloads.
html. David's snow applet simply requires the Java file that he has written,
snow.class, and a Web image file to present an image that looks like snow is
falling on it.

Be Careful with Java Applets

Some users may have Java turned off in their browser, so you should be careful
about including information that is vital to the Web page in a Java applet.

Watch Out!

Any Java applet that you intend to use in your Web page should come with
instructions on how to set it up. Be sure to read the instructions carefully and
enter all the parameters correctly, or the applet might not work. If you do not set
up the applet correctly, users will simply see an empty gray box on the page.

Dreamweaver will create the HTML code for you, but you need to pay attention to the parameter values that you need to add to the Java Applet object.

To insert an applet into a Web page, follow these steps:

1. Select the Applet object from the Media tab of the Insert bar or select Insert, Media, Applet. This opens the Select File dialog box.

2. In the Select File dialog box, navigate to the directory that contains the Java applet files. Select the appropriate file stipulated in the applet documentation. For the snow applet, for example, you select the file snow.class.

3. Enter all the parameters that are required by the applet documentation by first clicking the Parameters button to open the Parameters dialog box. The snow applet requires only one parameter: the address of the image file on which the snow will appear, as shown in Figure 9.14.

Parameters

FIGURE 9.14
A Java applet requires parameters specific to the applet.

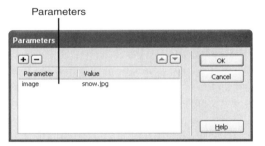

4. Save your Web page and preview it in a Web browser to make sure that it looks the way you want it. The snow applet, viewed in a browser, is shown in Figure 9.15.

HOUR 10

Managing Assets by Using the Assets Panel

What You'll Learn in This Hour:

▶ How to manage assets
▶ How to create favorite assets
▶ How to add assets to a Web site

After you have designed your Web page, you will populate it with page elements. The elements that make up your individual Web pages are likely to come from various sources and will be different types of objects. You might include Flash movies, images created in Fireworks, various colors, links, clip art, and photographs in your Web pages.

You need to gather and organize these page elements before you start to create a Web page. Dreamweaver MX 2004's Assets panel enables you to organize the elements of a Web site to quickly access and reuse items. The Assets panel can help you become more efficient and better organized!

What Are Assets?

Web pages are not just made out of text and code. You use images, movies, colors, and URLs to present information in Web pages. These Web page elements are called **assets**.

The Assets panel organizes these elements, enabling you to quickly find an image or a color that you want to use. You can preview assets in the Assets panel. You can also create a list of favorite assets—ones that you use often.

The Library and Templates panels are part of the Assets panel. These panels are covered in the next two hours.

Managing Assets in the Assets Panel

Dreamweaver automatically catalogs the assets for an entire site. When you open the Assets panel, you can select one of the category buttons from along the left side of the panel to display a list of all the assets of that type in your site. The Assets panel includes the following categories:

- ▶ Images
- ▶ Colors
- ▶ URLs
- ▶ Flash Movies
- ▶ Shockwave Movies
- ▶ Movies
- ▶ Scripts
- ▶ Templates
- ▶ Library

You can browse an asset category to preview the assets until you find the one you want. The Assets panel enables you to quickly add a selected asset to your current page. Later this hour you'll learn how to set some assets as favorites so that you can find them even more quickly.

Assets are specific to the current site that you are working in. Often you'll use certain page elements in multiple Web sites that you are working in. You can copy your assets to another Web site defined in Dreamweaver to use in that Web site.

Listing Assets in a Site

When you open the Assets panel, Dreamweaver goes through the cache and automatically catalogs all the assets within your current site. It places the assets into the correct categories by examining the file extensions of the files in the Web site. The Assets panel lists only the assets that are in the currently selected site. When you change sites, you might have a message box appear briefly while the Assets panel is being updated.

You can view all the assets in a category by selecting a category button along the left side of the Assets panel. Each of the categories except the Library and Templates categories has two radio buttons at the top of the panel, as shown in Figure 10.1, enabling you to select whether you want to see all the assets of that type or just your favorites. You'll learn how to create a favorite asset in a few minutes.

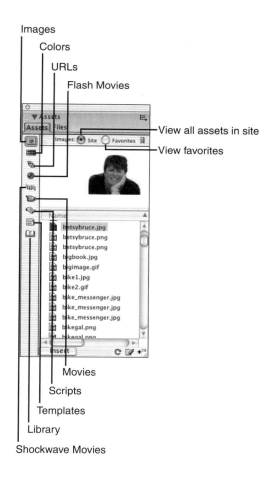

Images
Colors
URLs
Flash Movies

View all assets in site
View favorites

Movies
Scripts
Templates
Library
Shockwave Movies

FIGURE 10.1
The Assets panel has buttons for the different categories along the left side and radio buttons at the top to select whether to view all the assets or just your favorites.

After you add an asset to your site, you might need to click the Refresh button to see it listed in the Assets panel. You can refresh the list of assets anytime.

Previewing Assets

When you select a category in the Assets panel, the first asset in the list of that category is selected in the lower half of the panel, and a preview of that asset appears in the upper half. You can preview assets by selecting them in the list, as shown in Figure 10.2.

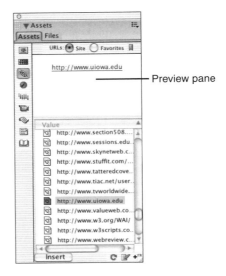

By default, the items listed in the Assets panel are sorted alphabetically. You can sort the items by any of the available column headings by clicking a column heading. For instance, if you want to sort your image assets by file size, you click the column heading File Size.

Sometimes you might want to locate the original asset file in the Site Manager window. In Dreamweaver you can open the Site Manager window with the asset file highlighted: In Windows you right-click on an asset item (in Mac you Control+click) and then select the Locate in Site command from the context menu. This works only on assets that are individual files, such as movies or images, and not on assets that are elements of Web pages, such as URLs or colors.

Exploring Image Assets

The Images category of the Assets panel displays all the images in your defined Web site (refer to Figure 10.1). Dreamweaver catalogs images in GIF, JPG, or PNG format. Dreamweaver displays a preview of the selected image in the top half of the Assets panel.

Instead of dragging and dropping, you can simply select the text and the color and then click the Apply button to apply the color to the text.

Jump Assets Alphabetically

To quickly jump to a section in the assets list, click within the assets list and then type the first letter of the name of the item you are looking for. You will jump to the first item that begins with that letter.

Did you Know?

Creating Favorite Assets

There are often assets in your Web site that you use repeatedly. You can assign these assets to the favorites list so that they are easy to pick out of the Assets panel. The favorites list is displayed when the Favorites radio button is selected at the top of the Assets panel.

To create a favorite asset, select the asset in the Assets panel and then select the Add to Favorites button. When you select the Favorites radio button, the favorite assets that you just added should be listed, as shown in Figure 10.8. You can give a favorite a different name by right-clicking it, selecting the Edit Nickname command, and typing a name that is easy to remember.

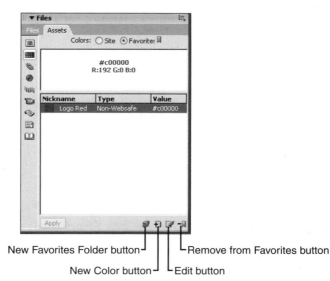

New Favorites Folder button
New Color button
Edit button
Remove from Favorites button

FIGURE 10.8
You can list only your favorite assets in a certain Assets panel category instead of all the assets in the site.

> ### No Templates or Library Favorites
>
> Favorites are not available for the Templates and Library categories of the Assets panel.

You can organize your favorites into groups by creating new folders within the favorites list. The New Favorites Folder button (shown in Figure 10.8) enables you to create a folder within the favorites list. After you create a folder, drag and drop items into the folder. Figure 10.9 shows favorite items organized into folders. Expand the folder to view the contents by selecting the + button next to the folder name. Collapse the folder view by selecting the – button next to the folder name.

FIGURE 10.9
Organize your favorite assets by creating folders in the favorites list.

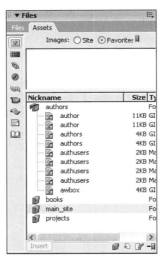

Remove items from the favorites list by selecting the Remove from Favorites button. The item is removed only from the favorites list and is not deleted from the Web site. You can also delete an item from the list by right-clicking the item and selecting the Remove from Favorites command from the context menu.

Creating New Assets in the Assets Panel

You can use the Assets panel to help design your Web site. Dreamweaver enables you to create new assets in certain asset categories. You can add a new color, URL, template, or library item. Hours 23, "Reusing Items in a Web Site by Using the

Library," and 24, "Creating and Applying a Template," describe how to create new library items and templates.

When you begin creating a Web site, you can organize your development effort with the help of the Assets panel. Organize your image assets into favorites so that commonly used images are easy to find. Define commonly used links and colors so that they can be quickly applied to Web pages.

The Assets panel catalogs the assets that already exist in your site. When you are in the favorites list, you can also create new URLs and colors to use in your site. These new assets are then available, even though they haven't yet been used in your Web site.

To create a new color or link asset, follow these steps:

1. Select the Favorites radio button at the top of the Assets panel. Select either the Colors category or the URLs category.

2. Right-click to launch a context menu and select the New Color or New URL command. Either the color picker appears, as shown in Figure 10.10, or the Add URL dialog box appears, as shown in Figure 10.11.

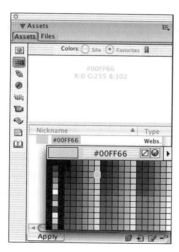

FIGURE 10.10
Use the color picker to create a new color in the favorite colors list of the Assets panel.

3. Pick a color from the color picker or fill in the URL and nickname in the Add URL dialog box.

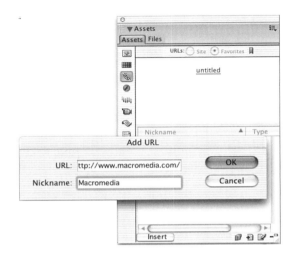

Copying Assets to Another Site

The Assets panel displays the assets of the current site. Sometimes you might want to share assets among different Web sites defined in Dreamweaver. You can copy a single asset, a group of assets, or a favorites group to another site.

To copy a single asset to another site, simply right-click (Control+click on the Mac) the item name and select the Copy to Site command. Select the defined site you want to copy the asset to. Dreamweaver copies the exact folder structure and the file for an image or movie asset.

To copy a group of assets to another defined site, select multiple asset items by holding down Shift while clicking (or Control+clicking on a Mac) on the item names. Right-click (or Control+click on a Mac) the group and select the Copy to Site command from the context menu. All the assets are then copied to the other site. You can also copy a group of favorites to another site by following these steps.

Summary

In this hour, you have learned how to use assets from the Assets panel. You have learned how to sort, add, and organize assets. You have explored the various types of assets and learned how to create favorites. You have also learned how to copy assets from site to site.

Q&A

Q. What is the best way to organize images?

A. Many Web developers divide images into logical directory structures so that they can more easily find the images they want. The Assets panel can help you organize images so that you may not need to use various directories for organization. You might want to use a naming convention so that you can sort your images. For instance, all the images for section 1 of a Web site can begin with the number 1 (1_image1, 1_image2, and so on). After you've sorted the images, you can create favorites and folders to organize the favorites so that you can quickly find the images you need.

Q. I have some URLs that begin with `file:///` listed in the Assets panel. How can I find and fix these?

A. When you notice in the Assets panel that you have links that begin with `file:///`, you know that you have a problem with your site. The way to identify the pages that contain these links is to run the Check Links report from the Site panel. Select each file that appears in the report as having a link that begins with `file:///` and change the URL to a document-relative address.

Workshop

The Workshop contains quiz questions and activities to help reinforce what you've learned in this hour. In case you get stuck, the answers to the quiz appear after the questions.

Quiz

1. Which asset categories list individual files that are referenced (or embedded) in a Web page?

2. How can you organize favorite assets?

3. When you copy assets to another site, Dreamweaver creates exactly the same folder structure in the site that the assets are copied to. True or false?

198

Quiz Answers

1. The Images and Flash Movies, Shockwave Movies, and Movies categories list actual files that are referenced in Web pages.

2. You create and name folders to organize your favorite assets so that they are easier to find and use.

3. True. The assets are stored in exactly the same folder structure.

Exercises

1. Create some favorite assets and then create folders. Organize the favorites in the folders you created.

2. Practice copying image assets to another site. Open the site you copied the files to in the Files panel and confirm that Dreamweaver created a new directory and copied the images to that directory.

PART III

Web Page Layout with Tables and Frames

HOUR 11   Displaying Data by Using Tables   **201**

HOUR 12   Designing Page Layout by Using Tables   **219**

HOUR 13   Understanding and Building Frames and Framesets   **235**

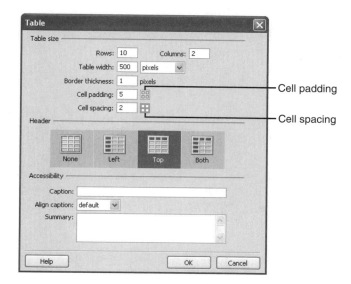

Cell padding

Cell spacing

FIGURE 11.7
Set the Cell
Padding and the
Cell Spacing set-
tings in the Table
dialog box.

Making a Table Accessible to People with Disabilities

Users who are visually impaired and using text-to-speech synthesizer software to read your Web page will have the most trouble reading large tables full of data. These users will greatly appreciate your small effort to design a table that is easier for them to navigate and extract data from. Dreamweaver has made this easy for you by placing the accessibility settings at the bottom of the Table dialog box.

You can add a caption for a table that appears in the browser and is visible to everyone. You can set the alignment for the caption so that it appears either above or below or to the left or right of the table. You should always add a sum-mary for your table, as shown in Figure 11.8. The summary is read only by text-to-speech browsers and helps the user evaluate whether to progress through the table data or skip the information.

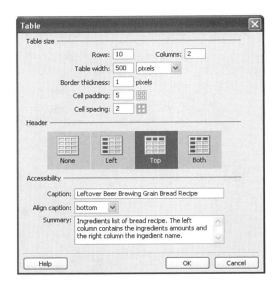

Modifying a Table and Adding Content

When you have your table structure determined, you can start adding text or images to the table. You can also fine-tune the structure as you work in Dreamweaver by using the Property inspector and selecting table cells or entire tables. Later in this hour you'll use some of the built-in table color schemes that are available in Dreamweaver.

Adding and Sorting Data

To enter data, you click in a table cell, type, and then tab to the next cell. You can press Shift+Tab to move backward through the table cells. When you reach the rightmost cell in the bottom row, pressing Tab creates a new row. Add data to your table until you have enough data to make it interesting to sort.

Creating New Table Rows

When you press the Tab key to create a new table row, Dreamweaver gives the new row the attributes of the previous row. This might be what you want. But if you use Tab to create a new row from a header cell row, your row will be more header cells!

Dreamweaver makes it easy to sort the data in your table by using Commands, Sort Table. To sort a table by using the Sort Table command, follow these steps:

the formatting to all the cells results in more HTML code in your Web page. The HTML code applied to the cells, however, takes precedence over the code applied to rows.

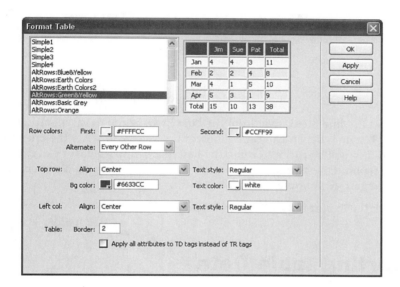

FIGURE 11.13
The Format Table dialog box contains the commands to format all the cells, rows, and columns in a table.

You can use the Format Table command even if you use a custom color scheme for your Web page. Select one of the formats available but enter custom hexadecimal numbers for specific colors into the boxes for the first and second row colors. You can also use a custom text color and add a background color for the header row.

Exporting Data from a Table

You can export table data from an HTML table. You can then import the data into a spreadsheet, a database, or another application that has the capability to process delimited data; that is, data separated by a delimiter. A **delimiter** is the character used between the individual data fields. Commonly used delimiters are tabs, spaces, commas, semicolons, and colons. When you are exporting a data file, you need to pick a delimiter that does not appear in the data.

To export table data from Dreamweaver, follow these steps:

1. Select a table or place your cursor in any cell of a table.

2. Select File, Export, Export Table. The Export Table dialog box appears, as shown in Figure 11.14.

FIGURE 11.14
Open the Export
Table dialog box by
selecting File,
Export. You use
this dialog box to
export delimited
data that can be
imported by other
applications.

3. Select the data delimiter from the Delimiter drop-down menu.

4. Select the line break style from the Line Breaks drop-down menu. The line break style is dependent on the operating system, so select the operating system that will be running when the data file is imported. For example, if you are sending the data file to someone who will be running a spreadsheet on a Macintosh computer, select Macintosh.

5. Click the Export button and save the file.

Importing Table Data

If you already have data in a spreadsheet or database, why retype it or paste it into Dreamweaver? You can import data exported from spreadsheet or database applications into Dreamweaver by using the Import Tabular Data command. Most spreadsheets and database applications can export data into a text file that Dreamweaver can import. You need to know what character is used in the data file as a delimiter before you can successfully import data into Dreamweaver.

Did you Know?

Exported Files from Excel

Microsoft Excel, a commonly used spreadsheet application, imports and exports files with the file extension `.csv` as comma delimited and files with the file extension `.prn` as space delimited.

Did you Know?

Create a Delimited Data File

Create your own data file to work with by opening a text editor, such as Notepad, and entering some data. Create a single line of text with multiple fields separated by tabs. Create multiple records by repeating this process on subsequent lines in the text file. Save your file and import it into Dreamweaver as a tab-delimited data file.

To import table data to Dreamweaver, follow these steps:

1. Place the insertion point in the Document window where you want the table located.

2. Select the Tabular Data object from the Common tab of the Insert bar or select Insert, Table, Tabular Data. The Import Tabular Data dialog box appears, as shown in Figure 11.15.

FIGURE 11.15
The Import Tabular Data dialog box enables you to import data files directly into a Dreamweaver table.

3. Select the Browse icon (which looks like a folder) to browse to the table data file to import it into Dreamweaver.

4. Dreamweaver attempts to automatically select the delimiter, or you can select the field delimiter manually from the Delimiter drop-down menu. If the delimiter isn't one of the four common delimiters listed, select Other from the Delimited drop-down menu and enter the delimiter.

5. In the boxes beside Table Width, select whether the new table should fit to the data or be a certain pixel or percentage value.

6. Enter values in the Cell Padding and Cell Spacing text boxes, if necessary. Remember, you can always change these values by editing the table later.

7. Select from the Format Top Row drop-down menu a value for the format of the first (header) row. You need to know whether the data file has column headings that will appear as header cells in your HTML table.

8. Enter a value for the table border size.

9. Click OK to import the table data.

Summary

In this hour, you have learned how to add a table to a Web page. You have also learned how to add and remove table cells and rows and how to set the column width and row height of a table. You have entered data into a table and then sorted the data by using the Sort Table command. You have learned how to import data into a Dreamweaver table and how to export table data for an external application to use.

▶ **Default**—This is usually the same as left for cell content and center for header cell content.

▶ **Left**—This aligns the cell contents on the left of the cell.

▶ **Center**—This aligns the cell contents in the center of the cell.

▶ **Right**—This aligns the cell contents on the right of the cell.

Adding Color to a Table

There are several places you can add color to a table:

▶ A background color for a table cell or group of cells

▶ A background color for the entire table

▶ A border color for a table cell or group of cells

▶ A border color for the entire table

Figure 12.11 shows where the different color settings are located in the Property inspector. Cell properties always have priority over the same properties in the table. For instance, if you applied blue as the table background color and then applied red to an individual cell, the one cell would be red and all the other cells would be blue. Set the table background and table border in the Property inspector. The Brdr Color setting determines the border color of the entire table.

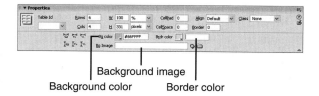

Background image
Background color
Border color

FIGURE 12.11
Adding colors in the Property inspector controls the table border and table background color attributes.

You can add a background image to a table cell or an entire table. Enter the URL for a background image in the box labeled Bg Image in the Property inspector. You can enter a pixel value in the Border text box to see a border; however, you don't usually add borders to a layout table. If you add a border color and don't see the border, you might have the border size set to zero. Set the cell background and cell border colors in the Property inspector with a cell or group of cells selected.

Nesting a Table Within a Table

Placing a table within a table cell creates a **nested** table. The dimensions of the table cell limit the nested table's width and height. To nest a table, place the insertion point inside a table cell and insert a new table (or draw a table when in Layout mode). Drawing a layout table by using the Draw Layout Table tool enables you to draw a table over an existing cell, as shown in Figure 12.12. The nested table will snap to the size of its parent cell.

FIGURE 12.12
A nested table in Layout mode snaps to the size of its parent cell.

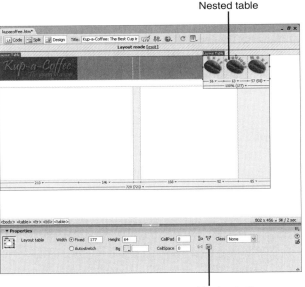

Nested table

Remove Nesting button

Don't Use Too Many Nested Tables

It's fine to nest tables within tables within tables. But if you nest too much, the browser may display the tables slowly. If the browser software has to labor to render your table, it might be better to format the information in a different way.

Using a Tracing Image to Transfer a Design to a Web Page

A tracing image is useful when you are creating a page design and you have an image showing all the completed page elements. You can use this image as a **tracing image**. Instead of estimating where the elements go onscreen, you can display a tracing image and lay the individual image and text elements over the tracing image perfectly. A tracing image makes it easy to align objects.

Load a tracing image into Dreamweaver in the Page Properties dialog box. The tracing image is visible only in Dreamweaver and is never visible in the browser. A tracing image covers any background color or background image. The background color or background image will still be visible in the browser.

Using a tracing image is very helpful when you are implementing a complicated design that has been created by a graphic artist. Usually page elements, such as buttons, titles, and logos, are sliced up in an image-editing program. The graphic artist (or you!) can export an image of the complete design (called *flattened* in graphic terms because all the visible image layers are merged into a single layer) to use in Dreamweaver as a tracing image.

To load a tracing image into Dreamweaver, follow these steps:

1. Open the Page Properties dialog box (by selecting Modify, Page Properties) and select the Tracing Image category. Click the Browse button beside the Tracing Image box to select the image that is a complete visual representation of your Web page.

2. Browse to the tracing image file. It needs to be a GIF, JPEG, or PNG.

3. Drag the Transparency slider to set how opaque (solid) or transparent the tracing image will be, as shown in Figure 12.13.

4. Click OK. Your tracing image appears in the background of the Document window, with the transparency setting you specified.

Tracing image

FIGURE 12.13
You can load a tracing image into the Page Properties dialog box. Set the transparency with the slider.

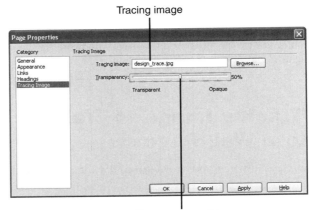

Transparency slider

5. Draw the design that you see in the tracing image, as shown in Figure 12.14. You also need to look in the Assets panel to see how the images in the design have been sliced up.

FIGURE 12.14
With a tracing image loaded, you can trace a design onto a Web page.

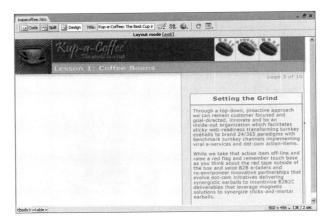

Did you Know?

View the Entire Tracing Image

If you use a tracing image with 0-pixel margins for the page, you will lose the 10 pixels at the top of the screen when you are in Layout mode. The Layout mode banner across the top blocks some of the tracing image. You can turn off the 10 pixels of the Layout mode banner by selecting View, Visual Aids, Hide All.

Turning a Table into a Group of Layers

During Hour 14, "Using Dynamic HTML and Layers," you will use layers to position objects on a Web page. **Layers** allow absolute placement of objects on the page. Whereas tables are also relative to the content on the page, layers can position content at any position on the page. Using layers is another effective way to position content on the screen, and Dreamweaver can convert a table into a group of layers.

To convert a table into a group of layers, follow these steps:

1. Select the table and make sure you're in Standard mode. The Convert Tables to Layers command is unavailable while you are in Layout mode.

2. Select Modify, Convert, Convert Tables to Layers. (Did you notice that there's also a command to convert layers to a table?) The Convert Tables to Layers dialog box appears, as shown in Figure 12.15.

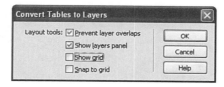

FIGURE 12.15
The Convert Tables to Layers dialog box creates a layer for every table cell.

3. Accept the defaults and click OK. (You'll explore the properties controlled by the check boxes in the Convert Tables to Layers dialog box in the next hour.)

The Layers panel, shown in Figure 12.16, lists all the layers that Dreamweaver created from the table.

FIGURE 12.16
The Layers panel
lists the layers that
were created from
a table.

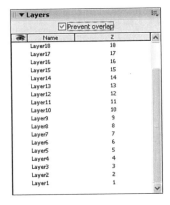

Summary

In this hour, you have learned how to use Layout mode to draw cells and tables
to create a page layout. You have used the column and row spanning properties
to merge and split individual cells and groups of cells. You have also learned
how to align the contents of cells both vertically and horizontally. You have
learned how to apply colors to an entire table, table cells, and table borders, and
you have learned how to convert a table into a group of layers.

Q&A

Q. *Why shouldn't I center objects in a table cell by using the text alignment buttons?*

A. You can use the text alignment buttons to center an object. Doing so will add an additional tag around the selected object and then apply the Center property. Everything in the table cell may not be centered when you do this, however. Only the objects within the added tags will be centered. If you later add an object to the cell, it might or might not be centered, depending on exactly where the insertion point was when you inserted the new object. Using the alignment properties of a cell is the way to make certain all objects in the cell will have the alignment you want.

Q. *Every time I position a table cell, everything in the table moves! How can I prevent this from happening?*

A. You can't prevent it from happening, but you can make it easier by first positioning images and text in the upper-left corner and then working to the right and down. The cells are relative to the upper-left corner of the table, so you need to solidify the positioning in that area first.

Q. *I like fine-positioning table cells by using the arrow keys, but it takes a long time to move the cells across the screen. Any way to make it go faster?*

A. Hold down the Shift key while using the arrow keys to position table cells 10 pixels per keypress instead of a single pixel per keypress.

Workshop

The Workshop contains quiz questions and activities to help reinforce what you've learned in this hour. In case you get stuck, the answers to the quiz appear after the questions.

Quiz

1. If you apply a background color to an entire table and you apply a background color to a cell, which color shows up in the cell?

2. What's the easiest way to add a row at the bottom of a table?

3. How do you horizontally align all the objects in a cell in the center?

Quiz Answers

1. The cell attributes take precedence over the table attributes, so the color you applied to the cell will show up.

2. Put the insertion point in the last cell (the one in the lower right) and press the Tab key. Or, with the table selected, add to the number of rows in the Property inspector. It's your choice.

3. Put the insertion point in the cell and select Center from the Horz drop-down menu in the Property inspector.

Exercises

1. Surf the Web, looking for Web page layouts that use tables. You might be surprised at how many Web sites use tables heavily. If you are not sure whether a site uses tables, select the View Source command in your browser and look for table tags in the code.

2. Insert a table and experiment with merging and splitting cells. Insert a new, nested table into one of the cells.

3. Find a Web page design that you like and take a screen capture of it (by pressing PrtScrn in Windows or Shift+Command+3 on the Mac—or use Mac OS X's Grab utility). Save this screen capture in a Web image format (GIF, JPEG, or PNG) and load it in Dreamweaver as a tracing image. Lay the page out by using layout tables and table cells.

Understanding and Building Frames and Framesets

What You'll Learn in This Hour:

▶ The difference between frames and framesets

▶ How to target content to load in a specific frame

▶ How to set frame attributes such as scrolling and borders

▶ How to use behaviors to load content into more than one frame at a time

Love 'em or hate 'em, many people seem to have strong opinions about frames. Creating a Web page with frames enables you to contain multiple Web pages in a single browser window. The user can select a link in one frame that loads content into another existing frame, enabling the user to stay in the same browser window.

Using frames can be an excellent way to present information on your Web site, but frames can also be a navigational nightmare for your users. Take care to make sure that your frames are carefully created so that the user can navigate to links that you provide in your site without being perpetually caught in your frames.

Certain types of Web sites are excellent candidates for a frame structure. A good example is a site with a table of contents constantly available so that the user can make multiple selections. Why make the user continually navigate back to a table of contents page? You can load the table of contents page into a frame and load the requested content into another frame so that both are present onscreen.

There may also be navigational issues that you can address with frames. If one part of the page never changes—for instance, the main navigational buttons at the top of the screen—then why continually reload them? You can put the navigational elements in a frame at the top of the page and allow the user to load new parts of your Web site into the bottom frame of the page.

There are several disadvantages to using frames. Because frames enable you to load Web pages without changing the Web page address in the browser, there is no way to bookmark the current state of the Web page. Your users may browse to a Web page within your frames and bookmark it, but when they return, they will return to the original Web page loaded into the frame instead of to the one they thought they bookmarked. Another disadvantage is that search engines may not properly index a Web site that uses frames, making it difficult for users to find content within the site by using a search engine. Visually impaired users visiting a Web site by using a text-to-speech browser may not be able to access framed content.

In spite of the disadvantages, there still may be valid reasons for creating Web pages that use frames. When it's necessary to view multiple Web pages at the same time, using a framed Web page is the only solution. It also may be advantageous to present one frame that remains visible while the user is scrolling content in another frame.

Creating a Frameset

Frames consist of individual Web pages—one for each frame—held together by a Web page that contains the frameset. The **frameset** defines the size and position of the individual frames. You can either load an existing Web page into a frame or create a new Web page. The frameset is like the "glue" that holds all the frames together. The frameset Web page isn't visible to the user; the user sees only the content held in the frames defined by the frameset.

Figure 13.1 shows an example of Dreamweaver's Top and Nested Left style of frameset. There is one Web page called `banner.html` that is displayed across the top of the framed page. The lower part of the page, below the banner, is split into two frames: the table of contents page on the left, made up of links, and the main display area on the right. The links in the left table of contents frame load content into the main display area. The banner and the table of contents remain constant, while different Web pages are loaded into the main display area.

Link loads in
frame to the right   Frames

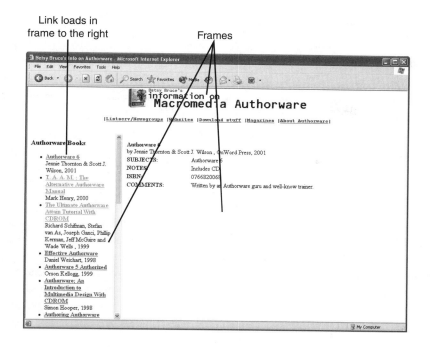

FIGURE 13.1
This Web page contains three frames: one at the top, one in the lower left that contains the table of contents, and one in the lower right that displays different Web pages when the links in the table of contents are selected.

When you are creating real projects, you'll probably use the prebuilt framesets that come with Dreamweaver. There are a variety of configurations available; you access them by clicking the icons in the Frames menu of the Layout category in the Insert bar (or by selecting Insert, HTML, Frames). This hour you'll begin by creating a set of frames in a frameset by hand. This will familiarize you with how frames work, how they are named, and how they are saved.

When you are working with frames, using the Save command becomes more complicated than it usually is. Are you saving the Web page in a frame, or are you saving the frameset? While you are working with frames, Dreamweaver activates the Save Frameset and the Save Frameset As commands in the File menu. You can also use the Save All command to save all the frame content and the frameset, too. There is also an additional Open command, the Open in Frame command, which appears in the File menu when you are working with frames. You can open an existing Web page in a frame by using this command.

There are three methods of creating frames:

- ▶ View the frame borders (by selecting View, Visual Aids, Frame Borders) and then drag the borders to divide the page into frames.
- ▶ Use the commands under the Frameset submenu in Dreamweaver's Modify menu. You might need to use these menu commands when the frame configuration you want to create is not possible by dragging borders.
- ▶ Use the prebuilt frame configurations that are available in the Frames menu of the Layout category in the Insert bar.

Viewing Frame Borders

You need to view the frame borders before you can drag them to create frames. Select View, Visual Aids, Frame Borders. You see a set of borders surrounding the page. These borders are visual aids within Dreamweaver and don't represent how the finished page will look in the browser. While you are working with your Web pages, you can move these borders to resize your design. When you are ready to turn them off, simply select View, Visual Aids, Frame Borders again to toggle the setting off.

Splitting a Page into Frames

To create frames, drag the frame borders. Create two frames, top and bottom, in an empty Web page by dragging the top frame border down, as shown in Figure 13.2. You now have three Web pages: the page in the top frame, the page in the bottom frame, and the Web page with the frameset. When viewers enter the URL of the frameset page, the browser automatically loads the individual pages that belong in each frame.

Get Rid of a Frame

If you change your mind about a frame, just drag the border off the edge of the page, and it will be deleted.

Frame borders

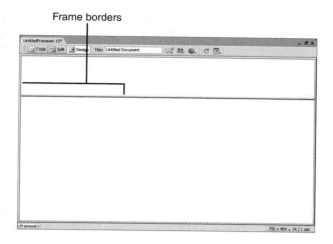

FIGURE 13.2
When you view the frame borders, you can simply drag one of the borders to create frames and a frameset.

Naming Frames

Naming and keeping track of frames can be confusing. Type the word **banner** into the top frame's Web page. With the cursor in the top frame, save the Web page as banner.htm after selecting File, Save Frame. When you are first working with frames, it's least confusing to save each frame individually. Repeat this procedure with the bottom frame: Type the word **main** in the frame and save it as main.htm. Your frames will look as shown in Figure 13.3.

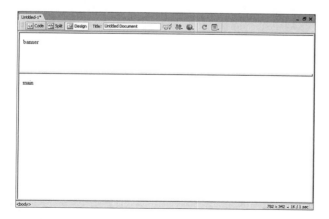

FIGURE 13.3
This Web page is divided into two frames named banner.htm and main.htm.

When the Frame Borders command is not checked under the Visual Aids submenu of the View menu, the Web page appears as it will in the browser. Later in this hour, you will change the actual border sizes and other attributes of frames. It will be helpful to turn off the frame borders to approximate how the frames will look in the browser. Turn off the frame borders in the Visual Aids submenu of the View menu to see what your Web page looks like without them and then turn the borders on again.

Now you will divide the bottom frame into two frames. If you drag the left frame border, you will end up with four frames—two on the top and two on the bottom. Instead, split the bottom frame into two frames by using the commands in the Frameset submenu under the Modify menu. To do this, follow these steps:

1. With the cursor in the bottom frame, select Modify, Frameset, Split Frame Right, as shown in Figure 13.4. This places the existing frame on the right and adds a new frame on the left. Or, you can drag the left frame border while holding down the Ctrl key (the Command key on the Mac).

FIGURE 13.4
The Frameset submenu in the Modify menu lists a number of commands you use to split frames into multiple frames.

2. Type **table of contents** into the Web page within the new frame.

3. Save the Web page contained in the new table of contents frame. Remember to place your cursor in the frame and then select File, Save Frame. You can name this Web page toc.htm.

You have created three frames and saved the Web pages that they contain. It's sometimes difficult to select the frameset. The easiest way is to place your cursor over one of the frame borders and click. You can tell you have the frameset selected when you see the frameset tag in the tag selector. Save the frameset Web page by selecting File, Save Frameset. You can name the frameset index.htm. The URL of the frameset is the only address the viewer will need to view all the Web pages.

While you have the frameset selected, give the Web page a title in the toolbar. Only the title of the frameset, never any of the individual framed Web page titles, appears in the title bar of the browser. Because the titles of the individual frames do not appear in the browser's title bar, it isn't necessary to give a frame a title. However, it's always good practice to give Web pages titles, and if you ever reference the Web page outside the frames, you will be assured that each page already has a title.

If you haven't already saved the Web pages in the frames and the frameset Web page, Dreamweaver will prompt you to save before you preview in the browser. The first time you save, it's less confusing to individually save the Web pages contained in each frame and the frameset Web page than to save all the files at once when Dreamweaver prompts you. Dreamweaver will prompt you to save the files every time you preview the frames.

Using the Frames Panel

The Frames panel (which you open by selecting Window, Frames), shown in Figure 13.5, enables you to select individual frames and set frame attributes. Notice that the Frames panel visually represents the configuration of the frames in a Web page. Select a frame by clicking the frame's representation in the Frames panel. You can also select a frame by holding down Alt while clicking (Shift+clicking on the Macintosh) inside the frame in the Document window.

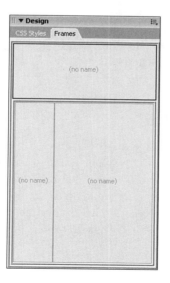

FIGURE 13.5
You select frames in the Frames panel. This panel visually represents the frame configuration in the current Web page.

When you click the representation of a frame in the Frames panel, the properties for that frame are available in the Property inspector, as shown in Figure 13.6. The Property inspector is where you set up the frame's scrolling and border attributes. You'll explore those in a few minutes. This is also where you give each frame a unique name.

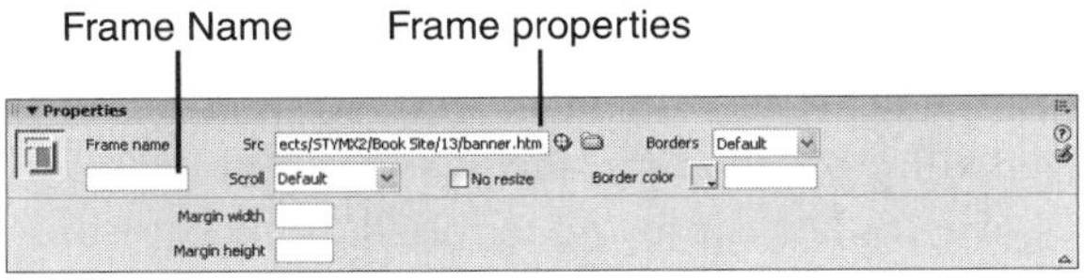

FIGURE 13.6
The Property inspector presents frame attributes, such as Frame Name, when an individual frame is selected.

Frame Name   Frame properties

It's important that each frame have a name. This is not the filename that you gave each frame a few minutes ago; this is an actual name for a frame. The frame name is used to target the frame, making a Web page load into the frame when a link is clicked in another frame. Click on each frame in the Frames panel and type a name in the Frame Name box in the Property inspector. You can name the top frame banner, the left frame toc (for table of contents), and the right frame main.

Name Your Frames Correctly

Frame names should not contain punctuation, such as periods, hyphens, or spaces. You can, however, use underscores in frame names. Also, you should not use the reserved names top, parent, self, and blank.

Nesting Frames

You can nest one frameset inside another frameset to have **nested frames**. Actually, that is what you just did! When you split the bottom frame into two frames, Dreamweaver created a frameset defining the bottom two frames. The original frameset now consists of a frame on top of the nested frameset. You nest framesets by nesting one frameset tag within another, within a single frameset Web page. If you'd like to see the code, select the frameset (by clicking the frame borders) and then look at the code in Code view.

To turn off the frame borders, make sure the frameset is selected and then select No from the Borders drop-down menu. You will need to turn the border off in all the framesets in the page. If the borders in the individual frames are set to Yes, they will override the frameset settings, and borders will be visible. To turn off a border, all the adjacent frames must have borders turned off, too. If you do not want borders to appear, you should also make sure there is not a border color assigned.

Setting the Frame Size

You can simply drag the frame borders in Dreamweaver to resize a frame. If you want finer control over the size of a frame, you can set frame sizes in the Property inspector while the frameset is selected, as shown in Figure 13.11. You can select the rows or columns in the frameset by clicking the small representation in the Property inspector. Often, the first frame has an **absolute** value (either pixel or percentage), whereas the second frame is defined as relative. When a frame is defined as **relative**, it takes up the remaining space either horizontally or vertically.

Selected frame

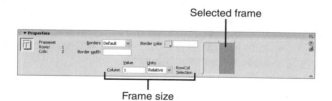

Frame size

FIGURE 13.11
A frame size value can be set to relative so that the frame takes up the remaining space in the browser window.

Creating an Alternative to Frames

All modern browsers support frames, and the large majority of users have modern browsers. One reason some people do not like frames has to do with usability issues. Some people with disabilities, such as the visually impaired, may use software that does not easily interpret content in frames. To respect viewers who cannot view frames, you should use the NoFrames Content command.

Select Modify, Frameset, Edit NoFrames Content. Note that a gray bar that says NoFrames Content appears across the top of the Document window, as shown in Figure 13.12. You can simply type in a disclaimer or, better yet, you can provide a non-frames version of the Web page. Turn off the NoFrames Content command by deselecting it in the Frameset submenu of the Modify menu.

NoFrames Content bar

FIGURE 13.12
NoFrames Content
appears to viewers
who have older or
text-based
browsers.

NoFrames tag

By the Way

No Way to Preview NoFrames Content

I don't know of any way to preview NoFrames Content in a browser other than by
installing an old version of a browser on your computer. You will probably have to
trust the WYSIWYG Dreamweaver display to be a true representation of what the
Web page will look like to those with very old browsers. When you preview the Web
page with a modern browser, you will see the frame content.

Dreamweaver automatically prompts you to add the title attribute for the frame
tag if you have enabled frames accessibility prompting in the Dreamweaver
Preferences dialog box. To turn on this feature, open the Preferences dialog box
(by selecting Edit, Preferences), select the Accessibility category, and select the
Frames check box. You can also turn on automatic prompting for the accessibility
attributes of form objects, media, and images. When you turn on the frames'
accessibility prompting, Dreamweaver asks you to give each frame a title that will
be read by text-to-speech browsers.

Using Frames Objects

The quickest way to create frames in Dreamweaver is to use the prebuilt frames
objects that are available in the Frames menu in the Layout category of the Insert
bar. The Insert bar has several common frame configurations that can quickly
get you going with a set of frames. If you are not quite sure what each of the
configurations looks like, look at the Framesets category in the New Document

dialog box, shown in Figure 13.13. This lists the same prebuilt frames objects as the Insert bar. There is a preview of the frames object's structure on the right side of the dialog box.

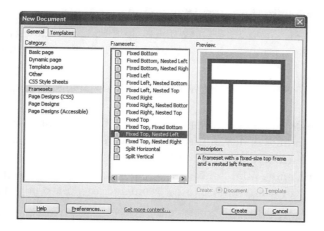

FIGURE 13.13
The Framesets category in the New Document dialog box enables you to preview what the frames will look like.

If one of these prebuilt configurations fits the way you want your frames to look, you'll have a head start by using the frames objects. You can fine-tune the frame settings by using the same methods you've used so far in this hour.

With a new Web page open, add a frames object by either clicking an icon from the Frames menu in the Layout category of the Insert bar or selecting Insert, HTML, Frames. The framesets in these frames templates all have the borders turned off. The individual frames are already named, but you need to select and save each file as you did earlier in this hour. Be careful not to preview the Web page before you save, or you will get caught in a series of confusing prompts to save Web pages when you have no idea which page you are saving!

Targeting Linked Pages to Open in a Specific Frame

One of the most exciting features of frames is their capability to load content in one frame after a user clicks a link in another frame. The frameset is the parent, and the frames or framesets it contains are its children. Understanding these concepts helps you understand **targeting**. You can load a Web page into a frame or window by targeting it. You add the target attribute to a hyperlink to send the linked content into a specific window or frame.

There are four reserved target names:

- ► **_top**—This opens a linked Web page in the entire browser window.

- ► **_self**—This opens a linked Web page in the same window or frame that contains the link. This is the default setting.

- ► **_parent**—This opens a linked Web page in the parent frameset. If the parent frameset is not nested, the linked page will fill the entire browser window.

- ► **_blank**—This opens a linked Web page in a new browser window.

The Target drop-down menu in the Property inspector lists all the reserved target names, plus the names of any of the frames you created that are currently open in the Document window, as shown in Figure 13.14. Creating a hyperlink and selecting a frame name from the Target drop-down menu will cause the linked page to load in that window. If no target is entered, the linked page will load in the frame that contains the link.

List of available frames to target

FIGURE 13.14
The Target drop-down menu lists the reserved target names, plus all the names of the frames in the current Web page.

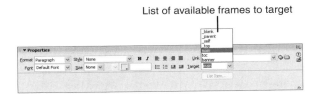

Use the original group of frames that you created at the beginning of this hour to target a hyperlink, as follows:

1. Create a hyperlink in the frame named toc. Add a link to an existing Web page or to an external URL.

2. Select main from the Target drop-down menu. This loads the hyperlink into the selected frame.

3. Use the Save All command (by selecting File, Save All).

4. Preview the frames in the browser. Click the link, and the Web page should load in the other frame.

PART IV

Dynamic HTML: Layers, Cascading Style Sheets, Behaviors, and Timelines

HOUR 14   Using Dynamic HTML and Layers   **257**

HOUR 15   Formatting Web Pages by Using Cascading Style Sheets   **271**

HOUR 16   Inserting Scripted Functionality by Using Behaviors   **289**

HOUR 17   Adding Advanced Behaviors: The Drag Layer Behavior   **309**

Use the Layer Fix Only If Necessary

Don't insert the Netscape layer fix unless it is absolutely necessary. The fix causes the page to reload and might be distracting to Netscape 4 users. Test your page by opening it in a small Netscape 4 window and then maximize the window. Do your layers stay small? If so, you need to apply the Netscape layer fix.

**Watch
Out!**

You'll notice the resizing handles on each border of your layer. You can drag these handles to make a layer bigger or smaller. You can also set the width and height of the layer in the Property inspector. The W and H properties in the Property inspector are the width and height of the layer. The default measurement unit is pixels.

It's a good idea to always name your layers. When you start adding behaviors, names will help you identify specific layers. You can specify a name in the Layer ID box in the Property inspector, as shown in Figure 14.3.

Layer name

FIGURE 14.3
Change the layer name in the Layer ID box of the Property inspector. It's important to give layers meaningful names.

No Punctuation in Layer Names

Don't use spaces or punctuation in layer names. If you later apply a behavior to the layer, sometimes JavaScript isn't happy with spaces or punctuation in a layer name. If you want to name your layer with multiple words, you can use capitalization or underscores to make the name readable. For instance, `CestLaVieBakery` and `Green_Grocer` are possible layer names.

**Did you
Know?**

You can also name Dreamweaver layers in the Layers panel. Double-click the name in the Layers panel Name column until it becomes editable and then type in a new name, as shown in Figure 14.4. Notice that when you select a layer in the Layers panel, the layer is selected in the Document window also.

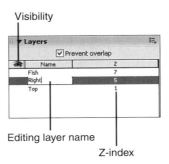

Visibility

Editing layer name

Z-index

Setting Layer Positioning

A layer has a drag handle in the upper-left corner. You can reposition a layer by picking it up and moving it with this handle. To select multiple layers, hold down the Shift key while clicking layers to add them to the selection. You can also use the arrow keys on your keyboard to move a selected layer.

Get in the habit of moving layers by picking up the drag handle. It's very easy to accidentally move items contained in a layer instead of moving the layer itself. If you become accustomed to using the handle, you won't make that mistake. If you can't use the layer drag handle because the layer is at the very top of the Document window, select it in the Layers panel and use the arrow keys to move the layer. Or enter positioning values in the Property inspector.

Use the Layers panel to select one or many layers. The Layers panel enables you not only to select layers, but also to see and set some layer characteristics. You'll learn about the two characteristics that you can set—the z-index and the visibility—in a few minutes. Notice that you can select a check box at the top of the Layers panel to prevent layers from overlapping. If you notice that you cannot place your layers on top of one another, this check box is probably selected.

The main reason you would want to prevent overlaps is if you were going to eventually convert the layers into a table; a table cannot have overlapping elements. In Hour 12, you learned how to export a layout table as layers by using the Tables to Layers command (by selecting Modify, Convert, Convert Tables to Layers). You can also use the Layers to Table command (by selecting Modify, Convert, Convert Layers to Table) to turn the layers in your page into a layout table.

You can use the drag handle to drag a layer anywhere on the screen, or you can use the Property inspector to set the exact positioning of a layer. The L and T properties stand for the left, the offset from the left edge of the page, and top, the offset from the top edge of the page. These positions are relative to the entire browser window. You can move a layer either by dragging it (with its selection handle) or by positioning it exactly by entering values in the L and T boxes, as shown in Figure 14.5.

Width

Left

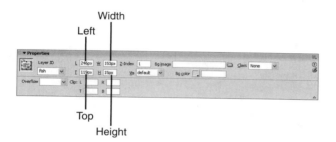

Top

Height

FIGURE 14.5
Position a layer exactly by entering values in the L (left) and T (top) boxes of the Property inspector.

Where Did the Layer Properties Go?

If you don't see layer properties in the Property inspector, it's because you don't have a layer selected. You might have accidentally selected the contents of the layer instead of selecting the layer itself.

Did you Know?

Adding a Background Color and Background Image

A layer can have a background color, as shown in Figure 14.6. You can use the color picker or type in a color in the standard HTML hexadecimal format, preceded by a #. Make sure you leave the Bg Color option blank if you want your layer to be transparent. If your page background is white and you make your layer background white, it will seem as if it's transparent until you position it over something else!

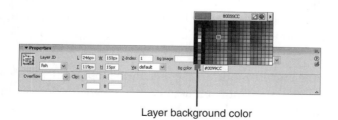

Layer background color

FIGURE 14.6
A layer can have a background color just as a table cell can. Enter a background color in the Property inspector.

You can also place a background image in a layer. The image will repeat multiple times (called *tiling*) within the layer if the layer is larger than the image. Any objects or text that you put within the layer will be on top of the background image. Select the Browse icon (the folder) beside the Bg Image box in the Property inspector and navigate to the background image file. Figure 14.7 shows the Property inspector when a layer that contains a background image is selected.

FIGURE 14.7
A background image will tile within a layer if the image is smaller than the layer.

Image tiled in layer

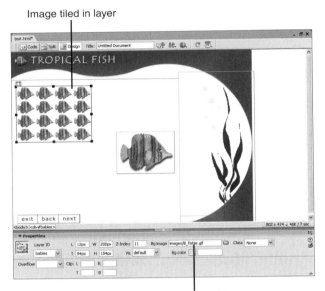

Layer background image

Exploring Layer Stacking Order

Not only can you position layers in exact places on the page, you can also allow layers to overlap one another. So, which layer is on top? The stacking order decides which layer is on top of other layers. The **z-index** value, in turn, determines the stacking order. The z-index can be either a negative or a positive number.

The layer with the highest z-index is the one on the top. The term *z-index* comes from the coordinate system that you used back in geometry class—remember x and y coordinates? Well, the z-index is the third coordinate that is necessary to describe three-dimensional space. Imagine an arrow coming out of the paper or screen toward you and another going back into the screen or paper. That is the z-index.

Q&A

Q. *The `<div>` tag is described as implementing CSS layers. I thought that CSS had to do with text. Am I right?*

A. The CSS standard does define many attributes for manipulating text. But it also defines *box elements*, which are what layers are. This might make more sense to you after you have completed the next hour, which is all about CSS. In that hour, you'll learn about the different attributes of layers that you will be able to set up in a style and how powerful that capability is.

Q. *Why would I want to use layers in my Web pages?*

A. You may decide not to use layers and may end up using other methods—tables, for instance—to position content on your Web pages. But if you'd like to have some content overlapping or sitting on top of other content, you'll need to use layers and set the layer z-index to a value higher than the underlying content's z-index. Alternatively, if you'd like to hide an image or text on the screen and then show it later by using the Show-Hide Layers behavior (see Hour 16), you'll of course need to use layers. In Hour 18, "Creating a Form and Using It to Collect Data," you'll learn how to animate layers to move around a Web page.

Workshop

The Workshop contains quiz questions and activities to help reinforce what you've learned in this hour. In case you get stuck, the answers to the quiz appear after the questions.

Quiz

1. How do you select multiple layers on a Web page?

2. What is the most common cross-browser tag used to implement layers?

3. The layer with the lowest z-index is the one on the top. True or false?

Quiz Answers

1. Hold down the Shift key while clicking the edges of the layers on the screen or when clicking their names in the Layers panel.

2. The `<div>` tag is the most logical choice. It is meant to logically divide sections of the page, and it works in most version 4.0 and higher browsers.

3. False. The layer with the highest z-index is the one on top.

Exercises

1. Create a Web page that has multiple layers. Experiment with inserting images and text into the layers. Change the background color of one of the layers. Be sure to make a few of the layers overlap so that you can see how the z-index works.

2. Create a banner and a navigation bar for a site by placing a layer across the top of the site for the banner. Place individual layers with the text Home, Previous, and Next in them. You can make these hyperlinks if you like. Now convert these layers into a table.

Exploring Style Settings

The CSS Style Definition dialog box has eight categories with numerous settings you can use to define a style. As you are defining a style, select the panels to gain access to the settings for each category. Any settings that you do not need to set should be left alone. The following categories are available:

▶ **Type**—This category defines type attributes, such as font and font size. These style settings can be applied to text or to objects that contain text.

▶ **Background**—This category defines background attributes, such as color and image. These style settings can be applied to objects, such as layers and tables, where you can set a background.

▶ **Block**—This category defines type attributes for paragraphs.

▶ **Box**—This category defines attributes, such as margin size, that are applied to box objects, such as layers and tables.

▶ **Border**—This category defines attributes that are applied to objects that have borders, such as layers and tables.

▶ **List**—This category defines list attributes, such as bullet type.

▶ **Positioning**—This category defines layer attributes, such as visibility and z-index.

▶ **Extensions**—This category defines miscellaneous attributes that are either future enhancements or for Internet Explorer only.

Table 15.1 lists the style settings available in the various categories of the CSS Style Definition dialog box.

TABLE 15.1   Style Settings in the CSS Style Definition Dialog Box

Setting	Description
Type Category	
Font	Sets the font family.
Size	Sets the font size and unit of measurement.
Style	Specifies the font as normal, italic, or oblique.
Line Height	Sets the height of the line of text and the unit of measurement. This setting is traditionally called *leading*. It is added before the line.

TABLE 15.1   Continued

Setting	Description
Type Category	
Decoration	Adds an underline, an overline, or a line through the text. You can set the text decoration to blink, or remove the decoration by choosing None.
Weight	Adds an amount of boldface to text. Regular bold is equal to 700.
Variant	Sets the small caps variant on text.
Case	Capitalizes the first letter of each word or sets all the text to lowercase or uppercase.
Color	Sets the text color.
Background Category	
Background Color	Sets a background color for an object.
Background Image	Sets a background image for an object.
Repeat	Controls how the background image is repeated. No Repeat displays the image only once, Repeat tiles the image horizontally and vertically, Repeat-x tiles the image only horizontally, and Repeat-y tiles the image only vertically.
Attachment	Sets whether the background image scrolls with the content or is fixed in its original position.
Horizontal Position	Specifies the initial horizontal position of the background image.
Vertical Position	Specifies the initial vertical position of the background image.
Block Category	
Word Spacing	Adds space around words. Negative values reduce the space between words.
Letter Spacing	Adds space between letters. Negative values reduce the space between letters.
Vertical Alignment	Sets the alignment of the object relative to objects around it (for example, the Alignment settings discussed in Hour 6, "Displaying Images on a Page").
Text Align	Aligns text within an object. Choices are left, right, center, and justify.
Text Indent	Sets how far the first line is indented. Negative values set outdent.
Whitespace	Sets how whitespace will appear in an object. Normal collapses whitespace, Pre displays all the whitespace, and Nowrap sets the text to wrap only when a tag is encountered.

Positioning a Layer by Using a Style

So far this hour, you've applied styles to text. When dealing with layers, it's useful to position objects on the page by using styles. If you need to position layers in a consistent place on the screen, it's an excellent idea to define a style for those layers. The other advantage to using styles is that if you'd like to move all the layers at once, you can simply edit the style definition.

To define a positioning style for a layer, follow these steps:

1. Create and name a new class, as you did earlier in this hour.

2. Select the Positioning category in the CSS Style Definition dialog box. Notice that the properties in this category are properties that you used in the last hour, when you created layers.

3. Select Absolute in the Type drop-down list at the top of the dialog box. Set the Left, Top, Width, and Height drop-down lists as shown in Figure 15.8.

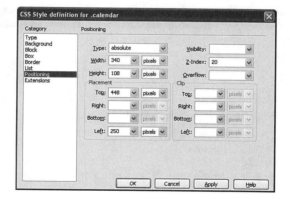

FIGURE 15.8
To create a positioning style, set the Left, Top, Width, and Height properties in the Positioning category of the CSS Style Definition dialog box.

4. Click the OK button to save your style.

Create a layer in your Web page. When you draw or insert a layer in your Web page, its positioning and other attributes are defined using an inline style, so layers already have CSS styles defined within them. First, you'll apply the new positioning style, and then you'll need to remove the existing inline style because it overrides the other style. Give this layer the name events.

You'll use a new method to apply this style to the layer. Select the layer and then right-click on <div#events> in the tag selector. Select the Set Class command in the tag selector menu, as shown in Figure 15.9, and select the new style you just created from the list. Next, delete the L (left), T (top), W (width), and H (height) layer properties, and the layer should hop to the position you defined in the style.

FIGURE 15.9
The Set Class com-
mand in the tag
selector menu
enables you to set
the style of a layer.

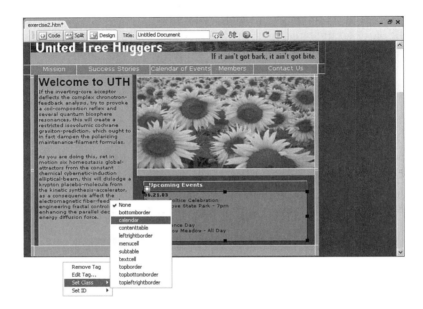

Moving a Layer Overrides a Style

Did you Know?

If you accidentally move the layer, you will override the style's top, left, width, and height attributes. To return the layer to its style-defined position, select the layer and remove the values in the Top, Left, Width, and Height boxes in the Property inspector. The layer should return to the location and size defined in the style. Also, you can always use the Undo command by selecting Edit, Undo.

Style Can Create Layers

Did you Know?

Instead of creating a layer first, you can simply apply a style you just created to a block of text in your Web page. The style will create a layer container around the text and position it according to the style settings.

Creating Advanced CSS Styles

The third type of style is advanced styles. This type of style can redefine a group of HTML tags instead of just one. For instance, you could use an advanced style to define what a specific heading tag looks like only within a table cell by entering the table cell tag, td, and then the paragraph tag, p. To do this, you enter all the tag names in the Selector box, as shown in Figure 15.10, and then define the style. The tags need to be in the correct hierarchical order, so if you create a style with a <p> tag nested within a <td> tag, <td> must come before <p> in the style selector.

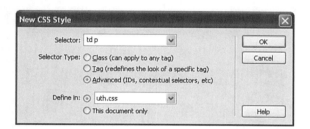

FIGURE 15.10
You can define attributes for a sequence of tags by using advanced styles in the New CSS Style dialog box.

Link Selector Styles

If you drop down the Selector menu instead of typing tags into the box, you will see a list of the selectors. These are the same CSS styles that you modified in the Page Properties dialog box in Hour 2 when you changed the link attributes.

Did you Know?

Creating an External Style Sheet

Adding styles to a single Web page is nice, but wouldn't it be great to apply the same styles to a number of Web pages? External style sheets allow you to do this. Instead of defining styles in the head of a Web page, you define all the styles in one text file. External style sheets end with the .css filename extension. When you update a style in an external style sheet, the changes apply to every page that is linked to that style sheet.

To create an external style sheet, follow these steps:

1. Create a new style and then select the top radio button in the Define In section of the New CSS Style dialog box. Select (New Style Sheet File) from the drop-down menu beside the radio button, as shown in Figure 15.11. Click the OK button.

2. The Save Style Sheet File As dialog box opens. Browse to the directory where you want to save your external style sheet. Enter a filename, as shown in Figure 15.12, and make sure it has the .css file extension. Click OK.

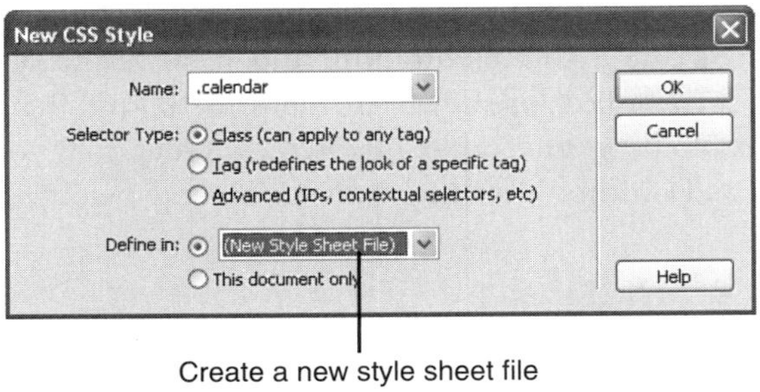

FIGURE 15.11
Select (New Style Sheet File) to define a new external style sheet.

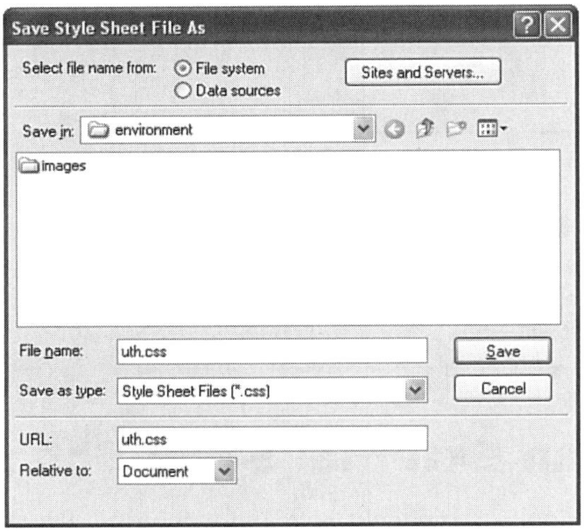

Create a new style sheet file

FIGURE 15.12
Create an external style sheet by browsing to the correct folder and saving a file with the filename extension .css.

3. The CSS Style Definition dialog box opens. Notice that the title bar says that you are defining this style in the external style sheet that you just created. Create and save your style as you did earlier this hour.

When you create an external style sheet, Dreamweaver creates a new file and places the style definitions in it. Dreamweaver also references the external style sheet in the head of your Web page. To add additional styles to the external style sheet, select the name of the external style sheet from the Define In drop-down menu when you are defining a new style, as shown in Figure 15.13.

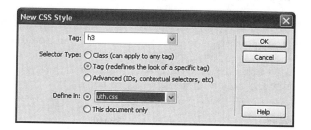

FIGURE 15.13
Select an external style sheet from the Define In drop-down menu to create a new style in the external style sheet.

Editing Styles

After you create styles, you may need to edit them. You can edit styles that are both internal to a Web page and contained in an external style sheet. Styles are listed as in the current document (the <head> section of the document) or in the external style sheet, as shown in Figure 15.14. Select any of the styles in the CSS Styles panel and click the Edit Style button to open the CSS Style Definition dialog box. Edit the style and save your changes.

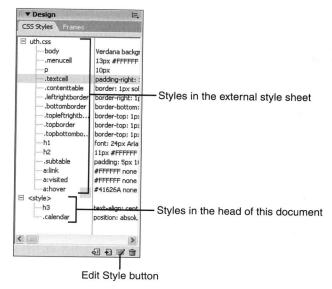

FIGURE 15.14
You can easily edit CSS styles by using the Edit Style button in the CSS Styles panel.

Did you Know?

Export Internal Styles

If you already created some styles in a Web page and then decide to use an external style sheet, select File, Export, Export CSS Styles to export the styles defined in the Web page into an external .css file. Link to the .css file using the Attach to Style Sheet button at the bottom of the CSS Styles panel.

Summary

In this hour, you have learned how to create and apply the three types of CSS styles: classes, redefined HTML tags, and advanced styles. You have also made an external style sheet that allows the same styles to be used throughout an entire Web site.

Q&A

Q. *Can I link more than one style sheet to a Web page?*

A. Yes. You can link as many different style sheets to a Web page as you'd like.

Q. *How can I remove the underline from hyperlinks by using CSS styles?*

A. Some people may advise against doing that, but if you feel your design demands it, it's your call. To remove the underline from hyperlinks, redefine the <a> (anchor) tag in the CSS Style Definition dialog box. Set Decoration (in the Text category) to None. All the hyperlinks on the page will no longer be underlined. You might want to define a:hover (select it from the Selector drop-down menu in the New CSS Style dialog box) with an underline so that the user can easily find the links when he or she places the cursor over them.

Q. *I know it's important to separate presentation from content, so how can I load a unique style sheet, depending on the browser that the user is using, so that I can optimize the user's experience of my Web page?*

A. In Hour 22, "Customizing Dreamweaver," you'll learn about extensions to Dreamweaver, files that you can download and install into Dreamweaver to extend its capabilities. There are a couple of extensions on the Dreamweaver Exchange, Macromedia's repository for extensions (www.macromedia.com/exchange), that add code to your page that loads different style sheets, depending on the user's browser and version. You can download one of these extensions, install it into Dreamweaver, and then use the extension to accomplish your goal of using different style sheets, depending on the user's browser.

Workshop

The Workshop contains quiz questions and activities to help reinforce what you've learned in this hour. In case you get stuck, the answers to the quiz appear after the questions.

Quiz

1. What are the three different types of CSS styles?

2. What should you create in order to use the same styles for all the Web pages in a Web site?

3. If you redefine the h3 tag as red in an external style sheet and then redefine the h3 tag as blue in the Web page, what color will h3 text be in that page?

Quiz Answers

1. The three types of CSS styles are classes, redefined HTML tags, and advanced styles (CSS selectors).

2. You need to create an external style sheet and link it to each page in your Web site.

3. The text will be blue because the internal style, the one defined in the page, is closer to the actual code and is dominant.

Exercises

1. Create a page as well as a class style that modifies text. Try applying this style to text in the page, table cells, layers, and other objects in the page.

2. Create different definitions for the four hover styles: `a:active`, `a:hover`, `a:link`, and `a:visited`. You can find these selectors under the Selectors drop-down menu when Advanced is selected in the New CSS Style dialog box. Create a unique style of each style. Write down the four colors you use and then figure out when each appears when you preview a link on the page with the style definitions in the browser.

HOUR 16

Inserting Scripted Functionality by Using Behaviors

What You'll Learn in This Hour:

▶ What a Dreamweaver behavior is
▶ How to apply a behavior to an object in a Web page
▶ How to use behaviors to add interactivity to a Web page
▶ How to select events to trigger behaviors

Dreamweaver behaviors add interactivity to Web pages. Interactivity usually requires coding in JavaScript, but Dreamweaver adds all the JavaScript for you, so you don't have to understand scripting to use behaviors. Behaviors enable you to make something happen when the user clicks the mouse, loads a Web page, or moves the cursor. You used your first behavior, the Go to URL behavior, in Hour 13, "Understanding and Building Frames and Framesets."

Because some JavaScript doesn't work with older browsers, Dreamweaver enables you to choose browser versions. When you target 4.0 or higher versions of Internet Explorer or Netscape, you have access to many more behaviors than if you target 3.0 browsers. Dreamweaver also enables you to select Netscape and Internet Explorer because these browsers sometimes capture different event triggers. Dreamweaver behaviors are written to work in the major browsers.

What Is a Dreamweaver Behavior?

When you add a behavior to a Web page, Dreamweaver inserts JavaScript functions and function calls, enabling users to interact with the Web page or make something happen. I like to think of a **function** as a little code machine—you send it some information, it processes it, and it sends you a result or makes something happen. A **function call** is the code added to an object that triggers the function and sends it any information it needs to do its job. For instance, a popular Dreamweaver behavior is the Swap Image behavior that you used in Hour 6, "Displaying Images on a Page." When you insert this behavior, Dreamweaver writes a function, called MM_swapImage(), in the head of the HTML document. The code in that function doesn't get called until some event on the page triggers it; the MM_swapImage() function is usually triggered by the onMouseOver event—the event fired when the cursor is placed over whatever object the function is attached to.

A **behavior** is an action that is triggered by an event, or you could look at it this way:

  event + action = behavior

Actions are the type of JavaScript code that Dreamweaver inserts into a Web page. **Events** are triggers that are captured by the browser. Table 16.1 lists examples of common browser events. Different browsers may capture different events. Also, different objects capture different events. This is just a small sampling of the events that are available, but luckily, most of the events are named so that the functionality is fairly obvious. The onDblClick event, for instance, is similar to the onClick event, except that the user clicks twice instead of once.

TABLE 16.1 Common Browser Events

Event	Description
onMouseOver	Triggered when the user places the cursor over an object. This event is often captured from images or hyperlinks.
onMouseDown	Triggered when the user presses the mouse button. This event is often captured from images or hyperlinks.
onMouseUp	Triggered when the user releases the mouse button. This event is often captured from images or hyperlinks.
onClick	Triggered when the user presses and releases, or clicks, the mouse button. This event is often captured from images or hyperlinks.

The Behaviors panel is not the same as the Server Behaviors panel. The Server Behaviors panel works with sites that use server-side scripting, such as ASP, ASP.NET, JSP, PHP, and ColdFusion. The Behaviors panel uses JavaScript, which is client-side scripting (and does not rely on a server).

You can attach multiple behaviors to an object. One event can trigger several actions. In Figure 16.3, you can see that the onClick event triggers a number of actions. The actions happen in the order in which they are listed. You can change the order in which the actions occur by moving the actions with the up and down arrow buttons on the Behaviors panel.

Events   Actions

FIGURE 16.3
One event—for example, the onClick event shown here—can trigger multiple actions, and you can have multiple behaviors attached to a single object in a Web page.

The biggest difference between the various browsers is the events that they support. When you use behaviors, you need to be aware of which browsers you are going to support. If it's crucial that you support every browser available—on a government Web site, for instance—then you will be very limited in the events available to you.

Dreamweaver enables you to set the browser events that it presents in the Behaviors panel. The Show Events For drop-down menu, shown in Figure 16.4, enables you to target specific browsers and browser versions. Depending on the selection in this menu, different events will be available. You access the Show Events For drop-down menu by clicking the + button in the Behaviors panel.

FIGURE 16.4
The Show Events For submenu enables you to choose browsers and browser versions. Only the actions and events that work with the browser and version you choose will be available.

Which Events Setting Is Best?

Did you Know?

You will have access to the largest number of events by choosing IE 6.0 and the fewest number of events choosing 3.0 and Later Browsers. The IE 4.0 and Netscape 4.0 events offer a good compromise between a useful number of events and compatibility with almost all browsers, so you'll generally want to choose the 4.0 and Later Browsers setting.

What Happens When the Event Isn't Supported?

Watch Out!

If you select an event that does not work in a certain browser, users using that browser will either have nothing happen or will receive a JavaScript error.

Showing and Hiding Layers

Now you're ready to add your first behavior. The Show-Hide Layers behavior has a name that pretty much says it all: You can use it to show or hide a layer on the Web page. You don't usually apply a behavior to the object that it affects, so you'll need to have another object on the page that triggers the behavior. For instance, Dreamweaver won't allow you to attach the Show-Hide Layers behavior

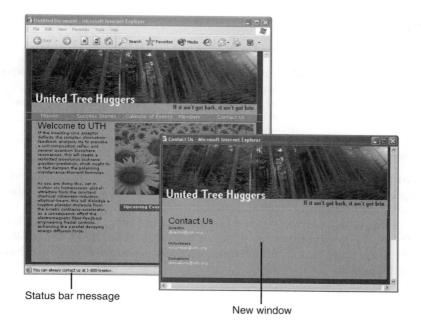

Status bar message

New window

FIGURE 16.14
All the behaviors execute after you click the image. The message pops up, the new window appears, and the text displays in the status bar.

Summary

In this hour, you have learned that a Dreamweaver behavior consists of an event that triggers an action. You have used the Show-Hide Layers behavior, the Open Browser Window behavior, the Popup Message behavior, and the Set Text in Status Bar behavior. You have captured events from a hyperlink and an image. And you have used the onMouseUp and onClick events as triggers for Dreamweaver actions.

Q&A

Q. *How can I apply a behavior to a layer that is hidden?*

A. You can select a hidden layer in the Layers panel. Switch to the Behaviors panel, without selecting anything else, and apply the behavior. Or you can temporarily make the layer visible, apply the behavior, and then hide the layer again.

Q. *How can I create a button that triggers a behavior?*

A. We'll cover forms and buttons in Hour 18, "Creating a Form and Using It to Collect Data." Basically, you place a button into the Web page to trigger a behavior. You insert a button from the Forms tab of the Insert bar. If Dreamweaver asks you if you'd like to add a form tag, you can click Yes. The trick is to make sure the button is not a submit or reset button. Select the None radio button in the Property inspector and then apply a behavior to the button.

Workshop

The Workshop contains quiz questions and activities to help reinforce what you've learned in this hour. In case you get stuck, the answers to the quiz appear after the questions.

Quiz

1. What is the equation that connects an event, an action, and a behavior?

2. You have the most behaviors and events available when you choose 3.0 and Later Browsers from the Show Events For submenu in the Behaviors panel. True or false?

3. What two events add up to an onClick event?

Quiz Answers

1. The equation that connects an event, an action, and a behavior is

    event + action = behavior.

2. False. Most Dreamweaver behaviors use DHTML, which requires 4.0 or later browsers. Selecting 4.0 and Later Browsers will enable you to use far more events and behaviors than will selecting 3.0 and Later Browsers. You will have the most events available when you select IE 6.0 as the target browser.

3. An onClick event consists of the onMouseDown and onMouseUp events.

Exercises

1. Create a second hyperlink for the Show-Hide Layers example that you did earlier in the hour. Type **Hide the Layer**, make it a hyperlink, and make clicking this hyperlink hide the layer you created.

2. Try using some behaviors that are similar to the behaviors you have used in this hour (for example, the Set Text in Layer behavior and the Go to URL behavior). What events are available for these behaviors? What objects do you need to have on the Web page for these behaviors to work?

HOUR 17

Adding Advanced Behaviors: The Drag Layer Behavior

What You'll Learn in This Hour:

▶ How to create a draggable layer
▶ How to create a target layer
▶ How to use the onLoad event

In this hour, you will apply a more advanced Dreamweaver behavior: the Drag Layer behavior. The Drag Layer behavior enables you to create layers that the user can drag around the browser window. You can even constrain the area within which the layer can be dragged. This capability is useful for creating sliders, puzzles, dialog boxes, and other interactions.

You can use the Drag Layer behavior to let users interact with objects on your Web page. For instance, you might have a layer that contains a map legend. You could make that layer draggable so that the user could move it out of the way if it happened to be blocking part of the map. Or you could create a blank face and let people drag different noses, ears, eyes, and so on, onto the face.

Check Out CourseBuilder!

Did you Know?

If you need to create complicated drag-and-drop interactions, you should investigate the CourseBuilder extension to Dreamweaver, which is available at the Macromedia Exchange (see Hour 22, "Customizing Dreamweaver," for information about extensions to Dreamweaver). The drag-and-drop interactions created by CourseBuilder have the capability to make an object return to its original position if dropped incorrectly.

Using the Tag Selector to Select the Body Tag

During this hour, you'll use a more complicated Dreamweaver behavior than you've used in previous hours. To get started, set up a Web page to use the Drag Layer behavior by first creating four layers that will be dragged. Then create a layer that will be the target. These layers can have anything in them, including text, images, and even other layers. Give each of these layers a meaningful name. The layers should look something like Figure 17.1. If you don't have any images handy, simply give the layers various background colors.

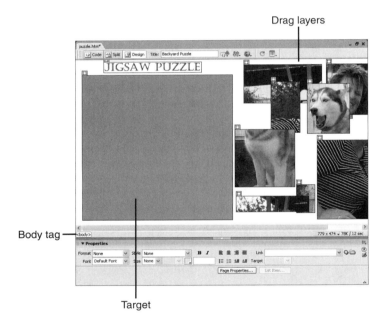

Drag layers

FIGURE 17.1
The user will drag layers onto the target layer to complete an interaction.

Body tag

Target

The Drag Layer behavior enables a layer to be dragged. You need to turn on this behavior before the layer can be dragged. This behavior can be triggered when the Web page loads by capturing the <body> tag's onLoad event. You select the <body> tag in Dreamweaver's tag selector. You should see <body> in the title of the Tag panel group.

The Body Tag Holds Everything Visible

You might notice that when you select the body tag, everything in your Web page is selected. That's because the body tag is the container within which all the objects on your Web page reside.

By the Way

Constraining the Movement of a Layer

After you've created your drag and target layers and given them all names, you're ready to apply the Drag Layer behavior. To use the Drag Layer behavior, follow these steps:

1. Select the <body> tag from the tag selector in the Dreamweaver status bar.

2. Click the + button in the Behaviors panel and select Drag Layer. The Drag Layer dialog box appears, as shown in Figure 17.2.

Basic tab   Advanced tab

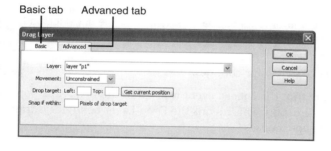

FIGURE 17.2
The Drag Layer dialog box has a Basic tab and an Advanced tab.

3. Select from the Layer drop-down menu the name of a layer to be dragged.

4. Optionally, select Constrained from the Movement drop-down menu. Four boxes appear for you to enter the pixel values for coordinates of an area. To constrain movement to only vertical, enter values for Up and Down but enter 0 for Right and Left. To constrain movement to only horizontal, enter values for Left and Right but enter 0 for Up and Down. To define a rectangular area, enter values in all the boxes. Values are all relative to the original position of the layer. The Drag Layer dialog box should look as shown in Figure 17.3. This layer is constrained to move 20 pixels up, 300 pixels down, 400 pixels to the left, and 20 pixels to the right from its original position.

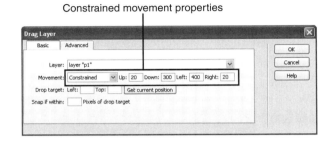

Constrained movement properties

FIGURE 17.3
When you select Constrained from the Movement drop-down menu, four new boxes appear. Enter pixel values to define the constrained movement area.

Did you Know?

Working with L and T Layer Attributes

An easy way to figure out which values to enter in the Movement boxes is to calculate them ahead of time. You can use Dreamweaver and a little math to decide on the numbers before you start to apply the Drag Layer behavior. Write down the original L (left) and T (top) values for the layer. Move the layer to the edges of the constraining area and write down those L and T values. Figure out the difference and enter those values into the Movement boxes when you set up the Drag Layer behavior. To return your layer to its original position, enter the original L and T values into the Property inspector.

5. Click OK to save your changes.

6. Make sure that the onLoad event is listed in the Behaviors panel next to the Drag Layer action. This means the Drag Layer behavior is triggered when the Web page loads.

Check to see that the Drag Layer behavior is working the way you want it to by previewing the Web page in a browser. The correct layer should be draggable, and other layers shouldn't be draggable yet. The drag area should be constrained the way you want it. You will go back and edit the behavior in a few minutes.

Capturing the Drop Target Location

You could calculate or guess at the exact target location, which might work some of the time. But the easiest way to capture the perfect target location is to take advantage of the Drag Layer behavior's built-in Get Current Position button. This button will capture the position of the layer and fill in the coordinates for you. To capture the drop target location, first make sure the Prevent Layer Overlaps check box in the Layers panel is not selected. Then follow these steps:

PART V

Collecting User Data by Using Forms

HOUR 18   Creating a Form and Using It to Collect Data   **323**

HOUR 19   Sending and Reacting to Form Data   **345**

You can add some text that appears in the text field when the user views the form. This could be instructions on what to enter into the field or a default value that the user could change if he or she wanted to. Enter text into the Init Val box in the Property inspector, as shown in Figure 18.10, so that text will be present when the user initially loads the form.

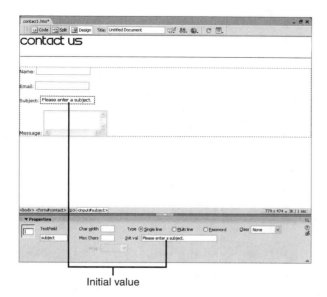

Initial value

FIGURE 18.10
Enter text into the Init Val box in the Property inspector so that it appears when the user initially loads the form.

Dreamweaver includes some form elements, along with other items, in the Snippets panel. You drag snippets from the panel and drop them on your Web pages. A useful snippet for your form might be Text Field Autoclear; this snippet places a text field containing default text into a form. When the user clicks the text field, the default text automatically disappears. You'll explore snippets further in Hour 22, "Customizing Dreamweaver."

Adding Radio Buttons and Check Boxes to Forms

Radio buttons are another type of form element that you can use to collect user input. Radio buttons are grouped so that the user can select only one button of the group at a time; when the user selects a different member of the group, the previously selected button is deselected. In order for radio buttons to be grouped, they all must have the same name.

To create a group of radio buttons, follow these steps:

1. Place the insertion point within a form where the radio buttons will be located.

2. Select the Radio Group object from the Forms category of the Insert bar or select Insert, Form, Radio Group.

3. Enter the name of the radio button group into the Name box of the Radio Group dialog box.

4. Enter a label name in the Label column and enter the value of the radio button when it is checked (called the *checked value*) in the Value column, as shown in Figure 18.11. The label is simply text that appears next to the button; it is not part of the form. Use the + and – buttons to add or remove radio buttons. At the bottom of the dialog box, select whether you'd like the buttons to be placed in a table or separated by line breaks. Click OK to save your settings.

FIGURE 18.11
Add a radio button group. Each button has a label and a value.

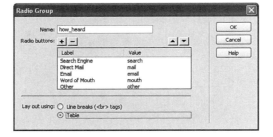

5. When you select an individual radio button, its properties are displayed in the Property inspector. Choose whether the button will be checked or unchecked when the user first loads the form by selecting either the Checked or Unchecked options, which are located beside Initial State.

Check boxes collect user input when the user either checks or unchecks them. They differ from radio buttons because they are not grouped; instead, they act independently. Radio buttons enable the user to select a single option, whereas check boxes enable the user to select any options that apply.

To add a check box to your form, follow these steps:

1. Place the insertion point within a form where the check box will be located.

2. Select the Checkbox object from the Insert bar or select the Insert, Form, Check Box.

3. Enter a name for the check box into the box in the far left of the Property inspector.

4. Enter a checked value into the Checked Value box. If you do not specify a checked value, the value "on" is sent for the check box when the form is submitted. If there is an entry for the Checked Value setting, that value will be sent instead of simply "on."

5. Choose whether the initial state of the check box will be checked or unchecked in the Initial State setting.

6. Type a text label beside the check box. The settings should look as shown in Figure 18.12.

FIGURE 18.12
The check box settings are similar to the radio button settings. Check boxes cannot be grouped like radio buttons.

Adding Lists and Menus to Forms

Some form objects work better than others in certain situations (for example, selecting 1 of the 50 states for a U.S. address). If you allowed the user to enter a state in a text field, you might get some users entering the full name, like Washington, other users entering the correct postal abbreviation, like WA, and other users entering anything in between. Allowing the user to select from a drop-down menu helps you collect consistent data. In Dreamweaver, you add drop-down menus by using the List/Menu object.

The List/Menu object inserts a list of values. You create the List/Menu object as either a list, displaying a set number of lines, or a menu, a drop-down menu displaying all the list values. Figure 18.13 shows a list and a menu in a form displayed in a browser.

To create a list, follow these steps:

1. Place the insertion point within the form where the list will be located.

2. Select the List/Menu object from the Insert bar or select Insert, Form, List/Menu.

3. Enter the name of the list into the box in the far left of the Property inspector.

FIGURE 18.13
Lists display a certain number of values. A menu drops down when the user clicks it, allowing the user to select a value.

Menu   List

4. After you select the List radio button, the Height and Allow Multiple attributes become active.

5. In the Height box, type the number of list items that you want to be visible at one time (see Figure 18.14). If there are more list items than can be shown, scrollbars will automatically appear.

Height option

FIGURE 18.14
You set a list's height in the Property inspector. You can also allow the user to select multiple values in the list by checking the Allow Multiple check box.

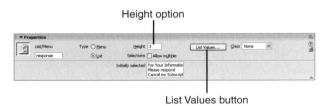

List Values button

6. Check the Allow Multiple check box if you want to allow the user to select multiple values in the list. You might want to add instructions that tell the user that he or she can select multiple entries by using the Ctrl key (or the Command key on the Macintosh) and clicking multiple selections.

7. Set up the list values by selecting the List Values button. The List Values dialog box appears, as shown in Figure 18.15.

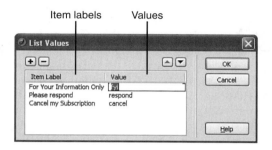

FIGURE 18.15
Select the + button in the List Values dialog box to add an item to the list.

8. Enter an item label and a value for each item in the list. The item label is what the user will see and select. The value is what will be sent back to a script on the server for processing. They can be the same, if appropriate. To add an item, click the + sign, enter the item label, tab to the Value field, and enter a value. You can tab forward and use Shift+Tab to go back if you want. Use the – button to delete entries, and use the arrow buttons to rearrange entries. When you are at the end of the list, pressing Tab creates a new item label and value pair.

9. Click OK in the List Values dialog box.

10. Select an item from the Initially Selected box if one of the items should be selected by default. Otherwise, the first item will appear.

11. Add a label beside the list.

Make the First List Item a Blank Value

Some people like to create a blank name and value pair as the first item in a list or menu. This keeps the first choice from being a default choice.

Did you Know?

Whereas a list can show a number of lines, a menu shows only one line until the user drops down the menu by clicking. Menus use less space than lists because a menu can drop down over other objects on the page when clicked, but it shrinks to only one line when it is inactive. You create a menu exactly the same way you create a list, except that you don't set the height and you cannot allow the user to select multiple entries. You can turn a list into a drop-down menu by selecting the Menu option as the type.

Controlling the Width of a List or Drop-Down Menu

There isn't an attribute to control the width of a list or a menu. However, to your advantage, the list or menu will expand to the width of the widest object. To make the list wider than the widest object, you need to add nonbreaking spaces to one of the list items to make it wider. Unfortunately, you cannot do this in the List Values dialog box. You need to add it directly to the HTML for the page.

Select the list or menu object and then open the HTML Source inspector. Because you have the list or menu selected, the HTML code for that object will be automatically selected in the HTML Source inspector. Place your cursor after one of the labels and insert some nonbreaking spaces. You can insert a nonbreaking space by using the keyboard shortcut Ctrl+Shift+spacebar (Option+Space on the Macintosh). The code for a nonbreaking space is . The HTML code will look like this:

```
<select name="select">
    <option value="1">1        </option>
    <option value="2">2</option>
    <option value="3">3</option>
    <option value="4">4</option>
    <option value="5">5</option>
    <option value="6">6</option>
</select>
```

For a quick and easy way to add standard menus, such as menus for years, numbers, or months, use the Snippets panel. The Forms section of the Snippets panel contains prebuilt menus and form elements that you can simply drag and drop onto your Web page.

Adding Push Buttons and Image Buttons to Forms

There are four different types of buttons that you can add to forms:

► **Submit**—This type of button sends the data the user has entered into a form to a script or an application on the server. The submit button triggers the action that you've set in the form's Action box in the Property inspector.

► **Reset**—This type of button erases all the data the user has entered in the form. It also reloads any initial values.

► **None**—This type of generic button has no automatic function. You can add functionality to a generic button by applying a behavior to it.

► **Image**—This type of button acts like a submit button. All the data in the form is submitted, and the coordinates of where the user clicked are sent, too.

The first three buttons are push buttons that you create by inserting Dreamweaver's Button object. They differ in the way they are configured in the Property inspector. The fourth button, the image button, is inserted using the Image Field object.

Adding Submit and Reset Buttons to Forms

In this section you'll add submit and reset buttons to your form. Usually, the submit button is on the left and the reset button is to the right of the submit button. To add a button to the form, follow these steps:

1. Position the insertion point and then select the Button object from the Insert bar or selecting Insert, Form, Button.

2. Select Submit Form as the action for this button.

3. Add another button to the right of the submit button.

4. Select Reset Form as the action for this button. The buttons should look like the buttons in Figure 18.16.

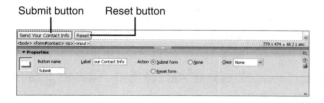

FIGURE 18.16
The submit button is usually placed on the left of the reset button. You need one submit button per form if you are sending this form to a script or to an application on a server.

You can accept the default names that Dreamweaver gives the submit and reset buttons or you can give them new names. You can change the label of either button; a button does not need to say Submit to function as a submit button. Each form must have a submit button to send the form data. The reset button is optional. You should have only one submit button per form with multiple text fields.

Adding Image Button to Forms

You can replace a submit button with an image button. When the user clicks the image, the form contents are submitted, and the coordinates of the location where the user clicked the image button are sent, too. You could capture and process the coordinate information if you wanted to.

To add an image field to a form, first make sure the insertion point is inside the form. Add an image field by selecting the Image Field object from the Insert bar or selecting Insert, Form, Image Field. The Select Image Source dialog box appears, enabling you to navigate and select a standard Web image file. The Property inspector displays the name, width, height, source, alt text, and alignment attributes for the field. You set these attributes as you would for any image.

Adding Generic Buttons to Forms

Add a generic button by selecting the Button object from the Insert bar or selecting Insert, Form, Button. Name the button, give it a label, and select None as the action. Now you can apply to this button a behavior that can be triggered by a button click.

Did you Know?

Deleting a Form

Sometimes it is difficult to delete a form from the page. The easiest way to delete a form is to right-click (or Command+click on the Mac) the form delimiter to view the context menu. Then choose the Remove Tag <form> command. If the Remove Tag command does not say <form>, you have the wrong object selected. You could, of course, always select the <form> tag in the tag selector to delete the form.

Creating a Jump Menu to Navigate to Different URLs

A **jump menu** is a list of links that allows the viewer to jump to other Web sites or different Web pages within the current site. Dreamweaver's Jump Menu object makes it easy to set up this type of jump menu. You can create a jump menu of email links, images, or any objects that can be displayed in a browser. The Jump Menu object uses JavaScript to redirect the browser.

Dreamweaver's Jump Menu object inserts a drop-down menu similar to the one you created a few minutes ago along with the JavaScript code contained in the Jump Menu behavior. You set up the list values in a special dialog box. The item labels appear in the drop-down menu, and the values contain the URLs to the Web pages where the user will jump. If you need to edit the jump menu after you have created it in the special dialog box, you will need to brush up on the form skills you've learned in this hour and the behavior skills you've learned in previous hours.

Quiz Answers

1. All the radio buttons in a group must have the same name.

2. After you insert a button into a form, select None as the action. You can then attach Dreamweaver behaviors to the button if you like.

3. A list displays a configurable number of items and may allow the user to select more than one item to submit. A menu displays only one line and drops down when the user clicks it so that an item can be selected. The user can select only one item at a time from a menu.

Exercises

1. Create a form to collect the user data of your choice. Format the form objects and labels with a table so that they line up nicely. Place the submit and reset buttons in the bottom row of the table and merge the cells so that the buttons are centered under the entire table.

2. Create a jump menu in a frame at the top of the page. Enter all your favorite URLs into the menu. Have the URLs load into a frame in the bottom of the page.

3. Experiment with using the form page designs and Snippets panel to quickly create forms.

Hour 22, "Customizing Dreamweaver," explains how you can download and install third-party extensions to Dreamweaver. One I particularly like is called Check Form, created by Jaro von Flocken (see www.yaromat.com).

Receiving Information from a Form

The standard way to process a form is to have an application on the server that parses the data and performs an action on it. **Parsing** data is the act of dividing and interpreting the name–value pairs that are sent to the server.

Each name–value pair contains the name of the form element entered in Dreamweaver and the value that the user has entered or selected for that field. A text field will have a name–value pair that contains the name of the text field and the value that was entered into the text field. A radio button group will send a name–value pair with the name of the radio button group and the value of the button that was selected when the user submitted the form. A list or a drop-down menu will send the name of the object and any items the user selected.

The name–value pairs are sent to a server via an **HTTP request** from the Web browser. The request is passed by the Web server software to the application server that handles the scripting language specified in the request, as shown in Figure 19.3. For instance, if the script is written in ColdFusion Markup Language (CFML), the ColdFusion application server handles the request. Depending on what is written in the script, the application server may request data from a database or send a request to an email server to send a specific email message. There are many ways scripts can be processed on the server. The application server usually returns some sort of output, usually HTML, that is sent by the Web server back to the browser. This all takes place in milliseconds!

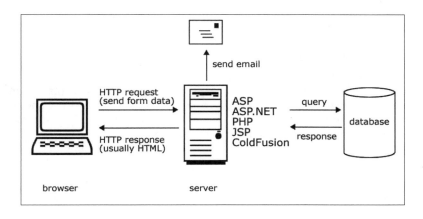

FIGURE 19.3
The browser sends a request to a script on the server and receives a response back. The script may control sending an email message or accessing and returning data from a database.

A popular way of processing forms on a server is by using a CGI script. Usually these scripts are written in Perl or other programming languages. Later in this hour, you will learn other ways of processing forms, with Active Server Pages (ASP), ASP.NET, JavaServer Pages (JSP), Hypertext Preprocessor (PHP), and CFML—proprietary processing systems that are powerful in creating Web applications.

Luckily, there are a number of places on the Web to download CGI scripts that are already written. Because programming CGI scripts is beyond the scope of this book, the examples in this hour use an existing script that processes form data and sends it to a specific email address.

Did you Know?

Get Free Scripts on the Web

The Web is an incredibly generous place, and you can download all sorts of free scripts to use. If you don't know how to program CGI scripts and you are willing to process your forms generically, you'll find a number of great scripts available from Matt's Script Archive (www.scriptarchive.com) and Freescripts (www.freescripts.com).

CGI stands for **Common Gateway Interface**, and it is the definition of the standard method of communication between a script and the Web server. The CGI script resides in a specific directory on the Web server. It is common for access to this directory to be limited to Webmasters for security reasons. You can contact your Webmaster and ask whether a script is already available on your server to do what you want to do or whether the Webmaster will install one for you. You may have a directory within your own Web directory that can hold CGI scripts. Often this directory is called cgi-bin or has cgi in the directory name.

You should double-check that your hosting service, if you are using one, supports CGI scripts. Sometimes you can use only the scripts that the service has available; check that a form mail script is available. Carefully review the features of the type of account you are signing up for and ask questions, if necessary.

Did you Know?

Use a Form Hosting Site

CGI scripts may expose a server to hackers on the Web, which is why access to the scripts directory is usually limited. If you don't have access to CGI scripts, you might want to use a form-hosting site (search for *free form hosting* on Yahoo! or any other search engine). The site www.formmail.com enables you to build and host forms without advertisements for less than a dollar per month.

Secure HTTP protocol

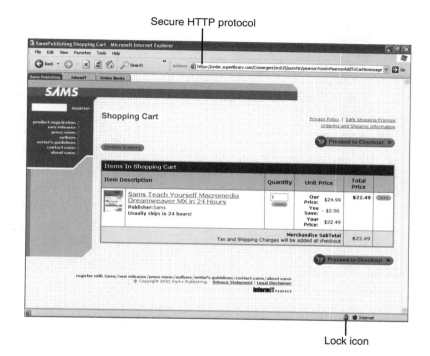

FIGURE 19.6
The browser displays a Lock icon in the status bar when the page is served via secure sockets.

Lock icon

You need to worry about secure submissions only when the user enters sensitive information, such as credit card numbers or other financial data. For polls, guest books, or feedback forms, you don't need to shield the information from potential thieves. Customers will expect you to protect only their sensitive data.

You need a server certificate to add security to your form submissions. A **certificate** is an electronic document that verifies that you are who you say you are. You might be able to use your Web host's certificate, or you might need to purchase your own. One of the major certificate vendors is VeriSign, and you can learn more about certificates at VeriSign's Web site: `www.verisign.com`.

Uploading a File from a Form

You might need to add a **file field** that enables users to upload files. You can collect images, homework assignments, or any types of files that you might need to have sent to you with a file field object. The user selects the Browse button, shown in Figure 19.7, to select a file from his or her local drive. When the user presses the Submit button, the file is sent to the server.

FIGURE 19.7
Use a file field to enable a user to upload a file to the server. However, make sure your server allows it before you create your form.

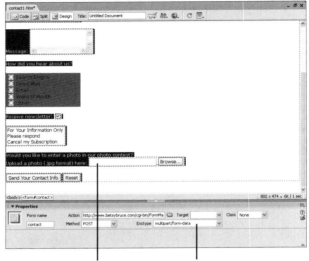

File field   Form Enctype property

A file field has attributes similar to those of a text field, which you used in the last hour. You can set the size of the file field by putting a value in the Char Width box in the Property inspector. You can also set the Max Chars attribute and the Init Val attribute in the Property inspector. You need to give the file field a unique name.

The important question you need to answer before you use a file field is, does your server allow anonymous file uploads? You also need to select multipart/form-data from the Enctype drop-down list for the <form> tag so that the file is encoded correctly. Also, you should use the POST method to submit your form; the GET method does not work with file fields.

Preparing a Page to Interact with ASP, ASP.NET, JSP, PHP, or CFML

Besides using CGI scripts, there are other ways to process forms and create dynamic Web applications. Like CGI scripting, these technologies interact with the Web server to process Web page information. Dreamweaver enables you to create dynamic Web pages that incorporate server-side scripting. When you create a new Web page, you create a dynamic page by selecting the Dynamic Page category in the New Document dialog box, as shown in Figure 19.8.

Q&A

Q. *I know an ASP programmer who will help me with my Web pages. What do I need to tell her about my Web pages so that she can write a script to process them on the server?*

A. She needs to know what you have called the items in your form and how you want them processed. If she is sending the data to a database, she needs to know what you call the items in your form so that she can parse the data into the correct place. She also needs to know if you need any validation or processing applied to the data. For instance, you might need to have individual prices added together as one total price.

Q. *Should I learn Perl, ASP, ASP.NET, PHP, JSP, or CFML?*

A. It depends on what you want to do when you grow up! Do you have a knack for coding? If so, having skills in any of these technologies might be fun and look great on your resume. Find out what technologies people at work are using. If you learn those technologies, your colleagues might be a good support system for your learning endeavor.

If you aren't very interested in coding but want to expand your Web skill set, maybe it's a better idea to specialize in something Dreamweaver excels at, such as Dynamic HTML. On the other hand, you can always learn more about databases. If you don't really enjoy coding, coding can be a real chore. Dreamweaver MX 2004 offers objects and server behaviors that make it much easier than before to code dynamic Web pages.

Workshop

The Workshop contains quiz questions and activities to help reinforce what you've learned in this hour. In case you get stuck, the answers to the quiz appear after the questions.

Quiz

1. What pair of items is sent when a user submits a form?

2. What is a hidden text field?

3. Dreamweaver allows you to add tag definitions for any type of code that can be inserted into a Web page. True or false?

Quiz Answers

1. The name–value pair is sent when a user submits a form. This is the name of the form object and the value the user either entered or selected.

2. A hidden text field contains a name–value pair that the user cannot change. Generally, this data is required by the script to properly process the form.

3. True. You can create a custom definition for any type of code you use in your Web pages so that Dreamweaver will recognize it.

Exercises

1. Add a Google search box to a Web page. You'll be adding a form that contacts the Google servers and returns results to the Web page. You can find the code at www.google.com/searchcode.html; paste this code in Dreamweaver's Code view and then change to Design view to examine and edit it.

2. Experiment with the FormMail fields that you did not explore in this hour. The script also offers validation functionality that you could use instead of using the Dreamweaver Validate Form behavior. You can find the documentation online at www.scriptarchive.com/readme/formmail.html.

3. Find a form on a Web and look at it critically. Select the View Source command to see the HTML. Does the form have any hidden fields? Where is the form being submitted? You should look for the <form> and </form> tags that contain the code for the form.

PART VI

Organizing and Uploading a Project

HOUR 20 Uploading a Project   **365**

HOUR 21 Managing and Editing a Project   **383**

HOUR 22 Customizing Dreamweaver   **397**

HOUR 23 Reusing Items in a Web Site by Using the Library   **415**

HOUR 24 Creating and Applying a Template   **429**

HOUR 20

Uploading a Project

What You'll Learn in This Hour:

▶ How to configure a remote site

▶ How to move your site onto a remote server

▶ How to import an existing site

▶ How to use Check In/Check Out

Finished Web sites reside on a Web server where many people access the Web pages. While you are working on your Web sites, you will want to move them onto the server for testing. At the end of the project, you'll need to move your Web pages to a public server so that other people can look at them. There are different ways to move the files onto a server and different methods for ensuring that the version of the files is correct and not accidentally overwritten.

Enabling Server Connection

When you define a Web site in Dreamweaver, you define a local site that exactly mirrors the final, public Web site. **Mirroring** means that the local site contains an exact copy of the files on the final site. Dreamweaver calls your final site the **remote site**. You work on the files in your local site and then upload them to the remote site by using Dreamweaver's file transfer commands.

When working in Dreamweaver, you don't need FTP transfer software or any other software in order to move your files onto the remote server. This capability is built right in to Dreamweaver! It's more convenient to set up your remote site and transfer files while working in Dreamweaver than to jump out to another application.

Adding Your Remote Site

You define a remote site by editing the Web site definition (which you get to by selecting Site, Manage Sites). Select a site and click the Edit button to launch the Site Definition dialog box for the selected Web site. In the Basic tab, click the Next button until you reach the Sharing Files section of the Site Definition Wizard, as shown in Figure 20.1.

FIGURE 20.1
You set up the remote site definition in the Sharing Files section of the Site Definition Wizard.

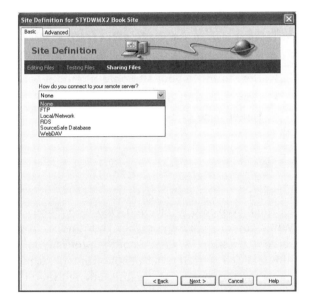

You can choose five transfer methods from the drop-down menu:

- ▶ FTP
- ▶ Local/Network
- ▶ RDS
- ▶ SourceSafe Database
- ▶ WebDAV

The transfer method you select depends on where your remote site is located. The site may be on your company's intranet, and if so, you can transfer the local site up to the remote site by using a LAN, or Local/Network, connection. The site may be at your ISP, the folks who provide you with an Internet dial-up service or a

Web hosting service. In this case, you will probably connect to its servers by using FTP. SourceSafe, RDS, and WebDAV connections are less common than the others but are sometimes used in professional Web development environments.

Setting FTP Information

You should select FTP access, as shown in Figure 20.2, if you need to transfer files over the Web to a remote server. The server could be physically located in your building, or it could be on the other side of the world. You need to enter the name of the FTP server into the text box What Is the Hostname or FTP Address of Your Web Server? Often this is in the following format: ftp.*domain*.com.

No Protocol Necessary

Do not enter the server name preceded with the protocol, as you would in a browser (such as ftp://ftp.*domain*.com).

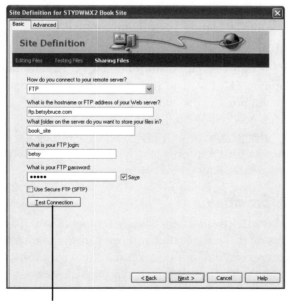

Test connection

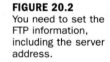

FIGURE 20.2
You need to set the FTP information, including the server address.

Enter the correct directory in the text box What Folder on the Server Do You Want to Store Your Files In? You might need to get the path for this directory from your Web or network administrator. If you are unsure what the root directory is on the remote site, try leaving the What Is the Hostname or FTP Address of Your Web Server? box blank. The FTP server might put you directly in the correct directory because your account may be configured that way.

You need a login and a password to access the FTP server. The standard anonymous login, often used to download files over the Internet, will probably not work to upload files to a Web site. You need to log in as a user who has access and permission to get and put files in the directories that will house your Web site. Dreamweaver saves your password by default. If other people have access to Dreamweaver on your computer and you don't want them to access your FTP account, deselect the Save check box.

Click the Test Connection button to make sure that you've entered everything correctly and are successfully connecting to the FTP server. You can troubleshoot FTP connection problems by first closing the Site Definition dialog box and then selecting Window, Results and clicking the FTP Log tab. The FTP log lists the reason you didn't connect successfully. For instance, if the log states that the password was incorrect or the directory you are targeting doesn't exist, you can change these in the Site Definition Wizard and try again.

If you are behind a firewall or using a proxy server, you might have difficulties with FTP. Consult the network administrator about which settings you need to choose when setting up FTP. If you go through a firewall to access the Internet, you may need to configure the firewall port and host in the Site category of the Dreamweaver Preferences dialog box, as shown in Figure 20.3. If you have a slow connection to the Internet, the default FTP timeout might be too short, causing your FTP connection to time out too often. You can increase this time in the Site category of the Preferences dialog box.

Setting LAN Information

You should select Local/Network in the Site Definition Wizard, as shown in Figure 20.4, if the server is on a computer that you can connect to directly by using a network. If you can access files on the server the same way you access your hard drive, moving files to and from it with ease, you have LAN access. You need to know the correct Web-accessible directory; your Web administrator should be able to give you that information.

Set up LAN access to the remote server by entering the path to the remote directory. Use the Browse icon to browse to the directory or type in the path. Checking the Refresh Remote File List Automatically may slow down Dreamweaver's performance a bit, but you will always have an up-to-date reflection of the remote site.

by selecting the Get button, and you can transfer files to the remote site by selecting the Put button. Later this hour, you'll learn about using the Synchronize command, which is a better way to transfer files. The Synchronize command detects whether a local file (or remote file) is newer and transfers it only if necessary, thus saving transfer time.

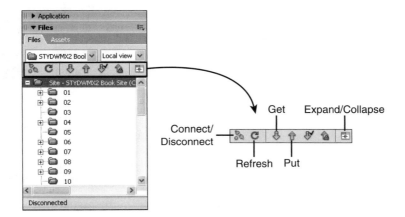

FIGURE 20.8
The buttons at the top of the Files panel help you transfer files between the local and remote sites.

These are the buttons at the top of the Files panel:

- ▶ **Connect/Disconnect**—This button establishes a connection to an FTP server. The button has a little green light that is lit when you are connected to the FTP server. This button is always lit when you have LAN access to your remote site.

- ▶ **Refresh**—This button manually refreshes the list of files in the Files panel.

- ▶ **Get**—This button retrieves files from the remote site and moves them to your local site.

- ▶ **Put**—This button places files from your local site onto the remote site.

Click the Expand/Collapse button on the far right of the Files panel to expand the panel, as shown in Figure 20.9. The expanded Files panel not only shows the local site, as does the Files panel, but it also shows the remote site. A list of the files on the remote site appears when you are connected. When you want to collapse the expanded Files panel, click the Expand/Collapse button again.

FIGURE 20.9
Use the
Expand/Collapse
button to expand
the Files panel.

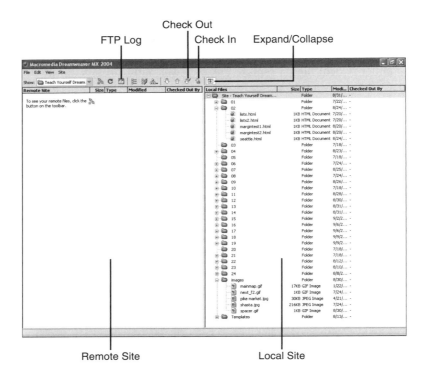

Understanding Dreamweaver's Web Site Management Capabilities

Understanding Dreamweaver's Web Site Management Capabilities

You use the Check In/Check Out tools in Dreamweaver to make sure that only one person is working on a file at a time. When you have a file checked out, no one else can check that file out until you check it back in, just like when you have a DVD or video checked out from the video store. Dreamweaver marks the file as checked out by you so that your collaborators know who to bug if they also need to make changes to the file!

When you check out a file from the remote site, Dreamweaver retrieves a copy of that file from the remote server to ensure that you have the most up-to-date version of the file in your local site. When Dreamweaver gets the file, it overwrites the file that exists on your local drive. The checked-out file appears to Dreamweaver users with your name beside it on the remote server, signaling to your collaborators that you have checked it out. The file has a green check mark beside it in your local site, showing that you currently have that file checked out.

Enabling Check In/Check Out

After you define the remote site in the Site Definition Wizard and click Next,
Dreamweaver asks if you'd like to enable Check In/Check Out. Because you overwrite files when you transfer them from the local site to the remote site, you need
to be careful. You can use Check In/Check Out functionality so that you do not
overwrite files that others have recently edited and uploaded to the remote site.

When you turn on Check In/Check Out on the Advanced tab of the Site
Definition dialog box, options appear, as shown in Figure 20.10, that enable you
to configure this feature. You choose whether you'd like to check out a file when
you open a file in your local site that isn't currently checked out. I suggest you
choose to view it as a read-only copy because then you can look at a file without
checking it out; if you then need to edit it, you can quickly check it out.

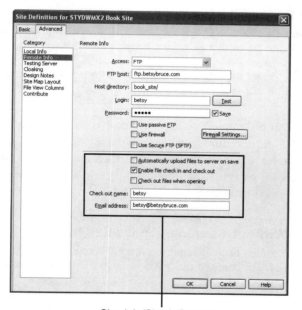

Check In/Check Out setup

FIGURE 20.10
Enable Check
In/Check Out so
that you can control
collaboration with
others.

Enter a name and an email address so that others accessing the remote site can
see who has the file checked out. They'll be able to click your name and send you
an email message about the file you have checked out.

Transferring Files

When you check in a file to the remote site, Dreamweaver transfers the file back to the remote server to make it available for others to work on or view. The file will no longer appear to other Dreamweaver users with your name beside it.

Dreamweaver's Locking Mechanism

Dreamweaver creates a file on the remote server with the .lck (for lock) file extension. This file contains the name of the person who has checked out the file. You don't need to worry about creating these .lck files, but I mention them because you might get questions about these files from others who examine the remote site without Dreamweaver.

Drag and Drop May Be Dangerous

You can drag and drop files back and forth between the local and remote sites. However, you need to be careful where you drop the files. You might drop them in an incorrect directory. Dreamweaver automatically transfers files into the mirror image location when you select a file and use the buttons to transfer the file. This way, the file remains in its correct location.

Check In/Check Out is designed to help you manage a collaborative environment. The Check Out procedure forces you to download the most recent version of the file. While you have the file checked out, others cannot work on it. After you check the file back in, you can open the file but cannot save any changes because Dreamweaver marks it as read-only.

Don't Leave Without Checking Your Files In!

Remember to check files back in when you are finished with them! Don't go on vacation with a bunch of files checked out if you want your co-workers to happily welcome you back when you return.

Dreamweaver enables you to circumvent some of the Check In/Check Out safeguards. You can, for instance, override somebody else's checked-out file and check it out yourself. You can also turn off the read-only attribute of a file and edit it without checking it out. However, why would you want to do any of these things? Dreamweaver's Check In/Check Out process is fine for a small environment where you don't expect mischief. If you need tighter security and version control, however, you should use one of the products on the market, such as Microsoft Visual SourceSafe, that enable very tight control.

Everyone Needs to Use Check In/Check Out

Your project will work more smoothly if everyone who is collaborating on the project turns on the Check In/Check Out functionality for the site. Otherwise, it's too easy to overwrite a file that someone else has updated. Check In/Check Out works only if everyone on the team uses Dreamweaver and enables the Check In/Check Out functionality.

Did you Know?

You can still use Get and Put when you have Check In/Check Out enabled. The Get command will move a file from the remote server and overwrite the local file. The file will be read-only on your local machine because you won't have it checked out. If you try to put a file that someone has checked out onto the remote server, Dreamweaver warns you that changes to the remote copy of the file may be lost if you go ahead and transfer the file. You can choose to do the action anyway or cancel the action.

The Synchronize Command

To get only the files that are more recent than the files on the local site onto the remote site, you use the Synchronize command, which will be discussed in Hour 21, "Managing and Editing a Project."

Did you Know?

To get or put files, first make sure the correct site is selected in the Site drop-down menu of the Files panel or the Site window. If you access your site via FTP, click the Connect button. If you are already connected or are accessing the files on a LAN, skip this step.

To get or check out files, follow these steps:

1. Select the files you want to transfer to your local site. You can also select an entire folder to transfer all of its contents.

2. Click the Get command, or click the Check Out command if you have Check In/Check Out enabled for this site.

3. Dreamweaver may display a dialog box, asking if you would also like to download dependent files. **Dependent files** are images and other assets that are linked to the files you are transferring. You can disable this dialog box by checking the Don't Ask Me Again check box. I prefer to transfer the asset files manually instead of having Dreamweaver do it automatically.

> **Don't Transfer Dependent Files Multiple Times**
>
> Continually getting and putting dependent files will slow down your transfers. Image files are usually much larger than HTML files and take longer to transfer. If the files haven't changed, you don't need to transfer them.

To put or check in files, follow these steps:

1. Select the files you want to transfer to the remote site.

2. Click the Put command, or click the Check In command if you have Check In/Check Out enabled for this site. If you transfer a file that is currently open, Dreamweaver will prompt you to save the file before you put it on the remote site.

3. Dreamweaver may display a dialog box, asking if you would also like to upload dependent files. You can disable this dialog box by checking the Don't Ask Me Again check box.

Importing an Existing Web Site

When a Web site already exists at a remote site, you need to define the Web site in Dreamweaver, connect to the remote site, and download all the files in the site to work on it. Remember, you can edit only files that are located on your own machine. You can download and edit an existing site even if it wasn't created with Dreamweaver.

Downloading a site for the first time might take some time, depending on how you are accessing the site and what your network connection speed is. After you initially download all the files, however, you should need only to download any files that change.

To import an existing Web site, all you need to do is mirror the existing site on your local drive. There is no conversion process, and the files will remain unchanged in Dreamweaver. To import an existing Web site, follow these steps:

1. Set up both your local and remote info in the Site Definition dialog box.

2. Get all the files on the remote site by selecting the top entry in the remote site of the Files panel. Selecting the top entry, the root folder, selects the entire site. If you select a file, you get only that file instead of the entire site.

3. Click the Get button to transfer all the files on the remote site to your local site.

You can also import and export a site definition, either to share with others or to back up your site definition. To do this, select the Export command from the Site menu in the Files panel. You can choose to either back up your site definition, saving your login, password, and local path information, or share the site definition with other users, without the personal information. Dreamweaver saves the file with the `.ste` extension. Select the Import command from the Site menu in the Files panel to import the site definition contained in the `.ste` file.

Summary

In this hour, you have learned how to connect to a remote site and transfer files. You have learned how to use the Advanced tab of the Site Definition dialog box and how to set up FTP, local/network, Visual SourceSafe, and WebDAV connections. You have also learned how to use Dreamweaver's internal version-control feature, Check In/Check Out.

Q&A

Q. *When is it appropriate to use Check In/Check Out?*

A. There are two major uses for Check In/Check Out: for working in a small group and for working on a site from two computers. Check In/Check Out isn't designed for use by enterprise-type projects (those with many developers), but it is perfect for a small group of developers who are working on the same sites. I use it all the time when I work on a site with two computers (home and work computers, for instance). It helps me know whether I have uploaded my changes.

Q. *Do you use the Site Definition Wizard or the Advanced tab of the Side Definition dialog box to define Web sites in Dreamweaver?*

A. I usually define a site initially by using the wizard because it's fast, but then I often tweak the site definition by using the Advanced tab.

Q. *One of my co-workers left for a two-week vacation with a bunch of files checked out in his name. How can I work on these files while he is gone?*

A. When you attempt to check out the files, Dreamweaver will warn you that someone else has them checked out. It will then ask you to override your co-worker's checkout. If you click the Yes button, the files will be checked out to you. Just hope that your co-worker hasn't made any changes to the files that he forgot to move onto the remote site.

Workshop

The Workshop contains quiz questions and activities to help reinforce what you've learned in this hour. In case you get stuck, the answers to the quiz appear after the questions.

Quiz

1. When you're working in a collaborative environment and using FTP, it doesn't matter if everyone is using Dreamweaver's Check In/Check Out functionality. True or false?

2. Why do you need to define a remote site for a Web site?

3. What is Dreamweaver's most useful tool for troubleshooting a connection to a remote site via FTP?

Quiz Answers

1. False. It's too easy for one member of your group to overwrite the work of another member if not everyone is using the Check In/Check Out functionality. The only time you don't need to use this functionality when working with a group is when you are using a third-party program to manage version control.

2. To define a remote site for a Web site, you need to put Web site files on a public server or share files with a group.

3. Dreamweaver's most useful tool in this situation is the FTP log. The FTP Log tab in the Results panel enables you to read the error messages sent back by the server.

Exercises

1. Define a remote site connection, using either the FTP setting or the Local/Network setting. If you don't have access to a remote computer, create a directory on your hard drive and name it remote. Pretend that this is a directory on a LAN and connect to it by using a local/network connection. Try transferring files back and forth between the local and remote sites.

2. Turn on Check In/Check Out functionality for a defined site and connect to the remote site. What changes in Dreamweaver?

HOUR 21

Managing and Editing a Project

What You'll Learn in This Hour:

▶ How to synchronize files on local and remote sites

▶ How to create a site map and manage links

▶ How to add design notes to document your project and share ideas with others

▶ How to generate reports about a Web site

Dreamweaver has a number of useful commands for managing an entire Web site. You can create (and even save) a site map that is a visual representation of the relationships of all the files in a Web site. There are commands to update links sitewide and to search and replace text in either the text or the HTML portions of a Web page.

Editing an Entire Site

Dreamweaver has a number of useful commands that can help you make sitewide changes. In the next few minutes, you will use commands that are very powerful and can save you a lot of time. You should be careful when changing items sitewide in case you make a mistake. But of course, you could just fix such a mistake sitewide, too!

The commands that you can apply to your entire site, such as the commands to transfer files, are available from the menus in the expanded Files panel. The expanded Files panel (showing both the local and remote sites) has File, Edit, View, and Site menus. When you don't have the Files panel expanded, these same menus and commands are available from the Files panel menu, shown in Figure 21.1.

FIGURE 21.1
The Files panel menu gives you access to the same menus available when the Files panel is expanded.

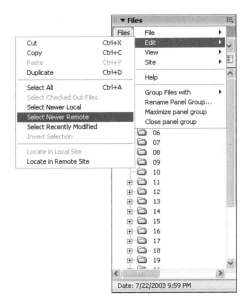

Synchronizing Your Files on the Local and Remote Sites

You should synchronize your files on the local and remote sites so that you are assured that you have the most up-to-date files in both places. Dreamweaver has three commands that are useful in determining which site has the newer files: Synchronize, Select Newer Local, and Select Newer Remote. You should select the Synchronize command to automatically synchronize files between the local and the remote sites, bringing both sites up-to-date with the most recent files. If you want to check whether new files reside on the local site or the remote site, use the Select Newer Local and Select Newer Remote commands, respectively, from the Edit menu in the Files panel.

To see which files are newer on the remote site, follow these steps:

1. Connect to the remote site by clicking the Connect button at the top of the Files panel if you are using FTP to access the remote site.

2. Select either the root directory or a section of files in the local site.

3. Select Edit, Select Newer Remote in the Files panel.

Dreamweaver searches through the files on the remote site to see whether any are newer than the same files on the local site. The files that are newer on the remote site are all selected. If files that don't exist on the local site exist on the remote site, Dreamweaver selects those, too. With all the files selected, you simply get the files from the remote site to update your local files. To select files that are newer on the local site, you follow the same steps, except you use the Select Newer Local command in step 3.

When you synchronize files, Dreamweaver analyzes the files on both the local and remote sites and gives you a report on which files need to be copied to synchronize the sites. You have total control over the process and can deselect any files that you do not want transferred. Dreamweaver will also tell you whether files are completely up-to-date and whether there is a need to synchronize.

To synchronize the files in the local and remote sites, follow these steps:

1. Make sure the site you want to synchronize is open in the Files panel.

2. If you want to synchronize only certain files or folders, select those files or folders.

3. Select Site, Synchronize from the Files panel menu. The Synchronize Files dialog box appears, as shown in Figure 21.2.

FIGURE 21.2
The Synchronize Files dialog box enables you to select which files to synchronize.

4. In the Synchronize drop-down menu, choose to synchronize the entire site or just the files you have selected.

5. Select how you want to transfer the files in the Direction drop-down menu. You can transfer the newer files to the remote site, get the newer files from the remote site, or get and put newer files in both directions.

By the
Way

Synchronize When Collaborating

Because I often collaborate with groups of people on Web sites, I am usually interested in what files are newer on the remote site. Others on the team may have changed files and uploaded them while I was doing something else. I like to make sure I'm looking at the most recent files in the project by synchronizing to get the newer files from the remote site.

6. Check the Delete Local Files Not on Remote Server check box if you want to get rid of any extraneous local files or the Delete Remote Files Not on Local Drive check box if there are extraneous files in the remote site. Careful! Maybe the files are newly uploaded to the site by someone else.

Watch
Out!

Delete Files Carefully

Be very careful about checking the Delete Local Files Not on Remote Server check box because you don't want to delete files you will need later. When you select this check box, you will be deleting the files from your hard drive. If the files do not exist anywhere else, you will not be able to restore them. Checking this box is a quick way to clean your local site of files that are not being used.

7. Click the Preview button. If your files are up-to-date, you get a message that no synchronization is necessary. If there are files that need to be synchronized, Dreamweaver displays the dialog box shown in Figure 21.3, which lists all the files that either don't exist or are newer than the site you are transferring to.

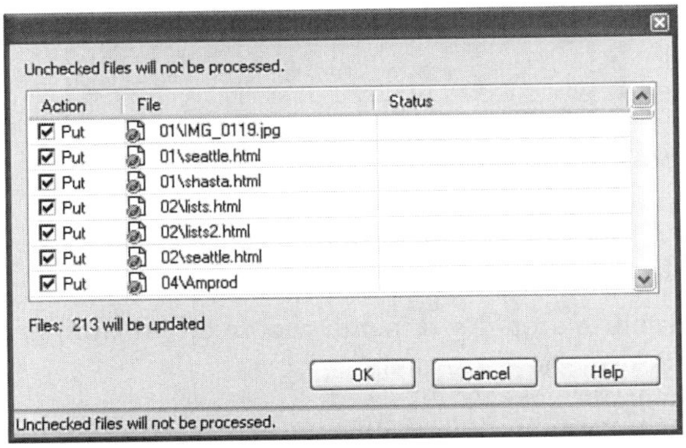

FIGURE 21.3
A dialog box listing the files that need to be synchronized appears when you click the Preview button in the Synchronize Files dialog box.

8. Look through the list and deselect any files that you do not want to transfer. When you are ready to transfer the files, click OK. During the transfer, Dreamweaver displays a status completion bar dialog box on top of the

Synchronize Files dialog box. After the synchronization is complete, the Synchronize Files dialog box displays the message "Synchronization complete" and gives the status of each file.

9. Click the Close button to finish synchronizing.

When you are updating and editing files on a live Web site, you will probably use the Synchronize command many times. It's a quick and mechanical method of deciding which files have been updated and need to be uploaded to the server. When you are collaborating with others, the Synchronize command is useful for helping you decide which files have been updated on the server and need to be updated on your local site. This saves you the trouble of downloading the entire site when only a few files have been updated.

Creating a Site Map

You can create a site map to visually represent the layout of your site. You can expand the Files panel by clicking the Expand/Collapse button to make it easy to create your site map. You can collapse the expanded Files panel after you are finished creating a site map by clicking the Expand/Collapse button again. After you've defined your map, you can view it in the Files panel by selecting View, Map View.

Before you view the site map, you need to define a home page for your site. The site map needs to know where "home" is in order to build the map. To define a home page, select a Web page as the home page in your local site and select Site, Set as Home Page. You can later change the home page if you need to by reselecting this command.

Site Map Layout

You can configure other attributes of the site map by opening the Site Map Layout category in the Site Definition dialog box. For instance, you can change how many icons (columns) appear per row in the site map.

By the Way

Select Click the Site Map button, shown in Figure 21.4, to display the site map. When you click the button, you can select to display the map by itself (Map Only) or with the local files (Map and Files). The site map appears along with the files in your local site, if you chose that option. Files appear as icons in the site map with lines drawn between related files to represent links. The following symbols appear next to the icons that describe the files:

► A broken link appears as red text with a small picture of a broken link of chain.

► A link appears as blue text with a small globe beside it.

► A file that is checked out to you appears with a green check mark beside it.

► A file that is checked out to someone else appears with a red check mark beside it.

► A file that is read-only appears with a lock beside it.

Site Map button

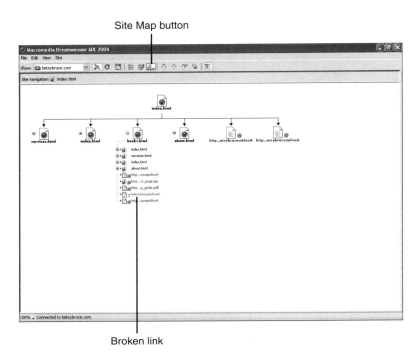

Broken link

Views in the Files Panel

You can view the site map in the collapsed Files panel instead of in the expanded Files panel. Select the Site Map command from the drop-down menu next to the Sites drop-down menu in the Files panel. It's more difficult to see all the files in the Files panel than in the expanded Files panel.

You can change the view in the site map by clicking any file and selecting View, View as Root. This places the icon you selected at the top of the site map. The files that are between the currently selected icon and the actual site root are displayed in the bar directly above the site map. You can click these files to jump to that level.

Select View, Layout to modify the way the way the site map is displayed; this command opens the Site Definition dialog box to the Site Map Layout category, as shown in Figure 21.5. You must display the site map in the Files panel in order for this command to be active. You can set the number of columns (how many files are display horizontally in the site map) and the column width. You can also set when the site map displays each file's filename or page title under the icon in the site map.

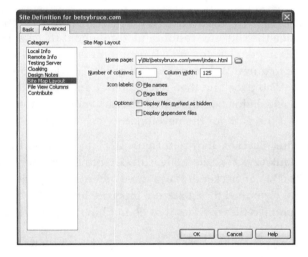

FIGURE 21.5
The Site Map Layout category of the Site Definition dialog box enables you to configure the number of columns and their width.

Save your site map as either a bitmap (.bmp) or a PNG file by selecting File, Save Site Map. You can embed a bitmap representation of your site map into a text document to send to a client or to save as documentation. You can also print the file as a reference or embed a PNG file in a Web page.

Managing Your Links

Dreamweaver automatically updates links when you move or rename a file within the current Web site. Make sure when you define the Web site that you create a cache to speed up the update process. By default, the cache is turned on, and it's best that you do not turn it off in your site definition. When you move or rename Web pages, Dreamweaver displays the Update Files dialog box. A list of linked files, as shown in Figure 21.6, is displayed in the dialog box. Click the Update button to update all the links or select individual files to update.

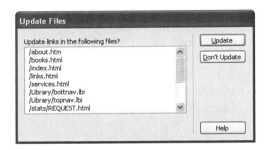

You can also change the URL of a certain link throughout the site. For instance, if you displayed links in your site for today's menu in the cafeteria, you would need to change the link to a new Web page every day. On Tuesday morning, you could select the Monday Web page and then select Site, Change Link Sitewide. The Change Link Sitewide dialog box that then appears enables you to enter the old link and then select the path for the new link.

You can use the Link Checker, shown in Figure 21.7, to check all the links in your site. To open the Link Checker, select Site, Check Links Sitewide command from the Files panel. The Link Checker displays three different categories: broken links, external links, and orphaned files. External links are links that Dreamweaver cannot check. Orphaned files are files that do not have any files linking to them.

Save Report button

An Orphan May Not Be an Orphan

Dreamweaver might say a file is an orphan even when that file is used in your site. The file may be referenced in a behavior, for instance, such as an image file used with the Swap Image behavior.

Broken links need to be fixed. Fortunately, Dreamweaver makes that easy. You just select the broken link, click the Browse icon, and navigate to the correct file to fix the link.

Save the Link Checker Report

You can save the report after running the Link Checker by clicking the Save Report button, the small floppy disk icon on the left side of the Results panel. Then you can easily refer to it as you fix any problems with your site.

Did you Know?

The Link Checker opens in the Results panel group, located directly below the Property inspector. You can hide the panel group by clicking the arrow to the left of the panel title (Results), or you can close the panel group by selecting the Close Panel Group command from the panel menu, the menu in the upper-right corner of the panel.

Adding Design Notes to Pages

Design notes enable you to add notes to your Web pages. You can use design notes to document your design process, share information with others, and keep any extra information that would be useful. Because design notes are not actually part of the Web page, you can use them to record sensitive information that you might not want people who view the Web page to be able to read.

You can add a design note to any file in a Web site, including templates, images, and movies. Web pages based on templates do not have the design notes attached; only the original template file keeps the design note. You might want to add a design note to each images to list the name and location of the original image file.

To attach a design note to a file, follow these steps:

1. When a file is open in the Document window, select File, Design Notes. Or right-click (Command+click on the Mac) a file in the Files panel and select the Design Notes command.

2. The Design Notes dialog box appears, as shown in Figure 21.8. Select the type of design note you want from the Status drop-down menu.

3. Click the Date icon to insert today's date in the Notes field. Type a note in the field after the date.

4. Check the Show When File Is Opened check box if you want this design note to appear when someone opens the file next.

5. Select the All Info tab in the Design Notes dialog box to see a list of the information in the current design note, as shown in Figure 21.9. Add a record to the list by clicking the + button, entering a name, and entering a value.

Date icon

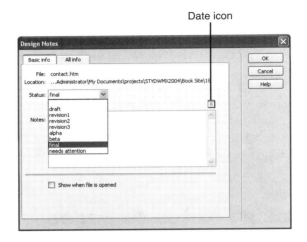

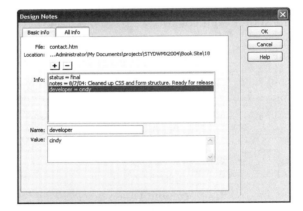

6. When you are done making changes in this dialog box, click OK.

*Did you
Know?*

Record the Author

When you are in a collaborative environment, a useful name and value data pair to
add to a design note is the name of the author of the note. To do this, select the All
Info tab in the Design Notes dialog box and click the + button. Name your new
record Name and put your name in the Value field.

A design note remains associated with files even if it is copied, renamed, moved,
or deleted. Dreamweaver saves your design notes in a directory called notes in

library item appears in the top half of the Library category of the Assets panel.

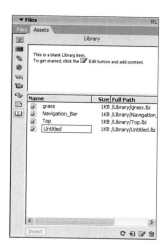

FIGURE 23.3
Create a new library item, open it, and add content.

2. Give the library item a name. For example, create a copyright statement that will go at the bottom of each of your Web pages. The name `Copyright` would be a good choice.

3. Double-click the library item in the Library category of the Assets panel. Dreamweaver opens the library item in a separate Document window. You can tell that you have a library item open because Dreamweaver displays <<Library Item>> along with the name of the library item in the title bar, as shown in Figure 23.4.

4. Insert objects into the library item's Document window just as you would in any Web page. Insert the copyright symbol (from the Text category in the Insert bar or by selecting Insert, HTML, Special Characters), a year, and a name.

5. Close the Document window and save the library item. Your changes will be reflected in the Library category of the Assets panel.

The Library category of the Assets panel has a pop-up menu that contains useful commands, as shown in Figure 23.5. This same menu also pops up when you right-click (Control+click on the Mac) a library item in the Library category of the Assets panel. Using the New Library Item command is another way to create a library item.

Title bar shows that you are in a library item

FIGURE 23.4
To add content to a library item, you open it in a separate Dreamweaver Document window. The window shows <<Library Item>> in the title bar.

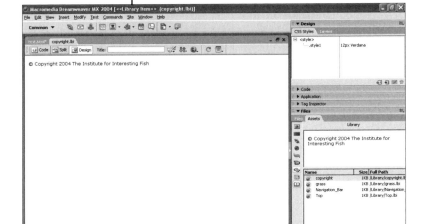

FIGURE 23.5
The Library category of the Assets panel pop-up menu has a number of commands to add, rename, open, and delete library items.

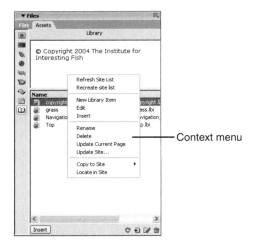

Context menu

Adding a Library Item to a Page

After you have created a library item, you simply drag it from the list in the Library category of the Assets panel and drop it onto your Web page, as shown in Figure 23.6. You can pick up the library item and move it to a different location in the Document window. You will not be able to select individual objects contained in the inserted library item. When you click any of the objects, you select the entire library item; the group of objects in a library item is essentially one object in your Web page.

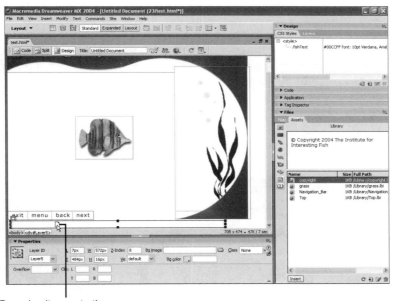

Dragging item onto the page

FIGURE 23.6
Drag a library item from the Library category of the Assets panel and drop it onto your Web page.

When you insert a library item into a Web page, a copy of its content is inserted. You no longer need to have the original library item present. When you upload your Web page onto a remote Web site, you do not need to upload the Library directory. It is a good idea to keep the directory, though, in case you want to make changes to library items throughout the Web site.

Sharing Library Items on the Server

Consider uploading the library onto your server so that others can use the library items, too. When collaborating with a group, you can share a library so that everyone creates consistent Web pages using the same library items.

The Property inspector, as shown in Figure 23.7, displays the library item attributes when a library item is selected in the Document window. The Src box displays the name of the library item (which you cannot change here). Three buttons in the Property inspector help you manage the library item:

▶ **Open**—This button opens the library item you wish to edit.

▶ **Detach from Original**—This button breaks the link between this instance of a library item and the original item. If the original library item is changed, a detached item will not be updated. If you detach a library item from its original, the individual objects contained in the item will be editable.

▶ **Recreate**—This button overwrites the original library item with the currently selected instance of the library item. This is useful if the original library item has been inadvertently edited or lost.

FIGURE 23.7
The Property inspector contains buttons to manage a library item. You can detach the item from its original or overwrite the item as the original.

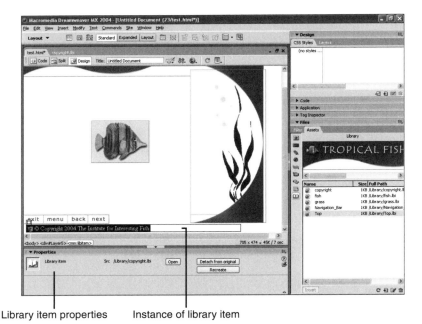

Library item properties   Instance of library item

You can apply a highlight to library items so that they are easy to see in the Document window. The highlight appears only in Dreamweaver and not in the browser. In addition, the highlight appears only if Invisible Elements is checked in the View menu. You set the highlight color in the Highlighting category in the Dreamweaver Preferences dialog box, as shown in Figure 23.8.

Library Items highlighting

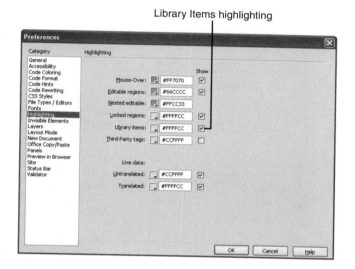

FIGURE 23.8
Set a highlight color for all library items in the Dreamweaver Preferences dialog box. The highlight appears only in Dreamweaver and not in the browser.

Making Changes to a Library Item

You edit a library item by opening the item to add or change objects in the Document window. Don't worry about the page background color when editing library items; the item will appear on the background color of the page it is inserted in. After you've inserted your previously created library item into a page, open the library item to edit it. Apply different formatting to some of the objects in the item.

After you are finished editing, save the library item. Dreamweaver asks you whether you want to update all the documents in the Web site that contain the library item, as shown in Figure 23.9. Click Update to automatically update all linked library items.

The Update Pages dialog box, shown in Figure 23.10, displays statistics on how many files were examined, how many were updated, and how many could not be updated. Check the Show Log check box if you want to see these statistics. Click Close to close the Update Pages dialog box.

FIGURE 23.9
Click Update to begin updating all the library items in your entire Web site that are linked to the selected library item.

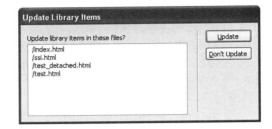

FIGURE 23.10
With Show Log checked, the Update Pages dialog box shows how many files were examined, how many were updated, and how many could not be updated.

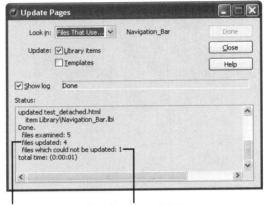

Four files updated   One file not updated

Watch Out!

Check Out Web Pages to Update

Certain library items in a Web site may not be updated if you do not have those items checked out. When you have Check In/Check Out turned on in your Web site, files that are not checked out to you are marked as read-only. Dreamweaver will not be able to update any library items in files marked read-only. Make sure you have all the appropriate files checked out before you update a library item.

You can manually update linked library items at any time. Right-click on the library item in the Library category of the Assets panel and select either the Update Current Page command to update the current Web page or the Update Site command to update the entire Web site. The Update Current Page command acts immediately, and no dialog box appears. When you issue the Update Site command, the Update Pages dialog box appears. Click the Start button to begin updating all the linked library items in the Web site.

Using Styles in Library Items

When you create a CSS style, Dreamweaver can insert the style definition into the head of the HTML document. A library item does not have a head section, as shown in Figure 23.11. You will be inserting a library item into a Web page, and the head of that Web page could have styles defined in it. When you know the name of the class that you'd like to apply to the library item, you need to add <span> tags around the item, with the class attribute set to the name of the class, like this:

```
<span class="greenText">Library Item here</span>
```

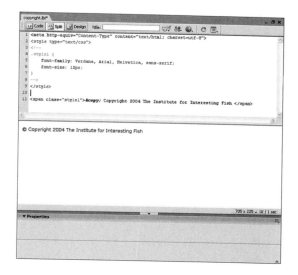

FIGURE 23.11
A library item is only HTML content and is not an HTML Web page. It doesn't include <head> or <body> tags.

You can apply styles to library items, but you need to link an external style sheet to the page. Make sure that every Web page that includes the library item is linked to the style sheet that contains the style definitions used in the library item. If you edit a style in the linked style sheet, all the library items will reflect any changes to the style.

Summary

In this hour, you have learned how to create library items, both from existing content and from scratch. You have learned how to use the Library category of the Assets panel to manage, open, and edit library items. You have learned how Dreamweaver automatically updates all the linked library items in a Web site and how you can launch the process manually.

Q&A

Q. *How can I apply edits I made to library items in only some of the linked files?*

A. I caution you to be careful if you are maintaining various pages, some with the newest version of the library item and some with an old version. You can select only the pages you want to update. But instead, why not open the library item, save it with a different name, apply your edits, and then replace it in the selected pages?

Q. *What types of objects are appropriate to put in the library?*

A. Here are some examples of objects that you might want to put in the Dreamweaver library: a company logo, a group of layers that appear on each page as a background, a search box (small form), a frequently used button, a custom bullet image, and a placeholder for content that isn't finalized (you can detach it later). You will find plenty of uses for the library.

Workshop

The Workshop contains quiz questions and activities to help reinforce what you've learned in this hour. In case you get stuck, the answers to the quiz appear after the questions.

Quiz

1. What is the file extension for library item files?

2. When you use library items, are they required to maintain the connection to the original item, reflecting updates to that item?

3. How do you unlink an instance of a library item from the original library item?

Quiz Answers

1. The file extension for library item files is .lbi.

2. No, library items may be detached from the original items so that they do not reflect any changes to the original items when pages are updated.

3. Select the Detach from Original button from the Property inspector with the library item selected.

Exercise

Create a library item and add it to a page. Experiment with reopening the library item, editing it, and then updating the page it's connected to. Try adding a CSS style to the library item and then insert the item into a Web page that has that style already defined.

HOUR 24

Creating and Applying a Template

What You'll Learn in This Hour:

▶ How to create templates from existing content and from scratch

▶ How to apply a template to a Web page

▶ How to edit an original template and update linked Web pages

▶ How to mark a selection as editable or optional

▶ How to use behaviors and styles with templates

You create templates to provide a foundation for consistent, controlled Web pages. **Templates** contain objects that you mark as editable; the rest of the template is locked. When you update an original template, the changes you make to it will update throughout your site.

Creating a Template

You can create a template, save it to the Template category of the Assets panel, and then use it to create a new Web page within a Web site. Anyone working on the same Web site can use the template, and you can use templates created by others.

You need to define a Web site before Dreamweaver can insert a template. Dreamweaver creates a directory called `Templates` in the root of your Web site where it stores the original template files. Dreamweaver keeps the code of a template in a file in the `Templates` directory and inserts a copy of the code when you insert a template in a Web page.

The Difference Between Templates and Library Items

A template differs from a library item in that a template is an entire Web page, not just a portion of one.

Using the Templates Category of the Assets Panel

To create and apply templates, open the Templates category of the Assets panel, as shown in Figure 24.1. The Templates category shows all the templates that exist in the current Web site. Each Web site that you create can have a different set of templates.

Download Templates from the Web

Does the Templates category of the Assets panel look bare? Copy one or more of the sites available in the Templates directory from the Dreamweaver CD-ROM to your hard drive and set it up as a site in the Files panel. These templates are also available for download from the Macromedia Web site, at www.macromedia.com/software/dreamweaver/download/templates.

FIGURE 24.1
The Templates category of the Assets panel displays all the templates in the current Web site.

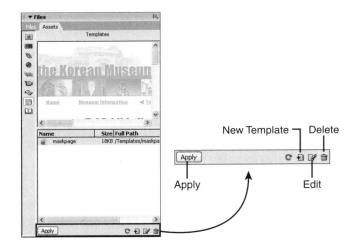

The Templates category of the Assets panel is divided into two halves. The top half displays the contents of the template, and the bottom half lists the names of the templates in the Web site. The buttons at the bottom of the panel include the following:

- ▶ **Apply**—You click this button to apply the currently selected template to the Web page.

- ▶ **New Template**—You click this button to create a new, blank template.

- ▶ **Edit**—You click this button to open the template in its own Dreamweaver Document window for editing.

- ▶ **Delete**—You click this button to remove the template from the `Templates` directory. This doesn't affect any instances of the templates except that the deleted template can no longer be updated throughout the site.

Creating a Template

There are two ways to create templates:

- ▶ **From an existing Web page**—When you decide to create a template out of a Web page, you can save the page as a template.

- ▶ **From scratch, as a new, empty template**—You can create a new template, open it, and then add objects to the template just as though it were a regular Web page.

When you apply a template to a Web page, a copy of all the content that the template contains is inserted into the page. You no longer need to have the original template present in order for the Web page to display. When you upload your Web page onto a remote Web site, you do not need to upload the `Templates` directory. You might want to upload the template onto your server so that others can use the templates, too. You should keep the directory in case you want to make changes to templates throughout your Web site.

Back Up Your Templates to the Server

Keeping the templates on the server ensures that you have a backup copy in case you accidentally change a template and need to restore the original.

By the Way

Did you Know?

Cloaking Affects Templates

Use Dreamweaver's Cloaking feature to prevent the Templates directory from being synchronized or uploaded when you are transferring files. You enable Cloaking in the Site menu and then right-click (Control+click on the Mac) the Templates directory and select Cloaking, Cloak. The folder will appear in the site with a red line through it.

Creating a Template from an Existing Web Page

To create a template from an existing Web page, follow these steps:

1. Select File, Save as Template.

2. The Save As Template dialog box appears, as shown in Figure 24.2. Enter a meaningful name for the template. Click the Save button to save the template to the Templates directory.

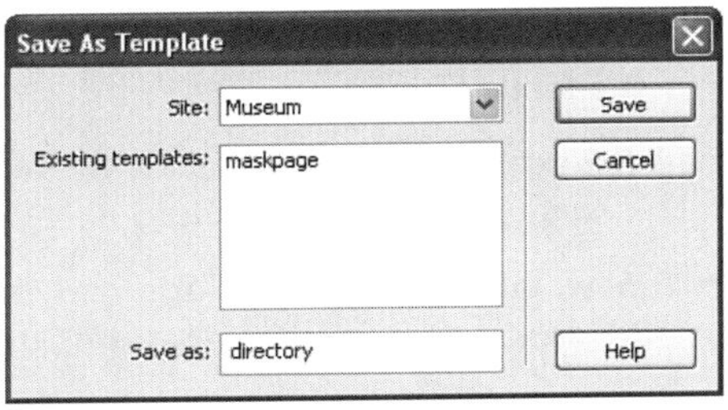

FIGURE 24.2
Give a new template a meaningful name in the Save As Template dialog box. This dialog box displays a list of existing templates in the current Web site.

3. A dialog box may appear, asking if you'd like to update links. Click the Yes button to agree. This tells Dreamweaver to make sure the document-relative links are correct when the template is saved to the Templates directory. If you plan on having all the linked objects, usually images, editable in the template, you do not need to worry about the path being correct for the linked objects.

By the Way

Template Files

Dreamweaver creates an individual file for each template. The file extension for templates is .dwt. In the Templates directory of your Web site, you will see one .dwt file for each template you have in your Web site.

Creating a Template from Scratch

To create a new, empty template and then add objects to it, follow these steps:

1. Click the New Template button at the bottom of the Templates category of the Assets panel. Dreamweaver creates a new blank template, as shown in Figure 24.3. A message appears in the top half of the Templates category of the Assets panel, telling you how to add content to the blank template.

— New template

FIGURE 24.3
A message appears in the Templates category after you create a new blank template. The message tells you how to add content to the new template.

2. Give the template a name. For example, create a template for displaying your CD or book collection and call it CD or book.

3. Double-click the template in the Templates category of the Assets panel. Dreamweaver opens the template in a separate Document window. You can tell that you have a template open because Dreamweaver displays <<Template>> along with the name of the template in the title bar, as shown in Figure 24.4.

4. Insert objects into the template's Document window just as you would with any Web page.

5. Close the Document window and save the template. Your changes will be reflected in the Templates category of the Assets panel. Don't worry right now about the message you receive about your template not having any editable regions. You'll add some editable regions in a few minutes.

Shows you are in a template

FIGURE 24.4
To add content to a template, you open it in a separate Dreamweaver Document window. The window shows <<Template>> in the title bar.

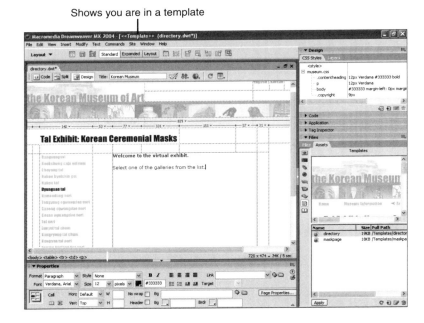

The Templates category of the Assets panel has a pop-up menu that contains useful commands (see Figure 24.5). Different commands are available, depending on what is currently selected.

FIGURE 24.5
The Templates category of the Assets panel context menu has a number of commands to apply, rename, edit, and delete templates.

Making an Existing Region Editable

Before you apply a template to a Web page, you need to mark regions of the template as **editable**. By default, all regions in the template are locked. Mark a region as editable if you will need to change, add, or update the content of this region in the pages you will create based on this template.

You should leave locked all regions that do not need to be changed. If you need to make changes to a locked region, you can change the original template file and update all the Web pages that are linked to that template. The commands for manipulating editable regions are located in the Templates submenu of the Modify menu, as shown in Figure 24.6.

FIGURE 24.6
The Templates submenu of Dreamweaver's Modify menu contains the commands needed to manipulate editable regions.

Placeholder Images

Use a placeholder image in your template to represent an image. You add a placeholder image to the page by selecting Insert, Image Objects, Image Placeholder.

Did you Know?

To make an existing region editable, follow these steps:

1. Open a template and select the region that needs to be editable.

2. Select Insert, Template Objects, Editable Region. The New Editable Region dialog box appears, as shown in Figure 24.7.

3. Give the region a meaningful name.

FIGURE 24.7
Name the new
editable region in
the New Editable
Region dialog box.

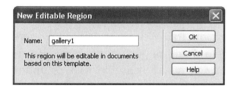

After you create an editable region, the name of the region is listed at the bottom of the Templates submenu of the Modify menu while you are working on the template. Select one of the region names in the menu to highlight that region in the Document window. Dreamweaver also automatically creates editable regions for the title of the document (called `doctitle`) and an empty region in the head of the document that is available for JavaScript code.

Dreamweaver gives you the ability to create editable regions on various objects in a template. For instance, you can make a layer editable. You can move the layer or change any of its properties after you apply the template to a Web page. Or you can leave the layer locked and create an editable region within the layer. Then you can't move the layer or change the layer properties when you've applied the template, but you can put content within the layer.

By the Way

Import XML into Templates

You can import or export the editable regions of a Dreamweaver template as XML. To do so, use the commands under the Import and Export submenus of the File menu. This is a useful way to automate importing objects, especially text, into templates. The difficult part of this is creating the XML files, files marked up with custom tags, in the first place. If you already have a source of XML files that need to go into Web pages, you should consider importing them into Dreamweaver templates.

Dreamweaver highlights editable regions so that they are easy to pick out in the Document window. The highlights are visible in Dreamweaver but not in the browser. To see highlights, select View, Invisible Elements. Set the highlight color in the Highlighting category in the Dreamweaver Preferences dialog box. The editable regions are highlighted only while you are editing the original template file. Just the opposite is true in a Web page with a template applied: The locked regions are highlighted.

Making a New Editable Region

You can create an optional editable region in a template. To do so, select Insert, Template Objects, Optional Region. Then name the new region in the New

PART VII

Appendixes

APPENDIX A Resources   **445**

APPENDIX B Glossary   **451**

APPENDIX A

Resources

You are in luck! You are learning about an information delivery medium—the World Wide Web—that contains a ton of information about itself. You as a Web developer will find many helpful Web sites on topics that interest you. You may even be inspired to create your own Web site to share your knowledge with others.

Web sites move and change quickly, so I apologize if some of these links are already out-of-date. Also, be aware that not all the information you get from the Web is accurate. It's a good idea to get information from trusted sources or to find sources to confirm the information that you find from unknown sources.

Dreamweaver Development

Macromedia's Dreamweaver MX 2004 Designer and Developer Center
www.macromedia.com/desdev/mx/dreamweaver

Macromedia's Dreamweaver Support Center
www.macromedia.com/support/dreamweaver

Dreamweaver Depot
www.andrewwooldridge.com/dreamweaver

Dreamweaver Resources
www.arrakis.es/%7Eandrewc/downloads/dream.htm

Dreamweaver FAQ
www.dwfaq.com

General Web Development

CNET Builder.com
www.builder.com

Webmonkey
hotwired.lycos.com/webmonkey

SiteExperts
www.siteexperts.com

Web Developer's Virtual Library
www.wdvl.com

World Wide Web Consortium (W3C)
www.w3.org

Netscape's DevEdge
devedge.netscape.com

Webreview.com—Cross Training for Web Teams
www.webreview.com

ProjectCool
www.devx.com/projectcool

The Spot for Web Site Builders
thespot.i-depth.com

Dynamic HTML (DHTML)

The Web Standards Project
www.webstandards.org/learn

Dynamic Drive
www.dynamicdrive.com

The Dynamic Duo—Cross Browser DHTML
www.dansteinman.com/dynduo

Dreamweaver Extensions

Macromedia Exchange
www.macromedia.com/exchange/dreamweaver

Massimo's Corner
www.massimocorner.com

Yaro's Yaromat
www.yaromat.com/dw

Rabi's Extensions
www.dreamweaver-extensions.com

Dreamweaver Extensions
www.cascade.org.uk/software/dreamweaver

Dreamweaver Supply Bin
home.att.net/%7EJCB.BEI/Dreamweaver

Scripting Resources: CGI, JavaScript, and Server-Side Scripting

CGI

Matt's Script Archive
www.scriptarchive.com

Free Stuff Center—Free Webmaster Tools
www.freestuffcenter.com/sub/webmastertop.html

JavaScript

JavaScript Tricks
home.thezone.net/~rbennett/utility/javahead.htm

Webmonkey JavaScript Code Library
hotwired.lycos.com/webmonkey/reference/javascript_code_library

Server-Side Scripting

ASP101—Resources for Web Professionals
www.asp101.com

PHP-Hypertext Preprocessor
www.php.net

CFAdvisor
www.cfadvisor.com

JSP Resource Index
www.jspin.com

Accessibility

Macromedia's Accessibility Center
www.macromedia.com/macromedia/accessibility

Bobby—Web Site Analyzer
bobby.watchfire.com/bobby/html/en

Anybrowser.org Accessible Site Design
www.anybrowser.org/campaign/abdesign.shtml

Usability

useit.com—Jakob Nielsen's Web site
www.useit.com

Microsoft Usability Research
www.microsoft.com/usability

Downloads

CNET Download.com
www.download.com

Chank Fonts
www.chank.com/freefonts.php

CoolGraphics—Free Cool Graphics
www.coolgraphics.com

Getty Images
creative.gettyimages.com

Browsers

Netscape Navigator
channels.netscape.com/ns/browsers

Microsoft Internet Explorer
www.microsoft.com/windows/ie

Opera
www.opera.com

Apple's Safari Browser
www.apple.com/safari

Organizations

HTML Writer's Guild
www.hwg.org

Macromedia User Groups
www.macromedia.com/support/programs/usergroups

Geek Cruises
www.geekcruises.com

can be embedded into Web pages and viewed in a browser with the Flash player.

Flash Button object   One of a number of buttons that are configurable in Dreamweaver and that are Flash .swf files. These buttons include the standard button states and can use various fonts. Many of the Flash buttons include animation.

Flash object   An object that places a Macromedia Flash movie at the insertion point.

Flash Text   One of a number of types of text that are configurable in Dreamweaver that are Flash .swf files. This text enables you to use various fonts in Dreamweaver without having those fonts available on the user's system.

font   A set of text characters in a specific style and size.

form   An object that enables the collection of information from Web site visitors via input elements such as text fields and radio buttons.

frame   One of multiple, separately controlled Web pages contained in a single Web browser window.

frameset   The Web page that defines the size, orientation, and source Web page for each of the individual frames it contains.

FTP (File Transfer Protocol)   An Internet protocol that is used to exchange files among computers over the Internet.

GIF   A standard Web graphic format that is good for line art that contains large blocks of the same color. This format also enables image animation and transparency.

Grayscale palette   A palette consisting of 256 tones of gray. It is not a Web-safe palette.

gripper   A dotted area in the upper-left corner of a panel group that enables you to drag the panel group in and out of its docked position.

H space   The horizontal space to the left and the right of an image, measured in pixels.

head   An element of a Web page that's not visible in the browser but that contains information and code (JavaScript, styles, meta tags, and so on).

header   The top row or left-most column, which describes the content of the column or row.

hexadecimal   A base-16 numbering system that is used to describe RGB values of colors. Hexadecimal numbers contain the numerals 0–9 and the letters A–F.

hidden field   A field that is not visible to the user and that contains information to be submitted with the other form elements.

HomeSite/Code-Style workspace
The workspace that approximates the HomeSite workspace and that shows the panel groups on the left with the Code view initially shown.

horizontal rule   A horizontal rule (line across the page).

hotspot   A region on an image map that has specific coordinates and contains a hyperlink.

.htm or .html file   An HTML file that is viewable in a Web browser.

HTML (Hypertext Markup Language)
A language that consists of paired and individual markup tags and is used to create Web pages.

Hyperlink object   An object that inserts a hyperlink, including the text and the link location.

image   A file that contains graphical information and is loaded into a Web page by a Web browser. The HTML tag for an image is the single <img> tag.

Image field   An image that acts as a submit button in a form.

image map   An image that has regions defined as hyperlinks. These regions can be circular, rectangular, or polygonal.

Image object   An object that places an image in a Web format at the insertion point.

Image Placeholder object   An image that inserts a placeholder for an image.

inline style   A style that is defined within the actual tag.

Insert bar   A Dreamweaver interface component that contains buttons for inserting objects into Web pages. The Insert bar contains all the same objects as the Insert menu.

insertion point   A blinking cursor that marks the location where new content will be inserted into a Web page.

Invisible Element   A visible representation in Dreamweaver of an object that is not visible in the Web page, such as forms and named anchors.

Java   A programming language developed by Sun Microsystems that can be used to program applications and create applets.

JavaScript   An interpreted scripting language originally developed by Netscape that is used to add scripted functionality to Web pages. Dreamweaver inserts JavaScript automatically by using behaviors. JavaScript is not related to the Java programming language.

JPEG (or JPG)   A standard Web graphic format that is good for photographs and images containing color gradients.

JSP (JavaServer Pages)   A scripting language that is embedded in Web pages and processed by servlets on the server. This technology can be used on a variety of Web servers.

jump menu   A drop-down menu within a form that enables viewers to navigate to multiple hyperlinks on the Web.

Justify Align   A setting that distributes the selected text across a container such as a Web page or a table cell.

keyword   A type of meta tag that contains keywords used by search engines to index the content on the page.

label   A text description that is added to a form element that contributes to an accessible Web page.

LAN (local area network)   A group of computers connected together to share data, applications, and other resources.

layer   A container that has positioning, visibility, and z-index attributes. Layers are elements of DHTML, and they are used in Dreamweaver timelines (animations). Most layers are created by using the HTML tags `<div>` and `</div>`.

layer object   An object that turns the cursor into a marquee tool to draw a layer onto the Document window.

Layout view   A view in Dreamweaver that enables you to draw cells and tables.

Layout View button   A button that enables you to display tables with selectable cells, with tables outlined in green and cells outlined in blue.

Left Align   A setting that aligns the selected text with the left margin of a container such as a Web page or a table cell.

Library   An Assets panel category that stores Web page objects, such as tables, images, or blocks of formatted text, to reuse throughout a Web site.

Line Numbers   A setting that is available in the View Options menu (in the Document toolbar) and by selecting View, Code View Options, Line Numbers while Dreamweaver is in Code view. This setting turns on line numbers to the left of the lines of code in Code view.

List/Menu object   An object that inserts a list or a drop-down menu into a form.

Live Data view   A view that is used in dynamic Web sites to display live data from a database in the Document window.

local site   The development computer on which Web site files are located.

loop   To repeat playing an audio clip or a movie file.

MacOS palette   A palette consisting of the 256 colors in the Macintosh OS palette. This is not a Web-safe palette.

meta tag   An HTML tag that encodes information about a Web page that is used to index the page in Internet search engines.

MIDI (musical instrument digital interface)   A compact sound format for recording and playing back music on digital synthesizers.

.mov file   A sound and movie file format that requires a player capable of playing QuickTime files.

.mp3 file   An audio file format that can create high-quality files that are small. It is a popular audio format on the Internet.

multimedia   A combination of multiple media, such as images, text, sounds, and video.

named anchor   An invisible element that is used to create hyperlinks within the same file.

Named Anchor object   An object that places a named anchor at the insertion point.

Navigation Bar object   An object that inserts a set of button images to be used for navigating throughout a Web site.

nested list   A list within another list.

nested table   A table within another table.

NoFrames content   HTML that is displayed when the viewer does not have a frames-capable browser.

Noscript   A command that inserts the <noscript> tags around HTML code that will be displayed by browsers that do not support scripts.

numbered list (or ordered list)   A list of items preceded by numbers or letters. The HTML tags for an ordered list are <ol> and </ol>.

palette   A set of colors that is available in Dreamweaver from the color picker.

panel group   A set of related panels that are grouped together.

PDF (Portable Document Format)   A file format for encoding printed documents with fonts and navigation elements. These files are created with Adobe Acrobat and are viewed through Acrobat Reader.

PHP (Hypertext Preprocessor)   A scripting language that is embedded in Web pages and processed by the server. This technology is freely available open source and can be used on a variety of Web servers.

player   A third-party program that is used to display nonstandard content in a Web browser.

Plugin object   An object that places any file requiring a browser plug-in at the insertion point.

plug-in   A type of player used in Netscape and other browsers to display nonstandard Web content.

PNG (portable network graphic)   A standard Web graphic format developed to replace the GIF format. Like the GIF format, the PNG format is good for line art containing large blocks of color and offers advanced transparency options.

pop-up message   A JavaScript alert message created by the Popup Message behavior in Dreamweaver.

Property inspector   A panel that enables you to set properties for the selected object. The Property inspector presents the properties of whatever object is currently selected.

protocol   A method of transferring information over the Internet. Examples are HTTP for Web pages and FTP for file transfer.

Quick Tag Editor   An editor that enables you to edit the content of a single tag.

QuickTime Player   A player created by Apple for viewing QuickTime sounds and movies along with many other formats.

radio button   A circular button inserted as a group into a form.

radio button group   A group of radio buttons that acts as a mutually exclusive group, enabling only one button in the group to be selected at one time.

RDS (Remote Directory Services)   A method of exchanging files on a ColdFusion server with a local site.

RealMedia   Multimedia content encoded with one of the methods available from RealNetworks and played with a RealPlayer application.

remote site   The Web site located on a remote computer, usually a Web server or staging area where groups can share project files.

Right Align   A setting that aligns the selected text with the right margin of a container such as a Web page or a table cell.

rollover   An image effect in which one image is swapped with another image when the cursor rolls over it.

Rollover Image object   An object that contains two images. One is the regular image and the other is the image that appears when the user puts his or her cursor over the image.

row   A horizontal group of cells in a table.

screen resolution   The number of pixels displayed on the horizontal and vertical axes of a monitor screen. Common screen resolutions are 800×600 and 1024×768.

script   A block of coded instructions.

server-side image map   An image map in which the code is located on the server. The Web page makes contact with the server to resolve the hyperlink. In Dreamweaver-generated client-side image maps, the map instructions are located within the Web page.

servlet   A small program that runs on the server and processes script commands.

`.shtml` **file**   A file that contains a server-side include.

Shockwave   Specially prepared Macromedia Director movies that play in Web pages by using the Shockwave player.

Shockwave object   An object that places a Shockwave movie at the insertion point.

site definition   The description of the configuration, directory structure, and preferences for a particular Web site.

Site Definition Wizard   A Dreamweaver wizard that guides you through the naming and configuration of a site definition.

site root-relative path   A path to a file that is relative to the root of a Web site. This type of path works only on a Web server that is configured properly. Only experienced Web developers should use this type of path.

snippet   Stored content that can easily be inserted into Web pages. Snippets are stored and accessed from the Snippets panel in Dreamweaver and are a handy place to store chunks of code that are used often.

SSI (server-side include)   A variable that is inserted into a Web page and processed by a Web server. A common use of an SSI is to load a header or footer from a separate file into the page at request time.

Standard view   The view in Dreamweaver in which tables are displayed as grids and cannot be drawn.

Standard View button   A button that displays tables as grids of cells.

status bar   The bar at the bottom of the Dreamweaver window that contains the tag selector, the window size drop-down menu, and the document size.

`.swf` **file**   A Flash file that is viewable in the Flash player. A `.swf` file cannot be edited in Flash.

table   A data structure that is made up of rows and cells and is used to organize information or a page layout.

Table object   An object that creates a table at the insertion point.

Tabular Data object   An object that creates a table at the insertion point and that is populated with data from a chosen file.

tag   An HTML element descriptor that is either a single tag or a pair of tags surrounding content. HTML tags are contained in angle brackets (for example, `<table>` and `</table>`).

tag selector   An element in the Dreamweaver interface, located in the status bar, that presents the hierarchy of tags, enabling you to select a tag and its contents.

template   A special type of Web page that is used in Dreamweaver to create locked regions. Templates enable you to control the layout of content and are designed to ensure consistency and ease of updating multiple Web pages at a time.

text field   A single-line form field for collecting text.

title   The name of a Web page that appears in the title bar of the browser and is saved as a favorite or bookmark. The HTML tags for title are <title> and </title>.

title bar   The bar at the top of the window that contains the filename and other window controls.

URL (uniform resource locator)   The address of a file that is accessible on the Internet.

V space   The vertical space on the top and bottom of an image, measured in pixels.

VB (Visual Basic)   A programming environment from Microsoft that is used to create code written in BASIC.

VBScript   An interpreted scripting language that is a subset of Microsoft's Visual Basic language. VBScript is commonly used when scripting ASP code.

visibility   An attribute of layers that enables the content of a layer to be either visible or hidden on the Web page.

Visual Basic .NET   The next generation of Visual Basic, used to write Windows applications, ASP.NET Web applications, and ASP.NET Web services. The primary alternative .NET language to Visual Basic .NET is C#.

VSS (Visual SourceSafe)   A version-control program from Microsoft that is used to share files in a group.

WebDAV   A standard version-control system that is used to exchange files over the Internet.

Web-safe palette   A group of 212 colors that can be displayed in both Internet Explorer and Netscape on both Windows and the Macintosh machines running in 256-color mode (8-bit color).

Windows Media Player   A player created by Microsoft to view many different formats of audio and sound files.

Windows OS palette   A palette that consists of the 256 colors in the Windows palette. This is not a Web-safe palette.

Word Wrap   A setting that is available in the View Options menu (on the toolbar) and in the Code View Options submenu of the View menu when in Code view. This setting wraps the lines of HTML code in Code view.

workspace   The Dreamweaver user interface. In Dreamweaver MX 2004 for Windows there are two workspace choices: an integrated interface and a floating interface. The workspace on the Mac uses the floating interface.

WYSIWYG (what you see is what you get)   A graphical interface that presents a Web page that is very close to what will appear in the Web browser. Pronounced "wiz-ee-wig."

XHTML (Extensible Hypertext Markup Language)   A more structured version of HTML that applies the strict syntax rules of XML to HTML. XHTML supports user-created tags for storing and structuring data within Web pages.

XML (Extensible Markup Language)   A structured, tag-based language for describing data. XML describes data but not the way the data is to be displayed.

z-index   An attribute of layers that enables the content of a layer to be stacked above objects with z-index attributes lower in value.

Index

Symbols

@referers variable, 352
(/) forward slash, 84
$mailprog variable, 352

A

absolute paths, 80, 84
accessibility resources, 448
Acrobat Reader (Adobe), 171
Acrobat Reader Web site, 171
Action attribute, 326
actions, 290
ActionScript (Macromedia), 165
activating
    Autostretch, 223
    Layout mode, 220
    software, 9
ActiveX controls, 164
Add Separator button, 407
Add to Favorites button, 193
adding
    advanced attributes to Drag
    Layer behavior, 315
    assets to Assets panel,
    192
    behaviors
        Set Text of Status Bar
        behavior, 304
        Show-Hide Layers
        behavior, 296

check boxes to forms,
    332-333
circular hotspot to image
    maps, 154-155
color to tables, 227
    background images,
    227-228
columns/rows in tables,
    210-211
contents to tables, 208
design notes to Web pages,
    391-393
effects to rollover images
    (Fireworks), 142-144
    slices, 144-147
files to Files panel, 70
header cells to tables, 206
hidden fields to forms,
    352-354
hyperlinks within Web sites,
    85-86
images to Web pages,
    117-118
    properties display,
    118-119
irregular hotspot to image
    maps, 155
Java applets to Web pages,
    179-180
JavaScript to Drag Layer
    dialog box, 315, 317
keyboard shortcuts,
    402-403
layout cells to Web pages,
    220-222

layout tables to Web pages,
    220-222
library items to Web pages,
    421-423
links to
    graphics, image maps,
    151-152
    PDF files, 171
lists to forms, 333
menus to forms, 333
objects to favorites
    category, 406-407
polygon hotspot to image
    maps, 155-156
Popup Message behavior to
    objects, 302
radio buttons to forms,
    331-332
rectangle hotspot to image
    maps, 153-154
sound files to Web pages,
    172
tables to Web pages, 202
    table headers, 203
text fields to forms,
    326-328
text to images, 122-123
    Fireworks, 137-138
Adobe Acrobat Reader (Acrobat
Reader), 171
advanced CSS styles, creating,
282
Advanced tab (Drag Layer dialog box), 314-315

Advanced tab (Site Definition dialog box), 62
  editing site definitions, 72-73
  remote sites, 371
advantages
  CSS, 271
  frames, 236
Align drop-down menu (Property inspector), 120-122
aligning
  cells in tables, 226-227
  hotspots, 156-157
  images, 120-122
  layers, grid commands, 265
All Info tab, 391
alt (alternative) text, 122-123
Alt drop-down menu (Property inspector), 122-123
anchors, named, 88
  creating long pages, 88-89
  invisible elements, 89
  linking to, 90
antialiasing, 137
Applet object, 180
applets (Java)
  adding to Web pages, 179-180
  browsers, 179
  snow, 180
Apply button, 193, 431
ASP (Microsoft), 357
ASP Script icon, 358
ASP.NET (Microsoft), 357
assets, 185-186
  Assets panel, 192
  copying to other sites in Assets panel, 193
  copying to sites, 196
  favorites list
    creating in Assets panel, 193
    removing assets from, 194

  links, 189
    naming, 190
  listing in sites, 186
  locating in Assets panel, 188, 193
  new, creating in Assets panel, 194
  previewing in categories, 188
  viewing in categories, 187
Assets panel, 185
  assets
    adding to Web pages, 192
    applying color to text, 192
    copying to sites, 193, 196
    creating new, 194
    favorites list, 193-194
    listing in sites, 186
    locating, 188, 193
    previewing, 188
    viewing in sites, 187
  categories, 186
  Colors category, 189
  Images category, 188
  Library category, 415-416
    buttons, 417
  Library panel, 186-187
    favorites, 194
  Movies category, 190
  Scripts category, 190-191
    external script files, 190
  Templates category, 429-431
    buttons, 431
  Templates panel, 186-187
    favorites, 194
  URLs category, 189
    naming URLs, 190

Attach to Style Sheet button, 286
attaching behaviors to objects, 294-295
attributes, 98. *See also* **properties**
  Action, 326
  Drag Layer behavior, 312
  Drag Layer dialog box
    adding attributes to behaviors, 315
    Advanced tab, 314-315
  Edit Tag mode (Quick Tag Editor), 105-106
  Form Name, 325
  frames, 244-245
  framesets, 244-245
  layers, 258
  Method, 326
  Open Browser Window behavior, 300-301
  pluginspace, 165
  text fields, applying to forms, 328-330
  title, 248
  Wrap Tag mode (Quick Tag Editor), 106
Authorware (Macromedia), 165
Autostretch, 222
  activating, 223
  setting spacer images in tables, 224
  stretching cells in tables, 222-224
Autostretch command, 223

B

Background category (CSS Style Definition dialog box), 276

backgrounds
color, adding to tables, 227-228
images, Web pages, 54-58
layers, 263-264
bandwidth, 163
Basic tab (Clean Up Word HTML dialog box), 111-112
Basic tab (Site Definition dialog box), 62
Site Definition Wizard, 62-64
behaviors, 289
actions, 290
Call JavaScript, 316
Drag Layer, 309
constraining layer movement, 311-312
dragging layers onto target layers, 310
Layer attribute, 312
target locations, 312-314
triggering with events, 317
events, 290
browser events, 290-291, 295
displaying, 299
Jump Menu, 340
Jump Menu Go, 340
objects, attaching, 294-295
Open Browser Window, 300
browser attributes, 300-301
inserting images, 301-302
overview, 290
Popup Message
adding to objects, 302
changing behavior order, 303-304

Set Text of Status Bar, adding behaviors to, 304
Show-Hide Layers behaviors
adding behaviors, 296
creating behaviors, 297-299
templates, editing, 440
types, 291-294
Validate Form, 346-348
Behaviors panel, 295
benefits
CSS, 271
frames, 236
_blank reserved target name, 158
Block category (CSS Style Definition dialog box), 276-279
<blockquote> tag, 50
body, Web pages, 99
<body> tag, 310
Border category (CSS Style Definition dialog box), 277
borders
frame, setting, 246-247
setting colors in tables, 211
Box category (CSS Style Definition dialog box), 277
break (<br>) tag, 43
broadband connection, 163
broken links, 390
browser events, 290
support, 295
types, 290-291
browser resources, 448
browser resources, 448
browser-safe palette, 46
browsers
frames, 247-248
Java applets, 179

previewing Web pages, 56
TTS, 122
Web page previews, 303-304
windows, opening, 300
browser attributes, 300-301
images, 301-302

C

caches, Web sites, 67
Call JavaScript behavior, 316
cameras, digital, 133
Cascading Style Sheets. See CSS
categories
assets
previewing, 188
viewing, 187
Assets panel, 186-191
CSS Style Definition dialog box, 275
Background category, 276
Block category, 276-279
Border category, 277
Box category, 277
Extensions category, 278
List category, 277
Positioning category, 277-278
Type category, 275-276, 279
Tracing Image (Properties dialog box), 229
Category button, 187

cell padding, setting, 206

cell spacing, setting, 206

cells

    aligning in tables, 226

        horizontally, 226-227

        vertically, 226

    Autostretch, stretching in tables, 222-224

    layout, adding to Web pages, 220-222

    merging in tables, 225-226

    splitting in tables, 225-226

centering text into Web pages, 42

certificates (server), 355

CFML (Macromedia), 357

CGI resources, 447

CGI script (Common Gateway Interface script), 350-351

Change button, 402

Change Link Sitewide dialog box, 390

check boxes, adding to forms, 332-333

Check In command, 378

Check In/Check Out tools, 374-378

Check Out command, 377

Choose Spacer Image dialog box, 223

Circular Hotspot tool, adding to image maps, 154-155

classes, 272-274

Clean Up Word HTML dialog box, 111-112

Clear History command, 405

Click the Site Map button, 387

client-side image maps, 152

client-side scripts, processing form data, 345

cloaking feature, 432

Close Panel Group command, 391

code

    HTML

        preferences, 106

        Word documents, 111

    snippets, creating, 400

Code Coloring category (Preferences dialog box), 106-107

Code Format category (Preferences dialog box), 106-109

Code Hints category (Preferences dialog box), 106

    setting, 109

Code Hints dialog box, 109

Code inspector, launching, 101

Code Rewriting category (Preferences dialog box), 106

    setting, 110

Code view (Document window), 97

    displaying, 100

    floating panels, 98

    View Options menu, 101

        displaying code, 101-102

Code View button, 98

Collapse button, 33

collapsing

    Files panel, 387

    inspectors, 33

    panel groups, 33

color

    adding to tables, 227-228

    customizing, 55

    layer backgrounds, 263-264

    library items, 423

    setting border colors in tables, 211

    tags, changing, 107

color picker, 45-47

Colors category (Assets panel), 189

columns, 210-211

Commands menu, 15

Common Gateway Interface (CGI), 350-351, 447

comparing

    Behaviors panel and Server Behaviors panel, 295

    Java and JavaScript, 179

    library items and templates, 416, 430

Connect/Disconnect button, 373

connections

    broadband, 163

    server, enabling, 365

Context menu, 36

controls

    ActiveX, 164

    playback, plug-ins, 173

    sizing, Plug-in object, 175-176

Convert Tables to Layers command, 231

Convert Tables to Layers dialog box, 231

converting tables into groups of layers, 231

copying

    assets (Assets panel) to sites, 196

    assets to other sites in Assets panel, 193

    images to Web pages, 118

    text into Web pages from files, 50-51

crawling (search engines), 168

creating

    behaviors, Show-Hide Layers behavior, 297-299

    buttons in forms, 336

CSS styles, advanced, 282

external style sheets, 283-284

favorite assets list in Assets panel, 193

Flash buttons, 169-171

Flash text, 167

forms, 323

Form object, 324-325

form properties, 325-326

framesets, 236-238

home pages, 82

image maps, 152-153

image rollovers, 126-127

images (Fireworks), 135-136

jump menus, 338-340

layers, 259-261

library items, 415

from existing objects, 417

from scratch, 417-418

Library directory, 416

linked images, 123

lists, 48-50

lists in forms, 333-335

long pages with named anchors, 88-89

mailto links, 92-93

menus in forms, 335-336

navigation bar, 159-161

nested layers, 267

new assets (Assets panel), 194

new files in Files panel, 70

radio buttons, 331-332

rollover images, 142

site maps, 387-389

slices, 146-147

snippets

code, 400

custom, 398-400

style classes, 272-274

tables for data, 201

templates, 429

from existing Web pages, 431-432

from scratch, 431-434

new editable regions, 436-438

Templates category (Assets panel), 430-431

Web pages

from templates, 438-439

new, 41

CSS (Cascading Style Sheets), 47. *See also* **styles**

advantages, 271

creating advanced styles, 282

HTML tags, 278-280

library items, applying styles, 425

overview, 271

templates, editing styles, 440

CSS Style Definition dialog box, 273, 281

categories, 275-279

CSS Styles panel, 280

classes, 272

Customize Favorite Objects dialog box, 406

Customize Favorites command, 406

customizing

colors, 55

Dreamweaver, 397

snippets, 398-400

D

.dcr file extensions, 165

data

exporting from tables, 213-214

forms

CGI script, 350-351

FormMail script, 351-352

parsing, 349

processing, 345

validating, 346-348

importing from tables, 214-215

sorting in tables, 208-210

tables, creating for, 201

databases (SourceSafe), connecting, 370

Date icon, 391

default pages, 82

defining

remote sites, 366-367

Web sites, 62-64

Delete button, 431

Delete Library Item button, 417

deleting

files, 386

forms, 338

delimiter, 213-214

deprecated, 47

design notes, adding to Web pages, 391, 393

Design Notes command, 391

Design Notes dialog box, 391

Design view (Document window), 97-100

Design Views button, 100

Designer workspace, 10-11

Detach from Original button, 422

Detailed tab (Clean Up Word HTML dialog box), **111**

development sites, 64-67

DHTML (Dynamic HTML), **257**
  CSS, 272
  overview, 257-258
  resources, 446

digital camera images, **133**

directories
  creating in Files panel, 70
  development files, 65
  Library, 416
  organizing structures of, 73-75
  parent, 84
  Templates, 429
    cloaking feature, 432

disadvantages, frames, **236**

displaying. *See also* viewing
  code (Code view), 101-102
  Code view (Document window), 100
  Design view (Document window), 100
  Document toolbar, 30
  events, 299
  Insert bar, 17
  PDF files, 171
  Web page image properties, 118-119

<div> tag, **258**

Document toolbar, **29-30**

document type declaration, **98**

Document window, **11**
  Code view, 97
    displaying, 100
    floating panels, 98
    View Options menu, 101-102
  Design view, 97-100
  Document toolbar, 28-29

Macintosh workspace, 11
  panels, 11
  Status bar, 30-32

Document window (Fireworks), Quick Export drop-down menu, **146**

document-relative paths, **80-82**
  linking files, 83-84
  URLs, 83

domains, URLs, **80**

downloading
  FormMail script, 351-352
  scripts from Web, 350
  templates from Web, 430

downloads resources, **448**

Drag Layer behavior, **309**
  constraining layer movement, 311-312
  dragging layers onto target layers, 310
  target locations, 312
    Get Current Position button, 313-314
  triggering with events, 317

Drag Layer dialog box, **311**
  advanced attributes
    adding JavaScript to, 315-317
    adding to behaviors, 315
    Advanced tab, 314-315

dragging
  layers onto target layers, 310
  library items from Library category (Assets panel), 421
    highlighted colors, 423

Draw Layout Cell button, **220-222**

Draw Layout Cell command, **220**

Draw Layout Table tool, **228**

Dreamweaver
  customizing, 397
  importing Fireworks files into, 147
  overview, 7-8

Dreamweaver development resources, **445**

Dreamweaver extensions resources, **446-447**

drop-down menus, Document toolbar, 29

Duplicate Set button, **401**

Dynamic HTML. *See* DHTML

dynamic Web pages, **8**

dynamic Web sites, specifying, 64

E

Edit button, 72, 359, 417, 431

Edit button (Fireworks), **147**

Edit button (Flash), **169**

Edit Coloring Scheme button, 107

Edit Contents dialog box, **359**

Edit menu, **13**

Edit Sites command, **67**

Edit Style button, **285**

Edit Tag Code command, **103**

Edit Tag mode (Quick Tag Editor), **104**-106

editing
  Flash buttons, 171
  images, commands, 125-126
  jump menus, 340
  keyboard shortcuts, 401-402
  library items, 423-424

linked images, 124-125
server-side scripting languages, 359
site definitions, 72-73
styles, 285-286
tables in Standard mode, 225
tags, 102
template behaviors, 440
template styles, 440
templates, from existing regions, 435-436
Web sites, 383
Editing Files section (Site Definition Wizard), 64
effects, adding to rollover images (Fireworks), 142-144
slices, 144-147
Effects menu, Property inspector (Fireworks), 143
elements
Form Delimiter, 323
forms, required, 348
invisible, 89
navigational, frames, 236
Web pages, 185. See also assets
email, sending to Web pages, 92
Email Link dialog box, 92
email links, 93
<embed> tag, 166
embedded player, 176
enabling Check In/Check Out tools, 375-378
entering text into Web pages, 42
events, 290
browser events, 290
support, 295
types, 290-291

displaying, 299
Drag Layer behavior, triggering, 317
OnClick, 299
onLoad, 310
OnMouseOver(), 290
OnMouseUp, 299
Expand/Collapse button, 373, 387
Expanded Files panel, 69
Expanded Tables mode, 222
expanding
File panel, 387
inspectors, 33
panel groups, 33
Property inspector, 35
Export button, 214
Export command, 379
Export dialog box, 144
Export Preview dialog box, 134
Export Table dialog box, 213
exporting
data from tables, 213-214
rollover images (Fireworks), 144
Extension Manager, installing third-party extensions, 408-410
extensions, 408
.dcr file, 165
.swf file, 165
files
.lck, 376
library items, 418
templates, 432
Flash movies, 165
Flash movies .dcr file extension, 165
third-party, installing, 408-410
extensions (behaviors), 291

Extensions category (CSS Style Definition dialog box), 278
external links, 390
external script files (Assets panel), 190-191
external style sheets, creating, 283-284
eye icon column header, 267

F

favorite assets list (Assets panel), 193-194
Favorites button, 194
Favorites category (Insert bar), adding objects, 406-407
fields
file fields, 356
hidden, adding to forms, 352-354
file extensions, .lck, 376
file fields, 356
File menu, 13
File Types/Editors category (Preferences dialog box), 124-125
filenames, 53
URLs, 81
files
adding to Files panel, 70
creating in Files panel, 70
deleting, 386
development files, sharing, 66
development sites
directory locations, 65
storing, 64
external script files (Assets panel), 190-191

Fireworks, importing into Dreamweaver, 147
library items, 418
link capabilities, 83
linking document-relative paths, 83-84
multimedia, 163-165
naming, 65, 72
    case-sensitive servers, 66
organizing directory structure, 73-75
PDF, 171
sound, 172-174
sound file formats, 174-175
synchronizing on Web sites, 384-387
templates, 432
transferring to remote sites, 376
    dependent files, 378
uploading from forms, 355-356
Files panel, 62, 68
adding files to, 70
buttons, 372-373
collapsing, 387
creating new files, 70
Expand/Collapse button, 69
expanding, 387
naming files, 72
fill settings, Property inspector (Fireworks), 140
Find All button, 410
Find and Replace command, 410
Find and Replace dialog box, conducting searches, 410-411

Find button, 410
firewalls, FTP servers, 368
Fireworks, 131
images
    adding shape to, 139-141
    adding text to, 137-138
    creating, 135-136
    optimizing, 133-135
importing files into Dreamweaver, 147
interfaces, 132
Photoshop plug-ins, 143
Preferences dialog box, 143
rollover images
    adding effects, 142-144
    creating, 142
    exporting, 144
    slices, 144-147
Slice tool, 144
Text tool, 137-138
Flash, 165
ActionScript, 165
buttons
    creating, 169-171
    editing, 171
search engines, 168
text, creating, 167
Flash movies, 165-166
Flash Text object, 167-169
floating panels, Code view, 98
Font drop-down menu (Property inspector), 44
<font> tag, 47
fonts, selecting, 44-45
Fonts category (Preferences dialog box), 99
form data
processing
    CGI script, 350-351
    client-side scripts, 345

FormMail script, 351-352
parsed data, 349
validating, 346
    Validate Form behavior, 346-348
Form Delimiter invisible element, 323
form elements, required, 348
Form Name attribute, 325
Form object (Forms category), 324-325
form properties, creating forms, 325-326
<form>tag, 326
form-hosting sites, 350
Format drop-down menu (Property inspector), 43
Format Table command, 212
Format Table dialog box, 212
formats
multimedia, 164
preset in tables, 212-213
sound files, 174-175
formatting text, 43
FormMail script, 351-352
FormMail Web site, 350
forms
buttons, adding/adding to, 336-338
check boxes, adding to, 332-333
creating, 323
    Form object, 324-325
    form properties, 325-326
deleting, 338
files, uploading from, 355
file fields, 356
hidden fields, adding to, 352-354
lists, adding to, 333-335

menus, adding to, 333-336

radio buttons, adding to, 331-332

text fields, 326

applying attributes, 328-330

collecting user information, 326-328

Forms category (Insert toolbar), 324

forward slash (/), 84

frame borders

removing, 238

setting, 246-247

viewing, 238

Frame Borders command, 239

frame sizes, setting, 247

frames, 235. *See also* **frame-**
sets

advantages, 236

attributes, 244-245

browsers, 247

NoFrames Content, 247-248

disadvantages, 236

frame borders, removing, 238

framesets, 236-238

loading Web pages into, 243

Go to URL behavior, 251-252

targeted linked pages, 249-251

naming, 239-242

navigational elements, 236

nesting, 242-243

nesting framesets into, 244

selecting, Frames panel, 241-242

splitting, 239-240

splitting pages into, 238

frames objects, 248-249

Frames panel, 241-243

framesets. *See also* **frames**

attributes, 244-245

creating, 236-238

nesting frames into, 244

Framesets category (New
Document dialog box), 248

Freescripts Web site, 350

FTP access, remote sites, 367-
368

G

generic button, 336-338

Get button, 373

Get command, 377

Get Current Position button, 313-314

GET method, 351

GIF format, 124

Go to URL behavior, 251-252

Go to URL dialog box, 251

graphics, adding links to image
maps, 151-152

grid commands, aligning layers, 265

Grid Settings dialog box, 265

guides, 137

H

<h3> tag, 278

H (Horizontal) space, 122

Flash movies, 166

hardware requirements, 9

head (Web pages), 99

header cells, adding to tables, 207

headers, tables, 203

heading properties, Web pages, 55

Help icon (Property inspector), 38

Help menu, 15, 37

hidden fields, adding to forms, 352-354

hiding

guides, 137

layers, 296

highlighted tags, 102

History panel, 404-406

home pages, 82

HomeSite/Coder-Style work-
space, 10-11

horizontal rule, 51

Horizontal Space (H Space), 122, 166

horizontally aligning table cells, 226-227

Horz drop-down menu, 226-227

hotspot tools, image maps, 152-156

hotspots, 151-152

aligning, 156-157

HTML (Hypertext Markup
Language), 7

code preferences, 106

paired tags, 8

Roundtrip HTML, 8

HTML code, Word documents, 111

HTML pages, 98

HTML tags, 278-280

hyperlinks, 79. *See also* **links**

adding within Web sites, 85-86

targeting, 250

Hypertext Markup Language.
See HTML

I

icons
- ASP Script, 358
- Date, 391
- Help (Property inspector), 38
- Lock, 354
- Point-to-File, 91, 123
- Quick Tag Editor, 103

image button, 336-337

Image command, 118

image editing commands, 125-126

image files, transferring, 378

image formats, 124

image maps, 151-152
- client-side, 152
- creating, 152-153
- hotspot tools, 152-156

Image Size dialog box, 133

images, 117
- adding text to, 122-123
- adding to Web pages, 117-118
  - properties display, 118-119
- aligning, 120-122
- copying to Web pages, 118
- digital cameras, 133
- Fireworks
  - adding shape to, 139-141
  - adding text to, 137-138
  - creating, 135-136
  - optimizing, 133-135
- JPEG format, 135
- layer backgrounds, 264
- linked, 123-125
- naming, 119

Open Browser Window behavior, 301-302
- optimizing, 124
- placeholder, templates, 435
- rollover, 126
  - creating, 126-127
  - creating navigation bar, 159-160
- rollover (Fireworks)
  - adding effects, 142-144
  - creating, 142
  - exporting, 144
  - slices, 144-147
- sizing, 119
- spacer, setting, 224-225
- tracing, 229-231
- WYSIWYG, 117

Images category (Assets panel), 188

Import command, 379

importing
- data from tables, 214-215
- Fireworks files into Dreamweaver, 147
- Web sites, 378-379
- XML into templates, 436

Indent button, 50

indenting text, 48-50

inline player, 176

Insert bar, 16
- displaying, 17
- drop-down menu, 16-17
- Favorites category, adding objects, 406-407
- objects, 17
  - Common category, 18-20
  - Forms category, 22-23
  - HTML category, 26-28
  - Layout category, 20-22
  - Text category, 24-26

Insert button, 192, 417

Insert Fireworks HTML dialog box, 147

Insert Flash Button dialog box, 169

Insert Flash Button object, 169

Insert Flash Text dialog box, 167

Insert HTML mode (Quick Tag Editor), 104

Insert Jump Menu dialog box, 339

Insert menu, 14-16

Insert Navigation Bar dialog box, 159

Insert Rollover Image dialog box, 127

Insert Table dialog box, 206

Insert Tabular Data dialog box, 215

Insert toolbar
- Forms category, 324
- Textarea object, 329-330

inserting Plug-in object, 172-174

inspectors, 32-33

installing
- ActiveX controls, 164
- software, 8
- third-party extensions, 408-410

interfaces (Fireworks), 132

invalid tags, 102

invisible elements, 89
- Form Delimiter, 323

Invisible Elements category (Preferences dialog box), 323

irregular hotspot, adding to image maps, 155

J

Java, compared to JavaScript, 179

Java applets, 179-180

JavaScript
adding to Drag Layer dialog box, 315-317
compared to Java, 179

JavaScript resources, 447

JavaServer Pages (JSP), 357

JPEG format, 124
images, 135

JSP (JavaServer Pages), 357

Jump Menu behavior, 340

Jump Menu command, 340

Jump Menu Go behavior, 340

Jump Menu object, 338

jump menus, 338-340

K-L

keyboard shortcuts, 401-403

Keyboard Shortcuts dialog box, 401-403

.lck file extension, 376

LAN access, remote sites, 368

languages, server-side scripting, 357-359

launching
Code inspector, 101
Quick Tag Editor, 103

layer fix (Netscape), 261

layers, 231, 257
aligning, grid commands, 265
attributes, 258
backgrounds, 263-264
converting tables into groups of, 231

creating, 259-261
eye icon column header, 267
hiding, 296
moving, 262-263
style definitions, 281-282
naming, 261, 297-299
nesting, 267-268
overview, 258
properties, 263
showing, 296
stacking order, 264
target
dragging layers onto, 310
Get Current Position button, 312-314
Transport layer (TCP/IP protocol system)
ports, 10, 175, 291-294
visibility settings, 266-267

Layers category (Preferences dialog box), 260-261

Layers panel, 231

layout, page, 219

layout cells, adding to Web pages, 220-222

Layout mode, 220-224

Layout Mode button, 220-221

Layout Table button, 220

layout tables, adding to Web pages, 220-222

Library category (Assets panel), 415-417

Library directory, 416

library items, 415
adding to Web pages, 421
highlighted colors, 423
buttons, 422

creating, 415
from existing objects, 417
from scratch, 417-418
Library directory, 416
CSS styles, applying to, 425
editing, 423-424
file extensions, 418
sharing on servers, 422
templates, comparing, 416, 430
updating, 424

Library panel (Assets panel), 186-187
favorites, 194

link assets, 189-190

Link Checker, 390-391

Link property (Property inspector), 123

linked images, 123-125

linked Web pages, 249-251

linking
external script files, 191
files, document-relative paths, 83-84
named anchors, 90

links. See also hyperlinks; URLs
adding to graphics, image maps, 151-152
adding to PDF files, 171
broken, 390
creating navigation bar, 159-160
email links, 93
external, 390
file capabilities, 83
mailto links, 92-93
orphaned, 390
updating, 389-390

Links category (Page Preferences dialog box), 87

List category (CSS Style
  Definition dialog box), 277
List Item button, 49
List Values button, 335
List Values dialog box, 335
List/Menu object, 333
lists
    adding to forms, 333
    creating, 48-50, 333-335
    ordered, 48
    unordered, 48
loading
    tracing images, 229-230
    Web pages into frames,
      243
        Go to URL behavior,
          251-252
        targeted linked pages,
          249-251
Local Files pane (Expanded
  Files panel), 69
local Web sites, synchronizing
  files, 384-387
locating assets in Assets panel,
  188, 193
Lock icon, 354
login, 368

M

Macintosh workspace, 11
Macromedia Authorware, 165
Macromedia CFML, 357
Macromedia Director, 165
Macromedia Dreamweaver
  Exchange Web site, 408
Macromedia Exchange Web
  site, 397
Macromedia Extension
  Manager, 408

Macromedia Fireworks. See
  Fireworks
Macromedia Fireworks Web
  site, 131
Macromedia Flash. See Flash
Macromedia Web site, 10, 430
mailto links, 92-93
Manage Sites dialog box, 62,
  68
maps, site, 387-389
margins, Web pages, 55
Menu bar, 13-15
menu commands, 403-404
Merge button, 225
Merge Cells command, 225
merging cells in tables,
  225-226
Method attribute, 326
methods, 351
Microsoft ASP, 357-358
Microsoft ASP.NET, 357
Microsoft Web site, 357
Microsoft Word, 111-112
MIDI sound files, 174
Missing Alt Text report, 123
MM_swapImage() function, 290
<mmtemplate: if> tag, 437
modes, Quick Tag Editor, 104
Modify menu, 14
Movie category (Assets panel),
  190
movies, Flash, 165-166
moving
    layers, 262-263
        style definitions,
          281-282
    sites onto remote servers,
      372
        Files panel buttons,
          372-373
MP3 sound files, 174
multi-line text fields, 329

multimedia files, 163-165
multimedia formats, 164

N

name-value pairs, 349
Named Anchor dialog box, 89
named anchors, 88-90
names, target, 158
naming
    classes, 273
    directory files, 65-66
    files, 72
    frames, 239-242
    images, 119
    layers, 261, 297-299
    objects, 354
    URLs in Assets panel, 190
    Web sites, 62
        Site Definition Wizard,
          64
navigation bar, creating,
  159-161
navigational elements, frames,
  236
nesting
    frames, 242-243
    framesets into frames, 244
    layers, 267-268
    tables within tables, 228
Netscape layer fix, 261
Netscape Navigator Web site,
  56
new assets (Assets panel), creating, 194
New CSS Style button, 272
New CSS Style dialog box, 273
    Tag drop-down menu, 279
New Document dialog box, 41,
  85, 136
    Framesets category, 248

New Editable Region dialog
  box, 435
New Extension button, 408
New Favorite Folder button,
  194
New File command, 70
New Folder command, 70
New Library Item button,
  417-418
New Library Item command,
  419
New Optional Region dialog
  box, 436
New Snippet button, 399
New Snippet command, 400
New Snippet Folder button, 398
New Template button, 431-433
NoFrames Content command,
  247-248
none button (generic button),
  336-338

O

<object> tag, 166
objects
  adding to Favorites
    category, 406-407
  Applet, 180
  behaviors, attaching,
    294-295
  Flash Text, 167
    inserting into Web
      pages, 167-169
  frames, 248-249
  Insert bar, 17
    Common category,
      18-20
    Forms category, 22-23

HTML category, 26-28
Layout category, 20-22
Text category, 24-26
Insert Flash Button, 169
Jump Menu, 338
library items, creating from,
  415
List/Menu, 333
naming, 354
Plug-in
  inserting, 172-174
  sizing controls, 175-176
Popup Message behavior,
  adding to, 302
Textarea (Insert toolbar),
  329-330
onClick event, 299
onLoad event, 310
onMouseOver event, 290
onMouseUp event, 299
Open Browser Window behavior, 300-302
Open Browser Window dialog
  box, 301
Open button, 422
Open SourceSafe Database dialog box, 370
opening
  browser windows, 300-302
  inspectors, 32
  panels, 32
operating systems, scripts, 352
optimizing images, 124
  Fireworks, 133-135
ordered lists, 48
organizations resources, 449
orphaned links, 390
Outdent button, 49

P

packets, 354
page appearances, 53-58
page layout, 219
Page Preferences dialog box,
  87
page properties, 52-58
Page Properties button, 52
Page Properties dialog box, 52
page titles, 52-53
paired tags, 8
panel groups, 33-34, 391
panels, 32
paragraph (<p>) tag, 43
parameters, 178
Parameters button, 173, 177,
  180
Parameters dialog box,
  177-178
parent directories, 84
password text fields, 329
passwords, 368
pasting text into Web pages
  from files, 50-51
paths
  absolute, 80, 84
  document-relative, 80-82
    linking files, 83-84
    URLs, 83
  site root-relative, 84
  URLs, 81
PDF files, 171
PhotoDisc Web site, 133
Photoshop plug-ins, 143
PHP, 357
pixels, sizing text, 44
pixilated, 135
placeholder images, templates,
  435
Play button (Flash), 166

playback controls, plug-ins, 173

players, 164-165, 176

playing movies, 190

Plg URL button, 173

plug-ins

    parameters, 178

    Photoshop, 143

    playback controls, 173

Plugin object,

    inserting, 172-174

    sizing controls, 175-176

pluginspace attribute, 165

PNG format, 124

PNG format (Fireworks), 141

Point-to-File icon, 91, 123

Pointer tool, Property inspector
(Fireworks), 142

polygon hotspot tool, adding to
image maps, 155-156

Popup Message behavior,
adding to objects, 302-304

Popup Message dialog box,
302

ports

    TCP/IP Transport layer, 10,
175, 291-294

    URLs, 81

    well-known ports, 10, 175,
291-294

Positioning category (CSS Style
Definition dialog box), 277-
278

POST method, 351

preferences, HTML code, 106

Preferences dialog box

    Code Coloring category,
106-107

    Code Format category,
106-109

    Code Hints category,
106-109

Code Rewriting category,
106

    setting, 110

File Types/Editors category,
124-125

Fonts category, 99

Invisible Elements category,
323

Layers category, 260-261

Layout Mode category. See
Layout mode

tag colors, 107

Preferences dialog box
(Fireworks), 143

preset formats, tables, 212-213

Preview button, 386

previewing. See also viewing

    assets in categories, 188

    Flash movies, 166

    NoFrames Content, 248

    Web pages, 56

    Web pages in browsers,
303-304

processing form data

    CGI script, 350-351

    client-side scripts, 345

    FormMail script, 351-352

    parsed data, 349

properties. See also attributes

    form, creating forms, 325-
326

    layers, 263

Properties dialog box, Tracing
Image category, 229

Property inspector, 34

    Align drop-down menu,
120-122

    Alt drop-down menu,
122-123

    displaying Web page image
properties, 118-119

expanding, 35

Flash movies, 165-166

Font drop-down menu, 44

Format drop-down menu,
43

Help icon, 38

image properties, 34

Link property, 123

Size drop-down menu, 44

    color picker, 45-46

    CSS, 47

Style drop-down menu, 274

Target drop-down menu,
158, 250

text properties, 34

Vis drop-down menu, 266

Property inspector (Fireworks),
140-143

protocols, URLs, 80

Put button, 373

Put command, 377-378

Q

query strings, URLs, 81

Quick Export drop-down menu,
Document window
(Fireworks), 146

Quick Tag Editor, 102-104

Quick Tag Editor icon, 103

R

radio buttons, creating,
331-332

RDS access, remote sites, 369

RealMedia sound files, 174

recording, menu commands,
403-404

Recreate button, 422

Rectangle Hotspot tool,
153-154

Reference panel, 291

Refresh button, 373

Refresh Site List button, 417

remote servers, 372-373

Remote Site pane (Expanded
Files panel), 69

remote sites
Advanced tab (Site
Definition dialog box),
371
Check In/Check Out tools,
enabling, 375-378
defining, 366-367
FTP access, 367-368
LAN access, 368
RDS access, 369
source/version-control
applications, 370
transferring files, 376-378
Web sites, importing,
378-379
WebDAV access, 370

remote Web sites, synchronizing files, 384-387

removing
assets, favorite assets list
in Assets panel, 194
columns/rows in tables,
210-211
frame borders, 238
guides, 137
styles, 274

reports, 393

Reports dialog box, 393

required form elements, 348

requirements, hardware/
software, 9-10

reserved target names, 158

reset button, 336-337

resources, Web sites, 445
accessibility, 448
browsers, 448
DHTML, 446
downloads, 448
Dreamweaver development,
445
Dreamweaver extensions,
446-447
organizations, 449
scripting, 447
usability, 448
Web development, 445-446

Results panel, 410

rollover images, 126
creating, 126-127
creating navigation bar,
159-160

rollover images (Fireworks),
142-147

root directories, 61

Roundtrip HTML, 8

rows, 210-211

Run button, 393

S

.swf file extension, 165

Save As Command dialog box,
404

Save As Template dialog box,
432

Save Selected Steps As a
Command button, 404

Save Style Sheet File As dialog
box, 283

saving
menu commands, 403-404
set of steps as commands,
History panel, 406

site maps, 389
templates to servers, 431
Word documents as Web
pages, 111-112

Script Archive Web site, 350

script files (Assets panel),
190-191

scripting, server-side, 356-359

scripting resources, 447

scripts
CGI, 350-351
client-side, processing form
data, 345
FormMail, 351-352
free Web downloads, 350
operating systems, 352

Scripts category (Assets panel),
190-191

Scroll drop-down menu, settings, 245-246

scrolling attributes (frames),
244-246

search engines
crawling, 168
Flash, 168
page titles, 52

searches, 410-412

security, Web servers, 354-355

Select Extension to Install dialog box, 408

Select File dialog box, 173,
180

Select Image Source dialog
box, 118

Select Table command, 203

selecting
fonts, 44-45
frames, Frames panel,
241-242
table elements, 203-205
text colors, 45-47

separators, adding to Favorites list, 407

Server Behaviors panel, comparing with Behaviors panel, 295

server certificates, 355

server connections, 365

server-side scripting, 356-359

server-side scripting resources, 447

servers
case-sensitive filenames, 66, 72
library items, sharing, 422
remote, 372-373
templates, backup copies, 431
Web
secure sockets, 354
server certificates, 355

Set Class command, 281

Set Text of Status Bar behavior, adding behaviors to, 304

Set Text of Status Bar dialog box, 304

settings, layer visibility, 266-267

shape, adding to images (Fireworks), 139-141

sharing
development files, 66
library items on servers, 422

Sharing Files section (Site Definition Wizard), 64

Shockwave, 165

shortcuts, keyboard, 401-403

Show All Events button, 300

Show Events For drop-down menu, 295

Show Grid command, 265

Show Set Events button, 300

Show Slices button, 146

Show-Hide Layers behavior, 296-299

Show-Hide Layers dialog box, 298

showing layers, 296

single-line text field, 329

site caches, 67

Site Definition dialog box, 62, 366-367
Advanced tab, 62, 371
editing site definitions, 72-73
Basic tab, 62
Site Definition Wizard, 62-64
Site Map Layout category, 387-389

Site Definition Wizard, 62-64, 366

Site Map Layout category (Site Definition dialog box), 387, 389

site maps, 387-389

Site menu, 15

site root-relative paths, 84

sites
moving onto remote servers, 372-373
remote, 366

Size drop-down menu (Property inspector), 44-47

sizing
frames, 247
images, 119
Plug-in object controls, 175-176
tables, 211
text, 44
text fields in forms, 329-330
Window Size drop-down menu, 31-32

Slice tool (Fireworks), 144

slices (Fireworks), 144-147

slider (History panel), 405

Snippet dialog box, 399

snippets, 398-400

Snippets panel, 398

snow applets, 180

software, 8-10
image optimization programs, 124
text-to-speech, 207

Sort Table dialog box, 209

sorting data in tables, 208-210

sound file formats, 174-175

sound files, 172-174

sound parameters, 178

source/version-control applications, remote sites, 370

SourceSafe databases, connecting, 370

South Park Web site, 172

spacer images, setting, 224-225

spam, mailto links, 93

Specific Tag search, 411

Split button, 225

Split Cell command, 225

Split Cell dialog box, 226

splitting
cells in tables, 225-226
frames, 239-240
pages into frames, 238

stacking layers, 264

Standard mode, 202, 225-226

Standard mode button, 225

Start page, 11

Status bar, 30-32

storing files, development sites, 64

stroke settings, Property inspector (Fireworks), 140

style classes, creating, 272-274

Style Definition dialog box, 272

Style drop-down menu, 274

Style drop-down menu
  (Property inspector), 274

style sheets, external, 283-284

styles. *See also* CSS

  CSS

    advanced, 282

    applying to library items,
      425

    editing, 285-286

    moving layers, 281-282

    removing, 274

    tags, 274

    templates, editing, 440

submit button, 336-337

summaries, development site
  definitions, 67

support, browser events, 295

Synchronize command, 377,
  384

Synchronize Files dialog box,
  385-387

synchronizing files on Web
  sites, 384-387

T

table cells, 226-227

Table dialog box, 202, 206

table headers, 203

tables, 257

  accessing by visually
    impaired users, 207

  adding color to, 227-228

  adding columns/rows,
    210-211

  adding contents, 208

  adding header cells, 206

  adding to Web pages,
    202-203

  Autostretch, 222-224

  creating for data, 201

  exporting data from,
    213-214

  importing data from,
    214-215

  layers, converting groups
    of, 231

  layout, adding to Web
    pages, 220-222

  modifying border colors,
    211

  modifying column/row
    sizes, 211

  modifying sizes, 211

  nesting within tables, 228

  preset formats, 212-213

  removing columns/rows,
    210-211

  selecting elements,
    203-205

  setting elements, 206

  sorting data, 208-210

  Standard mode, 225-226

tabs

  Advanced (Drag Layer dia-
    log box), 314-315

  Advanced (Site Definition
    dialog box), 62, 371

    editing site definitions,
      72-73

  All Info, 391

  Basic (Clean Up Word
    HTML dialog box),
    111-112

  Basic (Site Definition dialog
    box), 62-64

  Detailed (Clean Up Word
    HTML dialog box), 111

  Templates, 438

Tag drop-down menu (New CSS
  Style dialog box), 279

tag searches, 411-412

tag selector, 30

tag selector (Frames panel),
  243

tags, 8

  <blockquote>, 50

  <body>, 310

  <div>, 258

  <embed>, 166

  <form>, 326

  <h3>, 278

  <mmtemplate: if>, 437

  <object>, 166

  break (<br>), 43

  colors, changing, 107

  Edit Tag mode (Quick Tag
    Editor), attributes, 105-
    106

  editing, 102

  highlighted, 102

  HTML

    CSS styles, 278-280

    Web pages, 98

  Insert HTML mode (Quick
    Tag Editor), 104

  invalid, 102

  paragraph (<p>), 43

  styles, 274

  viewing, 102

  Wrap Tag mode (Quick Tag
    Editor), attributes, 106

Target drop-down menu
  (Property inspector), 158,
  250

target layers, 310-314

target names, 158

targeting linked pages to
  forms, 249-251

TCP/IP, Transport layer ports,
  10, 175, 291-294

Template Properties dialog box,
  439

How can we make this index more useful? Email us at indexes@samspublishing.com

templates, **429**
backing up, 431
behaviors, editing, 440
cloaking feature, 432
creating, 429
from existing Web
pages, 431-432
from scratch, 431-434
new editable regions,
436-438
Templates category
(Assets panel), 430-
431
CSS styles, editing, 440
downloading from Web, 430
editing, from existing
regions, 435-436
file extensions, 432
importing XML into, 436
library items, comparing,
416, 430
placeholder images, 435
Web pages, creating from,
438-439
Web pages, updating,
439-440
**Templates category (Assets
panel), 429-431**
Templates directory, 429
cloaking feature, 432
**Templates panel (Assets
panel), 186-187**
favorites, 194
Templates tab, 438
Test Connection button, 368
**Testing Files section (Site
Definition wizard), 64**
text
adding to images, 122-123
adding to images
(Fireworks), 137-138
break (<br>) tag, 43

centering into Web pages,
42
color assets, applying, 192
color picker, 45-47
copying/pasting into Web
pages from files, 50-51
CSS, 47
entering into Web pages,
42
Flash, creating, 167
fonts, 44-45
formatting, 43
horizontal rule, 51
indenting, 48-50
lists, 48-50
page properties, 52
background images,
54-58
heading properties, 55
margins, 55
page appearances, 53-
54
page titles, 52-53
paragraph (<p>) tag, 43
sizing, 44
**Text Align drop-down menu,
279**
text fields, 326-330
Text menu, 14
Text tool (Fireworks), 137-138
text-to-speech (TTS), 122
text-to-speech synthesizer software, 207
**Textarea object (Insert toolbar),
329-330**
third-party extensions,
installing, 408-410
tiling, 264
title attribute, 248
titles, 52-53

tools
Check In/Check Out,
374-378
Draw Layout Table, 228
editing image commands,
125-126
hotspot, image maps, 152-
156
Status bar, 30-32
**Tracing Image category
(Properties dialog box), 229**
tracing images, 229-231
**transferring files to remote
sites, 376-378**
Transparency slider, 229
**Transport layer (TCP/IP proto-
col) ports, 10, 175, 291, 293-
294**
TTS (text-to-speech), 122
TTS browsers, 122
**Type category (CSS Style
Definition dialog box), 275-
279**

U

uniform resource locators. *See*
URLs
universe (Web site), 61
unordered lists, 48
Update button, 390
**Update Current Page com-
mand, 424, 440**
Update Files dialog box, 389
Update Pages dialog box, 423
**Update Site command, 424,
440**
updating
library items, 424
links, 389-390
Web pages, templates,
439-440

uploading files from forms, 355-356

URLs (uniform resource locators), 79. *See also* links

CGI script, 351

document-relative paths, 83

domains, 80

paths and filenames, 81

ports, 81

protocols, 80

query strings, 81

security, 354

URLs category (Assets panel), 189-190

usability resources, 448

user forms, collecting user information, 326-336

V

V (vertical) space, **122**

Flash movies, 166

Validate Form behavior, **346-348**

Validate Form dialog box, **346**

validating form data, 346-348

variables, 352

VeriSign Web site, **355**

Vert drop-down menu, **226**

vertical space (V Space), **122**

vertically aligning table cells, **226**

View menu, **13**

View Options menu (Code view), **101-102**

viewing. *See also* displaying; previewing

assets in categories, 187

frame borders, 238

site maps, 388

tags, 102

tracing images, 231

Web page heads, 99

Vis drop-down menu (Property inspector), **266**

visibility, layers, **266-267**

W-Z

Web addresses. *See* URLs; Web sites

Web development resources, **445-446**

Web page elements, **185**. *See also* assets

Web pages

adding assets to, 192

adding Java applets to, 179-180

adding layout cells to, 220-222

adding layout tables to, 220-222

adding sound files to, 172

body, 99

creating, new, 41

creating from templates, 438-439

default pages, 82

design notes, adding to, 391-393

dynamic, 8

Flash Text object, inserting into, 167-169

head, 99

home pages, 82

HTML tags, 98

images

adding, 117-119

adding text to, 122-123

aligning, 120-122

copying, 118

editing commands, 125-126

linked, 123-125

sizing, 119

images, adding, 117

library items, adding to, 421

edits, 423-424

highlighted colors, 423

updates, 424

loading into frames, 243

Go to URL behavior, 251-252

targeted linked pages, 249-251

previewing, browsers, 56

previewing in browsers, 303-304

saving Word documents as, 111-112

splitting into frames, 238

tables, 202-215

templates, creating from, 431-432

text

break (<br>) tag, 43

centering, 42

color picker, 45-46

copying/pasting from files, 50-51

CSS, 47

entering, 42

fonts, 44-45

formatting, 43

heading properties, 55

horizontal rule, 51

indenting, 48-50

lists, 48-50

page properties, 52-58

How can we make this index more useful? Email us at indexes@samspublishing.com

paragraph (<p>) tag, 43
sizing, 44
updating, templates,
439-440
Web servers, 354-355
Web site maps, 387-389
Web site resources, 445
accessibility, 448
browsers, 448
DHTML, 446
downloads, 448
Dreamweaver development,
445
Dreamweaver extensions,
446-447
organizations, 449
scripting, 447
usability, 448
Web development, 445-446
Web sites. *See also* remote
sites
Acrobat Reader, 171
default pages, 82
defining, 62-64
development sites, 64-67
editing, 383
FormMail, 350
Freescripts, 350
home pages, 82
hyperlinks, adding, 85-86
importing, 378-379
Macromedia, 10, 430
Macromedia Dreamweaver
Exchange, 408
Macromedia Exchange, 397
Macromedia Fireworks, 131
Microsoft, 357
naming, 62-64
Netscape Navigator, 56
PhotoDisc, 133
reports, 393

root directories, 61
Script Archive, 350
South Park, 172
specifying dynamic sites,
Site Definition Wizard, 64
synchronizing files, 384-
387
universe, 61
VeriSign, 355
Web-safe colors, 189
Web-safe palette, 46-47
WebDAV (World Wide Web for
Distributed Authoring and
Versioning), 370
access, remote sites, 370
well-known ports, 10, 175,
291-294
Window Size drop-down menu,
31-32
windows, browser, 300-302
Windows Media Player, 175
Wizards, Site Definition, 62-64,
366
Word documents, 111-112
work areas, 10-11
Workspace Setup dialog box,
11
World Wide Web Distributed
Authoring and Versioning
(WebDAV), 370
Wrap property, 330
Wrap Tag mode (Quick Tag
Editor), 104-106
WYSIWYG (what you see is
what you get), 8
Web page images, 117

XML, importing into templates,
436

z-index, 264-265